GRUB STREET AND THE IVORY TOWER

Grub Street and the Ivory Tower

Literary Journalism and Literary Scholarship from Fielding to the Internet

EDITED BY
JEREMY TREGLOWN
AND
BRIDGET BENNETT

CLARENDON PRESS · OXFORD
1998

Oxford University Press, Great Clarendon Street, Oxford OX2 6DP
Oxford New York
Athens Auckland Bangkok Bogotá Buenos Aires Calcutta
Cape Town Chennai Dar es Salaam Delhi Florence Hong Kong Istanbul
Karachi Kuala Lumpur Madrid Melbourne Mexico City Mumbai
Nairobi Paris São Paolo Singapore Taipei Tokyo Toronto Warsaw
and associated companies in
Berlin Ibadan

Oxford is a registered trade mark of Oxford University Press

Published in the United States
by Oxford University Press Inc., New York

British Library Cataloguing in Publication Data
Data available

Library of Congress Cataloging in Publication Data
Data available

ISBN 0-19-818413-1
ISBN 0-19-818412-3 (pbk.)

1 3 5 7 9 10 8 6 4 2

Typeset by Best-set Typesetter Ltd., Hong Kong
Printed in Great Britain
on acid-free paper by
Bookcraft Ltd, Midsomer Norton, Somerset

Acknowledgements

We are grateful to the Humanities Research Centre (formerly the European Humanities Research Centre) at the University of Warwick and to its former director, Peter Mack, for sponsoring the seminars out of which this book grew. We also thank Marian Franklin, secretary of the HRC, and Andrew Biswell.

Contents

Contents

Introduction

'Literary journalism' has become so broad a term that it may soon have to be abandoned in its traditional sense. It's often used, now, especially in the US, to mean not journalism about books but—perhaps by analogy with the publishing concept of 'literary fiction'—any journalism which can be thought of as having lasting value. The subject of this book is arguably both. Most of the contributors treat it as defined here by Stefan Collini: journalism whose primary concern is 'those cultural and intellectual discussions that are carried on in the "literary" pages of newspapers and periodicals'—forums which Marjorie Perloff sees as being rapidly superseded (and radically transformed) by the Internet. The core is good writing about writing, with an emphasis on the vexed but at best mutually beneficial relationship between academic work on literature and a more public sphere.

The book's main argument is that there has rarely been as sharp a distinction between Grub Street and the academic Ivory Tower as has often been supposed (or wished by some people on both sides). Literary journalism and literary scholarship grew up together in the same neighbourhood and both can be found there still. Historically, the study of English literature began in Grub Street. Jenny Uglow's comparison between aspects of eighteenth-century literary culture and that of today implicitly recalls the fact that projects such as the early editorial work on Shakespeare by Nicholas Rowe, Lewis Theobald and Edward Capell, or Johnson's *Dictionary* and his *Lives of the English Poets*, were undertaken outside the universities of the time, in which literary study was confined to the Bible and the ancient classics. When English literature finally began to be taught as a university subject, as John Sutherland and Valentine Cunningham show, Victorian journalists were powerful in the profession and, long before 'research assessment' was thought of, brought to it their own demanding models of productivity. Stefan Collini considers the journalistic qualities of that

castigator of Grub Street, F. R. Leavis, who wrote his Ph.D.
thesis on the relations between early English journalism and
literature. Two notable amphibians, Karl Miller (a pupil of
Leavis) and Lorna Sage, write personally about how working in
Grub Street has enhanced what they and others have had to
offer to the Ivory Tower—and vice versa.

Such reciprocities have been an essential part of literature's
ecostructure. Grevel Lindop reveals how much De Quincey
owed to his academic connections in a Scottish intellectual
economy in which 'authors, editors, publishers and professors
changed roles with the greatest of ease'. In the other direction,
many serious imaginative writers have found in journalism an
opportunity, an escape, a stratagem. However squeamish
Coleridge felt about the medium, Zachary Leader shows that it
gave him fluency, unlocking his intellectual stammer. (To Gosse,
writing a piece in ten and a half hours on a Flemish novelist
whom he had never read before was 'a pleasant fillip: I am better
today than I have been for days.') Some of the essays here
exhibit such links primarily by applying academic expertise to
the historiography of cultural journalism: for example, David
Finkelstein's description of *Blackwood's Magazine* in its early
twentieth-century propagandist mode. Most are by scholars
who also command a non-academic readership, not least as
reviewers. Hermione Lee, for example, writes on Virginia
Woolf's complex and changing relationship with journalism and
other aspects of the literary market-place, and the links between
her non-fiction and her fiction; Edna Longley exposes the difficulties of book reviewing in present-day Ireland; and John
Stokes discusses Kenneth Tynan's theatre criticism—a genre
which, as Stokes points out, has a unique place in scholarship
because it offers the most vivid records we have of long-lost
performances. A purpose of the book is to show how rewarding
research can be in areas like these. While there are corners of
Grub Street where some residents of the Ivory Tower have
always liked to gather, British archives of literary magazines and
of publishing houses—such as the one at Reading University, a
treasure-store of material on individual authors as well as on the
institutions of cultural history—are still relatively unfrequented.

Grub Street and the Ivory Tower also assumes the value of
value-judgements in writing about books. Marjorie Perloff puts

herself on a limb by arguing with characteristic brio that poets aren't qualified to review academic books on poetry, or even poetry itself, both of which she sees as the proper preserve of academics. (Edward Bond once tried to discredit James Fenton as a theatre reviewer on similar grounds of demarcation.) Taken to their logical limit, such exclusions would have deprived readers of most of the work discussed in this book. However dominant the Ivory Tower has become, the Grub Street tradition of non-specialist, intellectually freelance, opinionated evaluation which Jenny Uglow sees Henry Fielding as having originated continues to hold its own and it remains true that, in Karl Miller's words, 'a high proportion of the most valuable and truthful literary criticism'—whether by freelance writers, salaried journalists or tenured academics—appears 'not in books initially, or ever, but in journals'.

Fielding also pioneered the other main impulses behind the kinds of criticism discussed in these pages, especially humour, exuberance, a sense of performance, a desire to be read. As Val Cunningham writes: 'if, as many recent critics have suggested, criticism is a story of reading, it does help if it has some of the charm and imaginative vigour, the verbal punch and push of the better kind of stories'. How these qualities can best be encouraged is a question with many answers, but one suggested here is that 'creative' writing should be put closer to the centre of literary syllabuses, with the aim of helping to produce not only better writers but better readers. John Sutherland and Karl Miller speak of the centrality of the practice of writing at University College London, past and present, and Lorna Sage argues, partly from her experience of the Creative Writing programme at the University of East Anglia, that academic study benefits from a return to 'the personalities of writing, writing's character, the stories of how books are structured, received, sold, understood or not, *made*'. Virginia Woolf told an undergraduate audience at Cambridge, 'I believe one should try to read books as if one were writing them. Do not begin by being a critic; begin by being a writer.' It's a motto which, at their best, the Ivory Tower and Grub Street still share.

Fielding, Grub Street, and Canary Wharf

JENNY UGLOW

The name 'Grub Street' was originally applied to Milton Street, a warren of garrets and tenements in Moorfields where poor writers lived at the end of the seventeenth century. Their work included indexing, proofing, compiling dictionaries, translating and writing poems to order for special occasions. By the 1720s this milieu spread through the impoverished wards that clung to the edges of the city, curling round to Clerkenwell and St John's Gate—home of the *Gentleman's Magazine* in the 1730s and for a while, until recently, of *The Times Literary Supplement*. Canary Wharf, also on the city's margins, is a megalith of glass and steel and concrete, an emblem to many of over-reaching entrepreneurism, 1980s greed and spiritual (and financial) bankruptcy.

Such metaphorical sitings evoke a dubious hinterland, a value-laden geography. In the eighteenth century the areas that constituted Grub Street were full of narrow alleys, thieves' dens and brothels, and harboured their own literary fences and pimps, the much maligned printers and booksellers.[1] (The words 'hackney' and 'hack' were current from the 1720s, for coach-men, prostitutes and writers and anything over-used, hired-out or common.) In a different way, Canary Wharf has come to symbolize the precarious dependence of the newspaper books' section on advertising and sales, a small niche fighting for space. If it is hard to place the *London Review of Books* in Canary Wharf, either physically or metaphorically, it is still true to say

---

[1] Pat Rogers, *Grub Street: Studies in a Subculture* (London, 1972) remains a classic account of Grub Street topography, practice, literary treatment and mythology.

that the stubborn independents are rarely self-financing; in the eighteenth century they depended on patronage, today on the Arts Council.

The topographical tags also implicitly place literary journalism as inferior to 'high' appreciation. In Fielding's day that would mean the writings of the leisured man of letters, the 'disinterested' aristocrat, cleric or scholar. A hundred and fifty years later, when Gissing redefined the territory in *New Grub Street* in 1892, he drew a different division, between two elements *within* the aspiring literary world: the facile and unscrupulous reviewer who thrives on self-advertisement and succeeds, and the scholars and writers of true artistic conscience, who inevitably fall victim to jealousies and poverty. In the twentieth century, although many reviews are written by practising poets or novelists, the high moral ground is often ceded to the academic or the theorist, at the expense of the 'journalist' paid by the piece.

A distinction of value between the journalistic and the 'literary', or the ephemeral and the enduring, seems to appear, or at least to crystallize, as soon as literature leaves the court and enters the market-place. In 1758 James Ralph, the political journalist who had been Fielding's friend and collaborator at the Little Theatre in the Haymarket and in their journal the *Champion* twenty years before, wrote an explosive defence of authors, contrasting the 'trade' of the writer with the hypocrisy of other liberal professions:

A Man may plead for Money, prescribe for or quack for Money, preach and pray for Money, marry for Money, fight for Money, do anything within the Law for Money, provided the Expedient answers, without the least imputation. But if he writes like one inspired from Heaven, and writes for Money, the Man of *Touch*, in the right of *Midas* his great Ancestor, enters his caveat against him as a man of *Taste*; declares the two Provinces to be incompatible; that he who aims at Praise ought to be starved . . . [The author] is laugh'd at if poor; if to avoid that curse, he endeavours to turn his Wit to Profit, he is branded as a Mercenary.[2]

'Grub Street' and 'Canary Wharf' brand British literary journalism not simply as mercenary but as metropolitan. And so it is.

[2] James Ralph, *An Apology for Authors* (1758), quoted in John Brewer, *The Pleasures of the Imagination: Eighteenth-Century Culture* (London, 1997), 149.

Bracing blasts from outside like the *Edinburgh Review* can occasionally overturn its dominance, but London literary cliques have been the object of attack since 1700. Even when reviewers can fax or down-load a piece from anywhere in the world, it will still be filtered through the screens and perceptions of London literary editors.

Although the suggestive geographical metaphors are offered as a guide to the way we still 'locate' literary journalism, this essay focuses on Henry Fielding and the mid-eighteenth century. I do not intend—nor do I think it possible—to draw precise parallels between past and present practice. It seems to me that the term 'literary journalism' has a different resonance and reference when applied to different periods, shifting from the urbane cultural gloss of Steele and Addison (which made periodical writing itself 'literary'), to the sonorous inclusiveness of the big nineteenth-century journals, the sharp, diverse tones of the 'little magazines' of the early twentieth century and the very different approaches of reviews and review-essays in the broadsheets, weekly journals and literary periodicals of today. But one of the elements that drew me to this comparison of two eras was a feeling that today's technology and speed of communication, combined with our habits of intertextual allusiveness, our sense of the fragmentation of old forms and awareness of game-playing, somehow replicated the closeness and knowingness of eighteenth-century London. And a glance back to the beginning throws up some unexpected and recurring questions: the relation of the literary to the more broadly cultural and political; the ambivalent relation of idealistic writers to the periodical market-place; and the role of criticism itself in the 'circuit' of cultural production.

As a young man, exuberant, passionate, comic and principled, Fielding began writing for journals at the end of the 1730s. His experimental practice as an early denizen of Grub Street may provide a glimpse, at least, of the primordial soup from which modern literary journalism emerged.

Fielding was always combative, full of opinions and judgements. He was ambitious but spendthrift (even at the height of his fame as a dramatist in the mid-1730s, he was said to take his coats out of pawn to wear on first nights). So he was writing principally for money. He arrived briefly in the capital in 1728, aged 21, immediately staking his claim with a play, *Love in Several Masques*, and a long poem, *The Masquerade*. It was the year of the first *Dunciad*, the immortalizing of Grub Street, and of *The Beggar's Opera*. It was also, according to the *OED*, the year when the word *journal*, previously applied only to a private diary, a daily account book or an official report, was first used of a daily paper. The concepts of specialization and a separate profession were slower to arrive: the term *journalist* is first noted in 1833. In this aspect of his work, Fielding would have called himself a periodical essayist, one among many hopeful followers of Addison and Steele.

In 1730, returning to London after eighteen months at the University of Leyden, leaving his books and bad debts behind him, Fielding told his cousin, Lady Mary Wortley Montagu, that he had no choice except between becoming 'a Hackney Writer or a Hackney Coachman'.[3] By the age of 24 he was the most talked-about dramatist in London, but in 1737 this career was cut short by the stage Licensing Act, provoked partly by his own anti-Walpole satire. Fielding then turned to the law, but supplemented his income with typical Grub Street work such as the translation of a French edition of the three-volume *Military History of Charles XII King of Sweden*—a labour Fielding may have remembered when he described Mr Wilson in *Joseph Andrews*, who undertook translation for a pittance and was given so much to do, he says, 'that in half a year I almost writ myself blind'.[4]

In the same year, Fielding launched his first newspaper, the *Champion*, with Ralph Allen. Between 1739 and 1753 he would sporadically edit four papers, the *Champion* (1740–1), the *True Patriot* (1746), the satirical *Jacobite's Journal* (1747) and the *Covent-Garden Journal* (1752–4). His involvement is interesting in terms both of the trajectory of his own career and also of the context of public literary discussion. First, the *Champion* reads like a springboard for his fiction: in its targets, its ironic tone and dramatized mode, it paves the way for the parodic criticism of *Shamela* (1741), and for the statements of intent and principles of practice in *Joseph Andrews* (1742), *Jonathan Wild*

---

[3] *The Complete Letters of Lady Mary Wortley Montagu*, ed. R. Halsband (3 vols.; Oxford, 1966), iii. 66.
[4] Henry Fielding, *Joseph Andrews*, ed. Douglas Brooks (Oxford, 1971), 194.

(1743) and *Tom Jones* (1749). Secondly, the make-up of all his papers reflects the fact that literary journalism has, as yet, no separate sphere: these concerns are only one aspect of a wider cultural discussion, which in turn is linked to a political and ideological debate about the kind of society that should be fostered in a burgeoning commercial world. These were mixed, polemical papers and at times their particular concerns define so-called 'literary' priorities; the *Champion* was an opposition journal, but the *True Patriot* and *Jacobite's Journal* were written to support the government during the 1745 rebellion and its aftermath.

Fielding's journals were unusual because they included an unprecedented amount of discussion of books and writers. When he launched the *Champion* there was no such thing as a 'book review'. There had been specialized review journals since the late seventeenth century, beginning with the quarterly term catalogue, which was simply a list of new publications. Later ventures (such as Dunton's *Compleat Library* in the 1690s, Bernard Lintot's *Monthly Catalogue* 1714–15, or the *New Mirror of Literature*, 1725–7) gradually expanded the basic listing with brief descriptions, surveys and abstracts. But they did not judge. In fact the compilers emphatically denied that this was their job. An early editor promised 'not to make any large Harangue, either in the Praise, or Dispraise of any Book' and another, aiming to keep a measure between 'tedious Extracts and superficial Catalogues', added that 'our practice is that of *Historians* and not *Criticks*'.[5]

Furthermore, the catalogues concentrated on learned works—antiquarian, scientific, religious. Until the *Monthly Review* began in 1749, and the *Critical Review* seven years later, the middle ground of essays, poetry and the new genre of the novel, was badly served, and would-be readers turned for guidance increasingly to the opinions of the periodical essayists. A new, intimate circuit was set in motion between producer and consumer, publisher and reader. Criticism and market response both became defining factors in what was produced.

The essayists' judgement assumed great importance because

[5] *Mercurius Librarius* (1680) and Jean de La Crose, *A History of the Works of the Learned* (serial publication, 1699–1711), quoted in Richard P. Bond, ed., *Studies in Early English Periodicals* (Chapel Hill, NC, 1957), 32, 34.

by the 1740s there was a huge new public for culture, eager for informed opinion. Writers of the particular brand who wanted to follow in the footsteps of Addison and Steele's *Tatler* and *Spectator* or of Pope and Swift (as Fielding certainly did, although his politics were different) felt they were men with a mission, a duty to mould society, a concern related to anxieties concerning that new, uneasily consensual London world loosely described as 'polite society' or the 'Town'. The expansion of the city had brought a greater, cheaper provision of culture. As the squares and streets extended ever westward, the theatres moved westward too. Auditoriums were larger and prices dropped. Concert halls opened. Pleasure gardens expanded. Booksellers and print-makers flourished. Auctions of pictures and prints boomed.

This coincided with a huge proliferation of newspapers and journals. The Newspaper Licensing Act was repealed in 1695 and between 1700 and 1760 there were over 900 different papers in the press in Britain. In 1728 alone—the year Fielding came to London—over 100 saw the light of day. They ranged from news reports to miscellanies and question-and-answer magazines (very popular), and from political organs to learned journals. Sales of only 500 copies, plus advertising, were enough to keep a paper afloat. Bookseller publishers with capital and enterprise were eager to find gaps in the market and launch new variations. And there was an inherent sense of sociability about the press; papers lay around in all the coffee-houses and were intended for shared, not private reading, as spurs to conversation, argument and analysis.

The boom in cultural provision gave rise to a continual debate, throughout the reigns of Queen Anne and George II. The danger, as some saw it, was that culture itself was going to be defined by the new, 'vulgar' public. With this sense of alarm went a concern for the definition of national character and status. The argument which raged about Italian opera, for instance, was about both its nonsense and expense, and the displacement of old British drama by flashy foreign imports. Opera was seen as culture for snobs, funded by the court. (There is a parallel to be drawn with the row about the use of lottery money for Covent Garden today.) On one hand there was a drive to raise national cultural standards by introducing foreign models.

On the other there was an earthy, curmudgeonly, chauvinist assertion of so-called 'native' traditions.

By the 1730s, however, the importance of culture as a public good—not a private indulgence of the aristocracy—was almost a cliché. It was even seen as an indicator of the 'free' (i.e. Whiggish) character of British life. And, as John Brewer points out in his stimulating survey of the formation of eighteenth-century taste, public appreciation was thought to be a potential spur to finer work. In Shaftesbury's words:

Without a public voice, knowingly guided and directed, there is nothing which can raise a true ambition in the artist; nothing which can exalt the genius of the workman, or make him emulous of fame, and of the approbation of his country, and of posterity. . . . When the free spirit of a nation turns itself this way, judgments are formed; critics arise; the public eye and ear improve; a right taste prevails, and in a manner forces its way.[6]

Key issues emerged. First, that of setting the boundaries of the kind of public that men like Shaftesbury wanted to address, then of educating this public in what he called 'right taste'. The self-assumed role of director could *sound* democratic. It does, for instance, in Addison's famous opening claim in the *Spectator*: 'It was said of Socrates, that he brought Philosophy down from Heaven to inhabit among Men; and I shall be ambitious to have it said of me that I brought Philosophy out of Closets and Libraries, Schools and Colleges, to dwell in Clubs and Assemblies, at Tea-tables, and in Coffee-Houses.'[7] The comparison with Socrates bringing philosophy *down* from Heaven is itself suggestive. But if one adds another of Addison's dicta, 'A man of Polite imagination is let into a great many Pleasures that the Vulgar are not capable of receiving',[8] it begins to seem as though 'politeness' was a way of creating a new élite, based on taste rather than blood. And the public arena of this culture of politeness was, as Addison said, the world of assemblies and coffee-houses, of 'Conversation', not private talk but public interchange. So behind the birth of writing about literature in the public press lie the questions, 'Who is going to be allowed

[6] Anthony Ashley Cooper, 3rd Earl of Shaftesbury, quoted in Brewer, *Pleasures*, 95.
[7] *The Spectator*, ed. Donald F. Bond (5 vols.; Oxford, 1965), i. 10.
[8] Ibid. 288.

into this conversation? Who chooses the topics? Who is expected to speak, and who must keep silent?'

A tension developed very quickly when criticism and opinion-making were associated with the public press. Previously, the role of 'director and guide' had been assumed by the 'disinterested' men of letters, wealth and leisure. Once writing and critical judgement were associated with the market, and with making money, they became tainted. Judgement was undermined by the low Grub Street status of the writers, and the fact that their allegiances were often so factional, so political.

The *Champion* was born in this brew of discussion and heated feeling about culture, morality, manners and society, but it contained more criticism, of real perception and fire, than the other short-lived journals of the day. Fielding contributed general papers on wit and humour, on fame or on the abuse of words, as well as appreciations of particular authors from Homer and Lucian to Spenser, Pope or Massinger. But Fielding's position, half in and half out of the true Grub Street world, also highlighted some features which were to be an enduring part of literary journalism.

From the start, for example, questions of finance and circulation came into play and affected the content. Fielding only owned two of the sixteen shares in the *Champion*. The other shareholders included James Ralph and eight booksellers. The financial affairs were directed by three of these, headed by Francis Cogan, of Temple Bar.[9] The paper was published three times a week, growing after a few months from two to four pages. (It moved from morning to evening publication when established evening papers began filching its best articles.) It was cheaply priced, at three halfpence, but won little advertising and for the first two months circulation faltered. Commercial pressures forced changes in content: Fielding had planned to write on social and literary topics rather than politics, as the opposition already had two papers, *Common Sense* and the *Craftsman*. But politics was what people wanted, and as sales dipped the paper adjusted accordingly. Fielding may have been the first literary editor fighting grimly to hang on to his pages. By mid-1740 he had virtually handed over editorial control to Ralph.

The first page usually had an essay by Fielding, sometimes followed by a 'Literary Article' and then by a satiric digest of foreign and domestic news. The short 'Literary Articles' have that tone of casual authority which was to become, and remain, a hallmark of literary journalism. Here, for example is the notice of a new translation of Voltaire's essays in January 1740: 'Perhaps it cannot be called a perfect piece; for an accurate and severe judge may point out some blemishes; but this is beyond controversy, that 'tis written with great fire and Vivacity, abounds with forcible and pointed Passages and affords Half an Hours elegant, and useful, entertainment.'[10] All opinion and adjectives, bereft of quotation or analysis, it simply assumes readers' trust in the writer's personal views. Fielding rapidly imposed his voice and style—although not quite his *own* voice. In the long essays, as his mouthpiece, he followed the pattern of the club in the *Spectator*. But, typically, he adopted a more demotic, man-of-the-people idiom. He appeared not as the urbane Mr Spectator, the merchant Sir Andrew Freeport or the squire Sir Roger de Coverley, but as the ex-prize-fighter Captain Hercules Vinegar of Hockley-in-the-Hole (Hockley being an area of Clerkenwell known for its bear gardens and bare-knuckle fighting). Taking up his cudgels, the Captain summons his family to contribute: his scolding wife Joan (to represent the demands of women readers and to provide a joke at the expense of Addison's deliberate appeal to the 'fair sex' in the *Spectator*), his father Nehemiah (for politics), a lawyer uncle, a doctor cousin, a classical scholar brother and two sons, law student Tom (theatre criticism) and idle Jack (town gossip).

The Vinegar persona let Fielding be fierce without being solemn, while the family added further layers to his ironic judgements. Fielding deliberately, with great conviction, aligned literary with social criticism. He believed that the values that apply must be the same, and as a lawyer, he wanted to 'try' the issues before judging them. His Captain Vinegar thus holds his own court, where 'the Covetous, the Prodigal, the Bully, the

[10] The *Champion*, 5 Jan. 1740. Collected single-volume ed. (London, 1741), 164.

Vain, the Hypocrite, the Flatterer, the Slanderer, call aloud for the Champion's vengeance'.[11]

As the English love executions, he says, they will be staged at Drury Lane during the intervals. Fielding's adoption of the Vinegar family, however, also placed him firmly on the side of the city and the people, as opposed to the court and the Walpole government. (The *Champion* was thrown out of the coffee-houses round St James's.) By this date it was clear where his allegiances lay. Eleven years earlier, at the age of 21, principle had seemed less important to him than patronage. His hopes then lay with the court: he wrote odes to George II, and a long, unpublished satire found in Mary Montagu's papers shows that he was quite ready to decry Pope, Gay and the anti-Walpole factions.

As a cultural critic, however, Fielding rapidly aligned himself with Swift, Pope and the Scriblerians, even if he did not accept their Tory politics. His long poem of 1728, *The Masquerade*, takes the fashionable masquerades patronized by the court as a symbol and site of all current ills—vanity, gossip, coquetry, the triviality of current taste. The mask, or persona, is both a disguise and an unwitting revelation of the self through the liberation of anonymity.

> Known prudes there, libertines we find
> Who masque the face, t'unmasque the mind.[12]

Fielding's own masks are also unmaskings. He signed this work as 'Lemuel Gulliver, Poet Laureat to the King of Gulliver', and later took the pseudonym of Scriblerus Secundus. Many of the devices of his criticism, as well as its targets, were derived from the Scriblerians: the copious, comically pedantic notes to *The Tragedy of Tragedies* (1731); the madman as the just critic; the discovered document; the secret society; the crazy scientific invention. He cites Swift as one of his masters of humour, alludes admiringly to Pope's *Essay on Criticism* and frequently

---

[11] The *Champion*, 22 Dec. 1739, in *The Works of Henry Fielding*, ed. Leslie Stephen (10 vols.; London, 1903), v. 242. This edn. includes the principal essays but not the 'literary Articles'.

[12] Henry Fielding, 'The Masquerade' (1728), in *The Female Husband and Other Writings*, ed. Claude E. Jones (Liverpool, 1960), 7.

quotes the *Dunciad*. Pope proves a useful authority, too, in his frequent assertion that the author is the best judge:

> Let those teach others who themselves excell,
> And censure freely who have written well.[13]

Yet when Fielding writes about the world of literary production he writes from within, with a knowledge of the financial needs and the labour of the hacks that Pope and Swift did not share. This closeness to the trade, graphically dramatized in his first play *The Author's Farce* (1730), sometimes makes his attack on Grub Street all the fiercer. His awareness of the harsh reality of literary life, that words equal money, food and survival, makes him doubly passionate when he pleads the case of the author who is the victim of malicious, unthinking criticism. When he sneers that 'bad writers seem to have a Sort of prescriptive Privelege to abuse good ones', he is thinking of the critic's responsibility to a man making a living, as well as to the art of writing. Grub Street was never homogeneous or united—its feuds, petty squabbles and mud slinging are one of the *Dunciad*'s main themes—and Fielding's ferocity in the *Champion* comes partly from his fight not to be identified with hackery (a favourite line of attack from his enemies) and partly from his so often being attacked by the hacks themselves. Hence his strong Popeian line (following 'The Art of Sinking') where he attacks the doctrine of 'pertness' in young writers as 'the Art of Swaggering in print'. Or when he promises his own prose *Dunciad* to rescue modern writers from oblivion, praising Pope (sarcastically but not inaccurately) for 'dragging many out of the Kennels [gutters] to Immortality'.

Beneath the playful façade, Fielding was passionately serious in attempting to evolve a middle role for the critic between the market and the rigid conventions of high culture. In the *Champion*, to establish his credentials as a judge, he first has to demolish the false critics. And—perhaps because his training was in the theatre, where the pit, boxes and gallery were packed with loud critics—he stands out firmly against judgement by popular reception. He does think periodical criticism is still a

[13] Alexander Pope, 'An Essay on Criticism', in *Pope: Poetical Works*, ed. Herbert Davis (Oxford, 1966), 64.

top–down affair, and he does, to continue in the jargon of the
present, feel it is dangerous to leave judgements to the brat-pack
or the chattering classes. Under the deliberately comic, silly rules
that Vinegar lays down about who can and can't be a critic, runs
real feeling:

First I expect henceforward, that no Person whatever, be his Qualifications what they will, presume to give his Opinion against any literary
Production, without having first read one Word of it. Secondly, That
no Man under the age of fourteen, shall be entitled to give a Definitive
opinion (unless in the Play-house). Thirdly, That no Person shall be
allowed to be a perfect Judge in any Work of Learning, who hath not
advanced as far as the End of the Accidence; unless at the Coffee
Houses West of Charing Cross [*the smart world of the courts and
connoisseurs*] where such deficiences shall be supplied by a proper
Quantity of Lace and Embroidery.

He also bans open prejudice and 'Winks, Nods, Smiles and
other signs and Tokens'.

This determined exclusion of frivolous mass judgement is still
evident twelve years later. In 1752, in the *Covent-Garden Journal* (where he writes as Sir Alexander Drawcansir, 'Censor of
the Nation') he invents a record, found in the Censor's office.
This shows that while in Elizabeth's reign there were nineteen
critics enrolled in London and Westminster, the latest tally is
276,302.[14]

Here Fielding slyly confronts the issue of relativism, the argument that taste is personal and no one should dictate it. He
seems to be open, while actually defining literary bad taste:
'Why should a Man in this Case, any more than in all the others,
be bound by any opinions but his own? Or why should he read
by Rule any more than eat by it? if I delight in a Slice of
Bullock's liver or of Oldmixon, why shall I be confined to Turtle
or to Swift?' He insists, however jokingly, that a critic must give
a reason for his judgement. The reason can be as foolish as he
likes but there must *be* one: 'except only the Words POOR STUFF,
WRETCHED STUFF, BAD STUFF, SAD STUFF, LOW STUFF, PAULTRY
STUFF. All which STUFFS I do banish forever from the Mouths of
All Critics'. He raises the age of critical consent to 18 (except for

---

[14] *The Covent-Garden Journal (1752)*, ed. B. A. Goldgar (Oxford, 1988), 27–30,
no. 3, 11 Jan. 1752. All quotations are from this edn.

women, if they are pretty or have £50,000 a year). He excludes the immoral, the insane and those with vested interests or party allegiances, except in the criticism of pamphlets. He implies that critics should have standards (they must have read Horace, Longinus and Aristotle in the original) but also generosity, the latter to be proved by a testimonial that they have spoken well of some living author other than themselves. And 'Lastly, all Persons are forbid, under the penalty *of our Highest Displeasure*, to presume any criticism upon any of those Works with which WE OURSELVES shall think proper to oblige the Public.' This joyfully blatant undercutting of the whole by the last item illustrates the nice complexity of Fielding's stance. And by citing the conventional trio of authorities, Horace's *Ars Poetica*, Aristotle's *Poetics*, Longinus' *On the Sublime*, he simultaneously asserts their authority and points to their unthinking and often contradictory application.

At the time he wrote this, Fielding was smarting under the poor reception of his last, sombre novel *Amelia* (1751), which is itself the subject of a mock trial by the 'Town'. In two of the definitions in his 'Modern Glossary', also in the *Covent-Garden Journal*, his bitterness shows:

AUTHOR: a Laughing Stock. It means likewise a Poor Fellow and in general an object of Contempt.
CRITIC: Like *Homo*, a Name common to all the human Race.[15]

Fielding's anti-definition of a critic is, of course, part of a battle to clear the ground for him to develop his own writing, with its eclectic mosaic of modes, and its deliberate choice of 'low' characters and settings (a choice that also identified him with 'Grub Street' in many readers' eyes). The negatives are clear, but, as a literary journalist, what does he stand *for*?

From the beginning, Fielding's literary judgements are embedded in the social, his critical insights tied to moral or behavioural generalizations. One *Champion* paper begins, 'It will be found, I believe, a pretty just Observation, that many more Vices and Follies arrive in the World through Excess than neglect. Passion hurries ten beyond the mark, for one whom Indolence holds short of it.' He illustrates this first with regard

[15] *Covent-Garden Journal*, no. 4, 14 Jan. 1752, 35.

to excessive moral characteristics: modesty, civility, uxorious-
ness and ceremoniousness in religion and law. Only then does he
turn to the liberal arts: to Homer's epic overkill, to Ovid's
exuberance of fancy, to the modern practice of 'young authors
who heap Idea on Idea till they have tired and confused their
readers'.

Behind Fielding's socio-literary criticism of passion lies an
adherence to moderation and decorum which is noticeably and
splendidly absent from his own work. The language of taste,
whether in the *Spectator* or the *Champion*, is intertwined with
that of politeness and with two other complex eighteenth-
century terms 'Good-Nature' and 'Good-Breeding', the latter
being the mental discrimination which turns the possessor of the
former into a person of 'polite behaviour'. In Fielding's writing,
Good-Breeding is still inevitably associated with aristocratic
ease, but, like politeness, it can be defined as a classless, innate
quality, fostered by education:

That whoever, from the Goodness of his Disposition or Understanding,
endeavours to his utmost to cultivate the Good-humour and Happiness
of others, and to contribute to the Ease and Comfort of all his
Acquaintance, however low in rank Fortune may have placed him, or
however clumsy he may be in Figure or Demeanour, hath, in the truest
Sense of the Word, a Claim to Good-breeding.[16]

In both his journalism and his fiction, Fielding continued to
probe the meaning and implications of the term. Humour, Fielding claimed, was the most potent of critical tools, both literary
and moral, because it could chart the deviation from Good-
Breeding through excess and wild individuality, laughing
mankind out of their follies and vices. In the *Covent-Garden
Journal* he defines Good-Breeding as 'the Art of conducting
yourself by certain common and general Rules, by which
Means, if they were universally observed, the whole World
would appear (as all Courtiers actually do) to be, in their external Behaviour at least, but one and the same person'.[17] In
practice, he says, it means the restraint of 'all those violent and
inordinate Desires' which are the true seeds of humour (in Ben
Jonson's sense): 'The Ambitious, the Covetous, the Proud, the

[16] 'On Conversation', *Miscellanies*, i (1743), ed. Henry Knight Miller (Oxford,
1972), 152.
[17] *Covent-Garden Journal*, no. 55, 18 July 1752, 298.

Vain, the Angry, the Debauchee, the Glutton, are all lost in the character of the Well-bred Man'. Humour, on the other hand, comes from 'throwing the reins on the Neck of our favourite Passion'—a trope that leads straight to Uncle Toby's hobby-horse in *Tristram Shandy*. Indeed the argument about teaching through humour stemming from excess offers the perfect justification for Fielding—as for Hogarth, Smollett and Sterne—to introduce wild, grotesque, exuberant indecorum into his work.

Exuberance is a feature of Fielding's critical as well as fictional style. In his essays he employs a host of ironic, rhetorical devices, many borrowed from Swift. One is the story of the 'accidental discovery' of a secret invention, a thermometer of Wit that measures genius, from Stupidity or Dullness, up through Pertness, Gravity, Good Sense and Vivacity to 'True Wit or Fire'. When he reads Virgil, the spirits leap in the glass; when he picks up a volume of sermons given to him by an eminent divine, he finds, with 'great Astonishment that the liquor sinks down of a sudden to the very Bottom of the Tube'. This is not simply another advocacy of moderation, but a plea to judge a work on its internal qualities rather than its extra-literary claims, or its publishing context. Returning to the realities of the literary world, Fielding suggests that this invention might work better than the common ways of judging new books—the letters after an author's name, the dedication, the name of the printer or publisher.

Fielding is always shrewd and savage about the conditions that affect the reception of a book. He writes brilliantly on cliquery and puffery, the value of sensational publicity and opportunistic advertising, as in the case of the 'Newgate' vogue, typified by the case of Savage:

an Author whose Manufactures had long lain uncalled for in the Warehouse, till he happened very fortunately for his Bookseller to be found guilty of a capital crime at the Old Bailey. The Merchant instantly took the Hint, and the very next Day advertised the Works of Mr Savage, now under Sentence of Death for Murder. This Device succeeded and immediately (to use their Phrase) carried off the whole Impression.[18]

---

[18] *Covent-Garden Journal*, no. 51, 27 June 1752, 283. Richard Holmes points out that Fielding refers to the *Newgate Life* of Savage, not his 'Works', which are Fielding's invention. (Richard Holmes, *Dr Johnson and Mr Savage* (London, 1993), 248 n. 4.)

This did not, of course, stop Fielding simultaneously exploiting and satirizing the same vogue for criminal lives in *Jonathan Wild*. And he himself cleverly ensured that *Tom Jones* was puffed so well that the first edition sold out before it even reached the shops.

The governing tone of the *Champion*, however ironic, is that of a radical conservative, a defender of rights, liberties and standards. Literature is supremely important precisely because it mirrors and even feeds faults that vitiate society as a whole. Forget critical objectivity: Fielding selects and attacks. But he does play by certain rules, even when he seems merciless, as in his sustained critical assault upon Colley Cibber's *An Apology for the Life of Mr. Colley Cibber*, published in 1740. Part of his animosity was political: the book had defended Walpole's government. Part was personal: as a theatre-manager and as an abridger of Shakespeare, Cibber had long been a target of Fielding's plays. But the main thrust is against Cibber's ludicrous self-importance, revealed by his abuse of language, a literary flaw symptomatic of a wider disregard for accuracy. Language is the currency of moral and political, as well as artistic, exchange; if it is debased the values it signifies are debased too (the point made by his own satiric debasing of Richardson's 'virtue' to 'vartue' in *Shamela*).

In successive issues Fielding follows up his charge in detail. First he adopts the Swiftian logic of wit, the mock defence. Claiming to rebut the slander that whatever language the *Apology* was written in, it certainly could not be English, he proves it *must* be English, and written by a Master, 'for surely he must be absolute Master of that whose Laws he can trample under Feet'.[19]

In the next issue he gives hilarious lists of examples, complete with page numbers. In a third, he takes the saying that 'every Great Writer' must have a particular style, 'a kind of Touchstone used by Commentators, to try what Parts of a Great Man's Works are truly his own', and then plunges into lists of examples, complete with page numbers: of the wrong use of adverbs, of making passive into active verbs, of non-sequiturs and mixed metaphors. (The listing is so precise as to be almost

---

[19] The *Champion*, 22 Apr. 1740, ed. Stephen, 420–1.

obsessive, and makes me wonder if similar homework on *Pamela* may lie behind his deft twisting of Richardson's mannerisms.)

This particular article ends, however, with a flying metaphor of Fielding's own—a timeless favourite of reviewers, the kind of risky critical-parodic freedom that journalism allows but most academic analysis eschews (although happily one can think of vivid exceptions). This excellent work, he says, is a 'Suet Pudding full of Plums' and as to the style:

It is a fluid of the galacteous, or milky Kind; on which, as on Milk, there is a Cream, or rather Froth swimming on the Top: This being once skimmed off, the whole becomes quite clear, without any Sediment on the Bottom. A Circumstance in some measure owing to the Rapidity of its Current; by which, as in a rapid Stream, the Waves of Words pass by so quick, that it is very difficult to separate or fix distinct Ideas on any particular Body of Water; you cannot distinguish one Wave from another, and you have from the Whole, only an Idea of a River.

The culmination of this onslaught is a mock trial, with Cibber in the dock for murder of the English language. The literary court is one of Fielding's favourite devices, used again in the *Jacobite's Journal* and *Covent-Garden Journal*. It allows him to add to the weapons of ridicule adopted from the Scriblerians a parodic mode of judgement derived from his own legal training, but also harking back to the lengthy legalistic debates in Chaucer and other earlier writers. On the one hand, a court evokes an ideal of informed impartiality, of logical argument from evidence, of rules and precedents enshrining standards. This can be linked to Fielding's insistence in 'the Derivation of the Word Criticism, which is from a Greek word, implying no less than Judgment'. (The complexity and difficulty of 'right judgement' are also a cornerstone of value in *Tom Jones*.)

Although he plants these abstract standards at the back of the reader's mind, however, when Fielding takes the role of 'censor' in these literary courts—which make for highly entertaining journalism—he emphasizes not the legal objectivity of rules, but the subjectivity of opinion. The court is always rigged. The judge is always right, since he is usually Fielding himself in one or other fictional guise, and although the form is legalistic, the

procedure is all too human. Colley Cibber's case, heard in the
Champion in May 1740, is set among other ordinary cases,
giving it a 'newsworthy' context. It opens with an indictment
and a reading of the relevant statute; witnesses are called and the
prisoner speaks in his defence. But the witnesses are illiterate
and hopelessly vague. And just as Captain Vinegar is about to
find Cibber guilty, his wife Joan whispers in his ear—reminding
him that Cibber's publisher has taken out advertising in the
Champion. With a swift fudging of issues, Cibber is rapidly
acquitted of murder and found guilty on the lesser charge of
'Chance Medley'.[20]

There is no pretence in Fielding's early writings of the neutral
'review', whose purpose is to tell the reader what is currently
available and offer discriminating judgement. Furthermore,
the playful forms he invents make it plain that he expects his
readers to understand the artifice of supposed neutrality. His
literary journalism is propelled by anger and conducted through
wit. These qualities are still there in the *Covent-Garden
Journal*, which contains a splendid burlesque of Shakespearean
editing and a ridiculous series on the debating society 'the
Robinhoodians', as well as some sustained sniping at his Grub
Street antagonist John Hill. Between 1739 and 1752 however,
one can feel a shift in the grounds of discussion. As periodicals
proliferated they became more specialized and literature
achieved its own province. When Robert Dodsley began publishing periodicals in the 1740s and 1750s, for example, he hired
the poet Mark Akenside to compile, edit and proof *The
Museum: or, Literary and Historical Register*, with a fortnightly
essay surveying recently published books in English, Latin,
French and Italian, and one can see this tendency as a step
towards the greater systematizing of the arts by the Johnson
circle.

While Fielding saw no need to survey or 'inform', he did
become more specific, to the point where we find his first real
review, of Charlotte Lennox's *The Female Quixote* (1752).
Here he lays out clearly his methods of judgement in terms of
a comparison with the original, and also, interestingly, praises

[20] The *Champion*, 17 May 1740, ed. Stephen, 445.

Lennox for her emotional realism, the fact that the reader cares what happens to the heroine, that the adventures are 'less extravagant and incredible' than Cervantes, offering 'a regular Story'.[21]

Just before his death, Fielding seems to put sensibility before wit. Nowhere is this clearer than in his response to *Clarissa*, especially when one remembers his scorn for *Pamela*. In the *Jacobite's Journal*, without irony, he applauds Richardson for his originality and emotional power. 'Such Simplicity, such Manners, such deep penetration into Nature, such Power to raise and alarm the Passions.'[22]

That this reflects his real opinions can be seen from comparing it to his private letter to Richardson, on publication of the novel's fifth volume. This describes his switchback emotional response: 'Here my Heart begins its narrative', he writes, and goes on to employ a whole vocabulary of sensation: shock, terror, compassion, thunderstruck admiration, astonishment. He finds Clarissa's letter to Lovelace 'beyond anything that I have ever read. God forbid that the Man who reads this with dry Eyes should be alone with my daughter when she hath no assistance within Call . . . this scene I have heard hath been often objected to. It is well for the Critick that my Heart is now writing and not my Head.'[23]

In fact Fielding often writes with the heart, rather than the head, and his very self-contradictoriness and willingness to admit a variety of responses illuminate the importance of mixed values in literary journalism. His combination of aggression and principle, commercial cynicism and literary idealism, his impassioned antipathies yet generous championing of what he deemed good, could be seen to be leading characteristics of literary journalism. They may not always be responsible characteristics, but they infuse life and danger into literary debate and they are needed just as much in research and teaching as in the critical press. It is surely right that people should move back and forth

[21] *Covent-Garden Journal*, no. 24, 24 Mar. 1752, 159–60.
[22] *The Jacobite's Journal and Related Writings (1745–60)*, ed. W. B. Coley (Oxford, 1967), no. 5, 2 Jan. 1748, 119.
[23] Henry Fielding to Samuel Richardson, 15 Oct. 1748, quoted Battestin, *Fielding*, 442–3.

across the boundaries, from the academic to the journalist, from the writing of novels, poetry, biography, history or travel, to the pages of the journal and the newspaper.

If anything, the 'conversational' voice of today's reviews is closer to Fielding's century than to the long, educative essay-reviews of the nineteenth, as if we have somehow sloughed off the legacy of the nineteenth century in this respect—its richness of information, its earnestness and judicious weighing. Fielding can seem almost postmodern in his allusive self-referentiality, almost a Canary-Wharfer in his raised-eyebrow intimacy with the literary world, an intimacy he expects his readers to share. And while modern literary editors may not feel the same anxiety about mass values or see it as their role to guide and direct, they still feel these issues are important. 'It is also our policy to do our best to identify the books that matter most,' wrote Karl Miller of the young *London Review of Books*, 'conscious that we can't hope to succeed in every instance—and to devote ourselves at length to the questions raised by those books.'[24] Yet the question of who decides what 'matters most' is still often dodged.

Other echoes are the ever-precarious nature of new ventures (Karl Miller also noted that 'in the early days we were forever rumoured to be going out of business'[25]) and the structure and status of the 'profession'. Reviewing has always been a way for would-be writers to make their name known. In 1734 the young Samuel Johnson was writing (in vain) to Edward Cave at the *Gentleman's Magazine*, offering to write a regular column, with short literary essays and critical remarks on authors or forgotten works that he felt needed revival. And since its early days, literary journalism has also offered a financial lifeline while authors write their 'real' book. Even Virginia Woolf totted up her earnings, setting British against American journals, which paid better. There are still plenty of 'drudges of the pen', as Johnson called them, who look no further than the week's deadline, but there are also reviewers who agonize in search of the perfect phrase, the apposite verb. This kind of literary jour-nalist is ambitious, concerned not only with responsibility to the

---

[24] The *London Review of Books; Anthology I*, ed. Karl Miller (London, 1981), p. ix.
[25] Ibid. p. vii.

book under review but with the notion of the review as in itself literary, a performance that must please.

We should hang on to the commitment of Fielding, even if our principles are different and our practice is tamer. Responsible literary journalism can offer a space like no other, a place to fly, a chance to live dangerously in print. And for the past two and a half centuries, since Fielding was scribbling the *Champion*, the best reviewers have put energy, integrity and commitment into this passing public form. But book reviews have always been ephemeral. We may keep the *TLS* and *LRB*, meaning to read the longer pieces, but the daily and Sunday papers are scanned and binned. As a wry consolation, literary journalists might remember this passage from Virginia Woolf's diary, in which she envisages a rather different literary court to Fielding's:

When I read reviews I crush the columns together to get at one or two sentences; is it a good book or a bad? And then I discount those 2 sentences according to what I know of the book & the reviewer. But when I write a review I write every sentence as if it was going to be tried before 3 Chief Justices: I can't believe that I am crushed together & discounted.[26]

And the best reviewers are not.

---

[26] 18 Feb. 1922. *The Diary of Virginia Woolf*, ed. Anne Olivier Bell and Andrew McNeillie (5 vols.; London, 1975–80), ii. 69.

2

Coleridge and the Uses of Journalism

Zachary Leader

Coleridge had strong political as well as pecuniary motives for writing for newspapers and periodicals but the most important effect journalism had on him was psychological: it was good for his creative health.[1] This effect was most pronounced in the period of his deepest engagement with the editor and polemicist Daniel Stuart and the newspaper he had recently purchased, the *Morning Post*, from the years 1797 to 1803. These were the years in which the paper moved gradually from opposition to Pitt and the war against France, to a more independent, eventually pro-war stance.[2] Coleridge and Stuart were introduced in November 1797 by James Mackintosh, Stuart's brother-in-law, and Coleridge immediately agreed to supply Stuart with 'verses or political essays'[3] for a fee of a guinea a week; in mid-1803 Stuart sold the *Morning Post* and, after a period in Malta,

[1] For a statement of Coleridge's early faith in the democratic potential of political journalism see the 'Prospectus' to the *Watchman* (1796), ed. Lewis Patton (London, 1970), 4: 'A PEOPLE ARE FREE IN PROPORTION AS THEY FORM THEIR OWN OPINIONS. In the strictest sense of the word KNOWLEDGE IS POWER. . . . In the present perilous state of our Constitution the Friends of Freedom, of Reason, and of Human Nature, must feel it their duty by every means in their power to supply or circulate political information.' The political motives for Coleridge's several self-publishing ventures in journalism have been related to his attempts to create what he called a 'Clerisy', a class of 'the learned of all denominations; the sages and professors of . . . all the so-called liberal arts and sciences'. (*On the Constitution of Church and State*, ed. John Colmer (London, 1976), 46.) See Jon P. Klancher, *The Making of English Reading Audiences, 1790–1832* (Madison, Wis., 1987), 150–70.

[2] After Stuart sold the paper in 1803, it became too right-wing or pro-government even for Coleridge, already earning its later title, from *Punch*, as 'The Fawning Times'. See Samuel Taylor Coleridge, *Essays on His Times*, ed. David V. Erdman (3 vols.; London, 1978), i, p. cxviii.

[3] Samuel Taylor Coleridge to Josiah Wedgwood, 27 Dec. 1797, in *The Collected Letters of Samuel Taylor Coleridge*, ed. Earl L. Griggs (6 vols.; Oxford, 1956–71), i. 360; henceforth cited as *CL*, ed. Griggs.

Coleridge joined him on the *Courier*, an evening paper Stuart had acquired control of in 1799. During the *Morning Post* years, the short period in which most of his best poetry was written, Coleridge also supplied Stuart with non-political essays, profiles, leading paragraphs, even parliamentary reports.

Though Coleridge wrote for newspapers throughout his life, he experienced three other comparably intense periods of journalistic activity: in 1796, while at work on the *Watchman*, the first of two abortive attempts to produce a periodical of his own, one that would 'supply at once the places of a review, newspaper, and annual register'[4] (it lasted ten issues); in 1809–10, while at work on the *Friend*, the second such attempt (it lasted twenty-seven issues);[5] and in 1811–12, while serving a two-year stint as auxiliary or deputy editor of the *Courier* under Thomas George Street, the paper's managing editor and 'effectual ruler'.[6] Coleridge wrote ninety-seven pieces for the *Courier* during the years 1811–12—and could easily have written more had Street allowed him—but as a poet, rather than the author of poetical prose passages, he had pretty much dried up. The Oxford *Poetical Works*, edited by E. H. Coleridge, lists only seven poems for these years, filling a total of four pages. By 1811 the Muse had long deserted Coleridge: in 1809–10, while at work on the *Friend*, he produced only four poems; in 1808 only one; in 1807 two.[7] So for any consideration of the tension between journalism, with its direct or explicit editorial and commercial constraints, and poetry and philosophy, conceived of (at least by Coleridge) as above or apart from such constraints, the early period, the *Morning Post* period of 1797 to 1803, is what matters. How Coleridge negotiated that tension could be said to

---

[4] The phrase is from Erdman's Introduction to Coleridge's *Essays on His Times*, i.

[5] The contents of the *Friend* were anything but journalistic. According to an anonymous writer in the Oct. 1811 issue of the *Eclectic Review*, 'though coming with some of the exterior marks of a newspaper, [it] was yet to derive nearly as little aid from the stimulant facts and questions of the day, as if it had been a commentary on Aristotle or Plato' (quoted in John Colmer, *Coleridge: Critic of Society* (Oxford, 1959), 90).

[6] The phrase is from Erdman's Introduction to *Essays on His Times*, i, p. cxxviii.

[7] See *The Complete Poetical Works of Samuel Taylor Coleridge*, ed. E. H. Coleridge (2 vols.; Oxford, 1912). These figures will doubtless be upwardly revised by J. C. C. Mays in the forthcoming Bollingen edn. of the poems—but not substantially.

reflect upon comparable tensions experienced by contemporary academics within literary studies—as when balancing scholarly and journalistic commissions. If the attitudes Coleridge expressed towards journalism live on, they do so in the academy, not just because today it is the academy which shelters many poets and virtually all philosophers, but because academic writing in general—'scholarship'—is meant to be pure and disinterested, above mere market considerations, including those of readability or accessibility, as also above such contingencies as tight deadlines or word limits.

Coleridge's reputation for unfulfilled promise and procrastination was established early. 'I became a proverb to the University for Idleness', he writes of his Cambridge days, '—the time, which I should have bestowed on the academic studies, I employed in dreaming schemes.'[8] The problem, he continues, in the 'Prospectus' of the *Friend*, was 'overactivity of thought, modified by a constitutional Indolence, which made it more pleasant to me to continue acquiring, than to reduce what I had acquired to a regular form'.[9] In 1804, well into a period of deepest blockage and debility, this diagnosis remains unchanged. As Coleridge says in a Notebook entry, his mind is jammed with 'large Stores of . . . unwrought materials; scarcely a day passes but something new in fact or in illustration . . . rises up in me, like Herbs or Flowers in a Garden in early Spring; but the combining Power, the power to do, the manly effective *Will*, that is dead or slumbers most diseasedly'.[10] It is not so much that this power is *lacking*, he writes to Sir George Beaumont, also in 1804, as that he is 'weak—apt to faint away inwardly, self-deserted and bereft of the confidence of my own powers'.[11]

Among the several reasons Coleridge adduces for this lack of confidence, most prominent is his sense of the poet's elevated

---

[8] Samuel Taylor Coleridge to Thomas Poole, 31 Mar. 1800, in *CL*, ed. Griggs, i. 329.

[9] See the 1809 'Prospectus' to Samuel Taylor Coleridge, *The Friend*, ed. Barbara E. Rooke (2 vols.; London, 1969), ii. 16.

[10] Entry of 10 May 1804, in *The Notebooks of Samuel Taylor Coleridge*, ed. Kathleen Coburn (3 vols.; Princeton, 1957–73), iii. 2086.

[11] Samuel Taylor Coleridge to Sir George Beaumont, 1 Feb. 1804, in *CL*, ed. Griggs, ii. 1054.

stature. 'I have too clearly before me the idea of the poet's genius to deem myself any other than a very humble poet.'[12] This genius depends importantly on the poet's originality. It is not enough for Coleridge that Wordsworth 'stands nearest of all modern writers to Shakespeare and Milton'. He has to do so 'in a kind perfectly unborrowed and his own'.[13] By the end of 1802, Coleridge reveals in a letter to Southey, his own relative inadequacy is clear: 'all my poetic Genius, if ever I really possessed any *Genius*, and it was not rather a more general *aptitude* of Talent, and quickness in Imitation / is gone'.[14] That Coleridge's view of philosophy was comparably elevated is clear from the sorry history of the 'Opus Maximum', a vast philosophical synthesis first mentioned in 1796, and publicly advertised in 1814, and again in 1817. In 1814 Coleridge wrote a letter claiming that he was in the process of printing the work in Bristol. But he did not get down to writing any of it until 1816. The aim of this work could not have been more ambitious: to reconcile the truths of nature, mind, and Christianity; that is, of the organic or dynamic philosophy of Wordsworth and Kant and the religious orthodoxy that would condemn such philosophy as 'pantheist'. Understandably, the work was never completed, its products dispersed in a variety of lesser publications and unfinished projects, though several hundred pages exist in manuscript.

Journalism was always strictly segregated in Coleridge's mind from these more elevated pursuits, and often treated as inimical to them. Coleridge's powers as a journalist were clear early on, and on several occasions he received offers of full-time employment as a writer and editor. When James Perry offered him co-editorship of the Foxite *Morning Chronicle* in 1796, 'evidently impressed by his *Watchman* journalism',[15] Coleridge accepted with extravagant misgivings: 'Farewell Philosophy! Farewell, the Muse! Farewell, my literary Fame!' Need alone, he declared

[12] Samuel Taylor Coleridge to Thomas Curnick, 9 Apr. 1814, in *CL*, ed. Griggs, iii. 914.
[13] Samuel Taylor Coleridge, *Biographia Literaria*, ed. James Engell and W. Jackson Bate (London, 1983), ii. 151; henceforth cited as *BL*, ed. Engell and Bate.
[14] Samuel Taylor Coleridge to Robert Southey, 29 July 1802, in *CL*, ed. Griggs, ii. 831.
[15] Richard Holmes, *Coleridge: Early Visions* (London, 1989), 121.

to Thomas Poole, 'those two Giants, yclept BREAD & CHEESE',[16] induced acceptance. Earlier, in the course of canvassing for subscribers to the *Watchman*, he confesses (endearingly, to a potential customer) to being 'far from convinced that a Christian is permitted to read either newspapers or any other works of merely political and temporary interest'.[17] 'The *Press as a Trade*', Coleridge declares in 1798, promises neither 'fame to myself or permanent good to society—but only to gain that bread which might empower me to do both the one and the other on my vacant days'.[18] This is because, as he writes in chapter 11 of the *Biographia*, 'truly *genial*' writing (that is, writing instinct with genius) is invariably the product of inspiration or unforced labour, of 'three hours of leisure unannoyed by any alien anxiety'. Full-time journalists have no such leisure, nor do '*mere* literary men', the sort for whom writing is a profession. Coleridge's 'affectionate exhortation to the youthful literati' in the *Biographia*, an exhortation 'grounded on my own experience', is short and succinct: 'the beginning, middle, and end converge to one charge: never pursue literature to a trade'.[19]

Which is to say: though Coleridge may, indeed, have been among our first 'modern journalists' or 'professional intellectuals' or 'men of letters', as Marilyn Butler has rightly suggested, this was hardly a source of pride, let alone an ambition.[20] *Not* working for the press was a source of pride, as when Wordsworth, Coleridge's model in these matters, reminds Stuart, in a letter of 17 May 1838, 'that the last thing that could have found its way into my thoughts would have been to enter into an engagement to write for any newspaper'.[21] (Wordsworth had secured his own finances early, thanks in large measure to a legacy of £900.) Newspaper work had its place for Coleridge,

---

[16] Samuel Taylor Coleridge to Thomas Poole, 4 July 1796, in *CL*, ed. Griggs, i. 227. The job, in fact, never materialized.

[17] *BL*, ed. Engell and Bate, i. 183.

[18] Samuel Taylor Coleridge to John Prior Estlin, 16 Jan. 1798, in *CL*, ed. Griggs, i. 372.

[19] *BL*, ed. Engell and Bate, i. 223.

[20] Marilyn Butler, *Romantics, Rebels and Reactionaries: English Literature and its Background, 1760–1830* (Oxford, 1981), 69–71.

[21] William Wordsworth to Daniel Stuart, 17 May 1838, in *The Letters of William and Dorothy Wordsworth: The Later Years, Part 3. 1835–1839*, ed. Ernest de Selincourt, rev. edn. Alan G. Hill (Oxford, 1982), 590.

but that place was secondary, and tolerable because secondary; 'letters', mere literary odd-jobbery, was mostly not. When Byron mocked Coleridge's friend William Sotheby in *Beppo* (1817) for being 'an author that's *all author*' (that is, a 'professional'), Coleridge would have concurred.[22] In 1800, while at work on a wearying translation of Schiller's *Wallenstein*, Coleridge declares in a letter to Poole that 'there are but two good ways of writing, one for immediate, & wide impression, tho' transitory—the other for permanence— / Newspapers the first—the best one can do is the second—that middle class of translating Books &c is neither the one or the other—When I have settled myself *clear*, I shall write nothing for money but the newspaper.'[23]

Newspaper work, though, is hard to regulate. Coleridge's resolution to avoid a 'middle class' of writing (translating, compiling anthologies, writing biographies, travel books, 'sweating plays so middling, bad were better', to quote Byron again on Sotheby), comes at the end of a four-month stint on full salary at the *Morning Post*, one in which Coleridge describes himself as 'employed from I-rise to I-set—i.e. from 9 in the morning to 12 at night—a pure Scribbler'.[24] Stuart, determined that he stay on in London, then offers Coleridge half shares in the *Morning Post* and the *Courier*, his evening paper, an offer worth £2,000 a year (according to Coleridge).[25] To accept, though, Coleridge tells Poole, would require him to 'devote myself with him to them'— that is, to become 'all author'. Alternatively, 'without any straining', Coleridge claims, he could, if he wanted, earn 500 guineas a year as a freelance (more than twice the figure William St. Clair calculates, on the basis of Treasury tax returns for *c.*1800–15, as having been needed to support a London gentleman with a small household and a servant); but he'd have to 'give up poetry—i.e. original poetry'. The proper balance,

---

[22] 'Beppo', line 593, in the Oxford Authors *Byron*, ed. Jerome J. McGann (Oxford and New York, 1986), 335.

[23] Samuel Taylor Coleridge to Thomas Poole, 31 Mar. 1800, in *CL*, ed. Griggs, i. 329.

[24] Samuel Taylor Coleridge to Robert Southey, 24 Dec. 1799, in *CL*, ed. Griggs, i. 552.

[25] Erdman, in the Introduction to *Essays on His Times*, i, p. xcvi, thinks Coleridge 'was offered *shares* worth £2,000. But their annual yield would be only a fraction of that.'

Coleridge concludes, is 'three half Evenings in the week', which would earn him £250 per year; anything more would be 'a real evil'.[26]

The dangers of journalism are signalled by metaphors of addiction. As Coleridge warns in the *Biographia*: 'the *necessity* of acquiring [money and reputation] will in all works of genius convert the stimulus into a *narcotic*', a phrase that recalls Coleridge's biographer, Richard Holmes, himself at one time a prolific literary journalist, on 'the oblivion of newspaper work'.[27] Even when public feeling rather than personal gain turns him to the newspapers, danger lurks. Early on in his career as a journalist, in July 1796, 'local & temporary politics' are said to 'narrow the Understanding and . . . *acidulate* the Heart'.[28] Four years later he cannot do without them. 'The dedication of much hope and fear to subjects which are perhaps disproportionate to our faculties and powers, is a disease,' he writes to Thomas Wedgwood, 'but I have had this disease so long . . . that I know not how to get rid of it. Life were so flat a thing without Enthusiasm—that if for a moment it leave, I have a sort of stomach-sensation attached to all my Thoughts, like those which succeed to the pleasurable operation of a dose of Opium.'[29] The 'acidulating' effect comes now not from 'Enthusiasm' itself (proleptically, journalism, or writing on 'local and temporary politics') but from the attempt to withdraw from it; which makes journalism like opium. Or alcohol, as a comparably revealing letter to Josiah Wedgwood of the same period shows. 'We Newspaper scribes are true Galley-Slaves', Coleridge complains, after promising to bid London adieu 'for ever' (London being to the provinces for Coleridge what journalism was to the 'genial'—though to others, such as De Quincey, journalism was everywhere),

---

[26] The Coleridge quotations come from a letter to Thomas Poole, 21 Mar. 1800, in *CL*, ed. Griggs, i. 582. William St. Clair's calculation is quoted in Holmes, *Early Visions*, 176, from an unpublished lecture given at the Royal Institution, London, in 1988.

[27] *BL*, ed. Engell and Bate, i. 224. For Holmes's quote see *Early Visions*, 312.

[28] Samuel Taylor Coleridge to Thomas Poole, 4 July 1796, in *CL*, ed. Griggs, i. 227.

[29] Samuel Taylor Coleridge to Thomas Wedgwood, 2 Jan. 1800, in *CL*, ed. Griggs, i. 558.

yet it is not unflattering to a man's Vanity to reflect that what he writes at 12 at night will before 12 hours is over have perhaps 5 or 6000 Readers! To trace a happy phrase, good image, or new argument running thro' the Town, & sliding into all the papers! Few wine merchants can boast of creating more sensation.[30]

Here and elsewhere in Coleridge's correspondence, on the rare occasions when he writes approvingly of journalism he does so exuberantly, as if giddy, breathless, tipsy.

These suggestions of the intoxicating or narcotic properties of journalism call to mind Thomas De Quincey, a fellow addict in several senses. De Quincey's attitudes to authorship were quite different from those of Coleridge. To begin with, he frankly accepted writing as a trade, just as he frankly accepted his opium-eating as an addiction. He made little distinction in his own career between journalistic and more elevated forms, and as a consequence suffered less acutely from inhibiting notions of originality, autonomy, or perfectibility. Hence the figural or symbolic character of his accounts of local contingencies and constraints in the publishing process, as in the following passage from the 'Prefatory Notice' to the revised or 1856 edition of the *Confessions*, an apology for inevitable error:

Endless are the openings for such kinds of mistake—that is, of mistakes not fully seen *as* such. But even in a case of unequivocal mistake, seen and acknowledged, yet when it is open to remedy only through a sudden and energetic act, then or never,—the press being for twenty minutes, suppose, free to receive an alteration, but beyond that time closed and sealed inexorably: such being supposed the circumstances, the humane reader will allow for the infirmity which ever wilfully and consciously surrenders itself to the error, acquiescing in it deliberately, rather than face the cruel exertion of correcting it most elaborately at a moment of sickening misery, and with the prevision that the main correction must draw after it half-a-dozen others for the sake of decent consistency.[31]

De Quincey's sense of defeat and delimited authority in this passage derives, on the surface at least, from local contingencies

---

[30] Samuel Taylor Coleridge to Josiah Wedgwood, 4 Feb. 1800, in *CL*, ed. Griggs, i. 569.

[31] Thomas De Quincey, *Confessions of an English Opium Eater*, ed. Alethea Hayter (Harmondsworth, 1971), 138.

(such as 'the press being for twenty minutes, suppose, free to receive an alteration', or the author being reduced by need and overwork to a state of 'sickening misery'), contingencies familiar to journalists and other 'professional' writers. But the more general impression his words give rise to, one confirmed elsewhere in the 'Prefatory Notice',[32] is of inevitable imperfection. De Quincey cannot be bothered to exert himself here, at least in part, because he thinks the perfect text an illusion, like the illusion of authorial control or originality.

This impression is reinforced by a second account of supposedly local difficulties, again concerning the fate of the 1856 revision of *Confessions*, this time from a letter:

> I am much afraid—that in consequence of the very imperfect means for communicating with the Press which I now possess or ever *have* possessed (being at all times reduced to the single resource of *writing*—which, to evade misinterpretation and constant ambiguity, requires a redundancy of words—and, after all that is done on *my* part, requires in addition a *Reader* that is not only singularly attentive, but also has a surplus stock of *leisure time* [)]—*Premising* all this, I am and *have* been at all stages of this nominal reprint (but virtually *rifacimento*) of the Confession, in terror of mutual misunderstandings—consequetly [sic] of each party unintentionally thwarting or embarrassing the other by movements at *cross purposes*.[33]

On the surface, De Quincey is talking here about potential problems with the actual production of his book; but his subject is also, implicitly, reception in general, writing *per se*, presumably including the most refined or uncommercial writing. The Press's '*Reader*' may not understand De Quincey's instructions because De Quincey is 'reduced to the single resource of *writing*' (as opposed, in the local context, to communicating in person); moreover, this '*Reader*' may well be too busy to be 'singularly attentive'. In other words, like any writer, De Quincey is no more able to control reader response than he is the work's final

---

[32] De Quincey describes his revisions as 'chronic'; the 'misery' he speaks of is called 'a nervous malady, of very peculiar character, which has attacked me for the last eleven years'. Elsewhere he speaks of this misery as 'the wearing seige of an abiding sickness' (see *Confessions*, ed. Hayter, 137–8). It should also be noted that De Quincey is speaking here of the publication of *Confessions* as a book, not of journalistic or serial publication.

[33] Letter of 18 Sept. 1856 quoted in Edmund Baxter, *De Quincey's Art of Autobiography* (Edinburgh, 1990), 17.

or printed form. As the phrase 'reduced to the single resource of *writing*' suggests, the complaints of journalists and other 'professional' writers are merely intensifications of a more general writing condition.

Behind such attitudes to writing lie radical doubts about the possibility of *any* sort of control or agency in language and human behaviour. These doubts Coleridge himself shared—witness the many instances of inexplicable, unreliable, uncontrolled, and blocked utterance in his writing, or of motiveless crimes and correspondingly inexplicable redemptions. But at the same time Coleridge never relinquished a vision of the self as independent and autonomous, as did De Quincey. The *Biographia Literaria* is as flawed or 'immethodical' as the *Confessions*, as subject to distracting stops and starts, lost or unfollowed arguments, excuses, deferrals, digressions, alien voices. Yet its aim, unlike the *Confessions*, is to defend the freedom, unity and independence of the self (most immediately against David Hartley and other mechanistic philosophers). The doubts it registers about this aim are, as one critic argues, simultaneously doubts 'that in the course of his literary life [Coleridge] has become a mere man of letters'[34]—that is, a writer without integrity (in several senses) or autonomy. To collapse the distinction between journalism and other, more elevated forms of writing implies for Coleridge a collapse of personal identity, and with it the possibility of true or 'genial' writing. Thus, the first function or use of the category 'journalism' for Coleridge, a negative function to be sure, is to preserve the possibility of another and higher category of writing. This function lives on in contemporary literary scholarship, even, ironically, when such scholarship views writing as does De Quincey. To many a theoretically inclined academic, for example, the elevated category 'literature' is an illusion; yet saying so in a scholarly fashion requires the utmost elevation of manner, effectively excluding non-academic readers. The exclusion fosters precisely the distinctions 'advanced' scholarship claims to wish to efface.

A second function of the category 'journalism' is to forestall inhibiting self-criticism. Coleridge mostly thought of what he

[34] Jerome Christensen, *Coleridge's Blessed Machine of Language* (Ithaca, NY, 1981), 21.

published in newspapers and periodicals as provisional, put before the public out of financial need rather than any considered sense of achievement or completion. 'I dedicate three days in the week to the Morning Post,' he tells Thomas Wedgwood in a letter of 20 October 1802,

and shall hereafter write for the far greater part such things as will be of as permanent Interest as any thing I can hope to write. . . . The Poetry, which I have sent, has been merely the emptying out of my Desk. The Epigrams are wretched indeed; but they answered Stuart's purpose better than better things— /. I ought not to have given any signature to them whatsoever / I never dreamt of acknowledging either them or the Ode to the Rain.[35]

Earlier, in a letter of 26 August 1802 to Sotheby, he announces that the 'greater number' of the occasional verses to be sent to the *Morning Post* under the signature Εστησε (i.e. 'STC') 'will be such as were never meant for anything else but the peritura charta [*perishable or evanescent writings*] of the M. Post'.[36] Such poems were safe from criticism because they were not really poems, not appearing in a book, or a book with Coleridge's name on it.

A number of the 700 poems J. C. C. Mays will print in his forthcoming Bollingen edition of Coleridge's collected verse, the projected standard or variorum edition, fit this category. Yet even poems Coleridge put his name to and printed in books he had trouble calling poems. Besides 'thoughts punctuated by rhymes' and 'that which affects not to be poetry', Coleridge's list of substitutes for 'poem' includes 'effusions, vision, epistles, fragments, improvisation, translation, imitation, "a Desultory poem," and "a poem it ought to be." '[37] When Mays refers, in an

[35] Samuel Taylor Coleridge to Thomas Wedgwood, 20 Oct. 1802, in *CL*, ed. Griggs, ii. 876.

[36] Samuel Taylor Coleridge to William Sotheby, 26 Aug. 1802, in *CL*, ed. Griggs, ii. 857. Coleridge used the signature for essays and articles as well as poems. As he explains in a later letter to Sotheby, 10 Sept. 1802, *CL*, ii. 867: 'Εστησε signifies— *He hath stood*—which in these times of apostasy from the principles of Freedom, or of Religion in this country, & from both by the same persons in France, is no unmeaning Signature, if subscribed with humility, & in the remembrance of, Let him that stands take heed lest he fall.' Alan Liu, in *Wordsworth: The Sense of History* (Stanford, Calif., 1989), 422, asks 'what did it mean for *He hath stood* to take his stand? In essence, it meant that he slipped, slid, and desperately reversed himself in a balancing act that at last created, at great cost, a new stand.'

[37] Edward Kessler, *Coleridge's Metaphors of Being* (Princeton, 1979), 5.

essay on the principles underlying the Bollingen edition, to 'the few poems Coleridge wrote which aspire purely to literature', he's referring to a very few poems indeed.[38] Yet by exempting periodical and newspaper publication from the realm of the truly genial—by insisting on the second-class status of newspaper verse—he was at least able to produce something. Nor were the verses he printed in such venues always negligible. In the autumn of 1802, in what has been called the 'Indian summer'[39] of Coleridge's poetic creativity, he produced a series of poems for the *Morning Post*, including 'Dejection: An Ode', 'The Picture, or, the Lover's Resolution', 'The Day Dream', 'Hymn Before Sunrise in the Vale of Chamouni', 'The Keepsake' and, *pace* the August 1802 letter to Sotheby, the 'Ode to the Rain', which artfully distance themselves from an earlier, Wordsworthian sense of nature as anchor, guide, guardian. In addition, Coleridge also published, between 1798 and 1800, a handful of important political poems in the *Morning Post*, including 'France: An Ode' (originally titled 'The Recantation, an Ode'), 'The Raven', 'Fire, Famine and Slaughter', 'Recantation', 'The British Stripling's War-song', 'The Devil's Thoughts' (with Southey), and 'Tallyrand to Lord Grenville'.[40] The many and various virtues of this newspaper poetry call to mind Thomas McFarland's account of the relation of the *Biographia* to the 'Opus Maximum', an account applicable to Coleridge's creative life in general: 'by displacing the hope of classical status onto the conception of *magnum opus*, [Coleridge] was enabled to

---

[38] May's comment, from 'Reflections on Having Edited Coleridge's Poems', in Robert Brinkley and Keith Hanley, eds., *Romantic Revisions* (Cambridge, 1992), 149, recalls Coleridge on Southey, who has 'attempted almost every species of [poetical] composition . . . and if we except the highest lyric (in which how few, how very few even of the greatest minds have been fortunate), he has attempted every species successfully' (*BL*, ed. Engell and Bate, 191).

[39] Norman Fruman, *Coleridge: The Damaged Archangel* (London, 1972), 260.

[40] In addition to the poems listed one should mention the 'Ode to the Departing Year', published on 31 Dec. 1796 in the *Cambridge Intelligencer*. These poems of what Carl R. Woodring, in *Politics in the Poetry of Coleridge* (Madison, Wis., 1961), 161, calls 'pay, play, and party', are of more substance, if not always more clarity, than the earlier 'Sonnets (as it is the fashion to call them) . . . to eminent Contemporaries', published in Dec. 1794 and Jan. 1795 in the *Morning Chronicle*. Stuart was justly proud of the poetry printed in the *Morning Post*; he was not *just* puffing in 1798 when he printed an advertisement requesting 'the attention of the *Literati* to this department of our Paper'. Up to 1800, his principal poetical contributors, in addition to Coleridge, were Robert Southey and Mary Robinson, and he still had hopes of Wordsworth as a contributor.

produce casual and *ad hoc* writing that . . . is nevertheless
among the treasures of our language'; the *Biographia*'s 'provisional nature' or 'near-hackwork status . . . does not block the
revelation of Coleridge's insights but is in fact the necessary
condition under which they can be expressed'.[41]

Coleridge's prose contributions to the *Morning Post* involve
more straightforward uses. To begin with, there was the effect
journalism had on his style. To James Perry, editor of the rival
Chronicle, Coleridge's newspaper work was 'poetry in prose'.[42]
So too for Stuart:

To write the leading paragraph of a newspaper I would prefer him to
Mackintosh, Burke, or any man I ever heard of. His observations not
only were confirmed by good sense, but displayed extensive knowledge, deep thought and well-grounded foresight: they were so brilliantly ornamented, so classically delightful. They were the writings of
a Scholar, a Gentleman and a Statesman, without personal sarcasm or
illiberality of any kind. But when Coleridge wrote in his study without
being pressed, he wandered and lost himself.[43]

Coleridge was well aware of this opinion. As he reports in the
Biographia, his extended prose writings 'have been charged with
a disproportionate demand on the attention; with an excess of
refinement in the mode of arriving at truths; with beating the
ground for that which might have been run down by the eye;
with the length and laborious construction of my periods; in
short with obscurity and the love of paradox'.[44] In a letter of
9 October 1809, he himself concurs. At least in respect to The
Friend, 'there is too often an *entortillage* in the sentences & even
the thoughts, which nothing can justify; and, always almost, a
stately piling up of *Story* on *Story* in one architectural period,
which is not suited to a periodical Essay or to Essays at all'.[45]

[41] Thomas McFarland, *Romanticism and the Forms of Ruin* (Princeton, 1981),
49, 51.
[42] Quoted in Wilfred Hindle, *The Morning Post, 1772–1937* (London, 1937),
100.
[43] Quoted in *Essays in His Times*, ed. Erdman, i, p. lxvii.
[44] See *BL*, ed. Engell and Bate, i. 220. See also Colmer, *Coleridge: Critic of
Society*, 57: 'A comparison of the essays [in the *Morning Post*] with passages in
letters to friends exhibits the unexpected manner in which Coleridge, applying a
rigorous form of self-control, disciplined his mind to the task of commenting
publicly on public affairs.'
[45] Samuel Taylor Coleridge to Thomas Poole, 9 Oct. 1809, in *CL*, ed. Griggs, iii.
234.

Criticisms like these apply also to Coleridge's poetry, which he himself thinks of as weighed down by 'abstruse research' (a phrase from 'Dejection'), so that what little he produces seems 'crowded and sweats beneath a heavy burden of Ideas and Imagery'.[46] Whenever he sat down to write poetry, Coleridge complained in 1802, in language that recalls the *Biographia* passage on prose, he 'beat up Game of far other kind—instead of a covey of poetic Partridges with whirring wings of music . . . up came a Metaphysical Bustard, urging its slow, heavy, laborious, earth-skimming flight'.[47] Writing to deadline curbed bustard-like tendencies, and the most successful of Coleridge's *Morning Post* articles, such as the profiles of John Hatfield, the 'Keswick Imposter' (in which Coleridge assumes the persona of investigative reporter), or of Pitt (a 3,000-word piece, composed in a single day, 19 March 1800, while he was also translating fifty lines of *Wallenstein* into blank verse), proceed with confident dispatch. 'I am happy you begin to feel your power', comments Poole in late March 1800, contrasting Coleridge's present state with an habitual 'prostration in regard to Wordsworth' (a view Lamb and Wedgwood seem to have shared). Coleridge begs to differ (it is only later that he questions Wordsworth's 'sole divinity', returning to London at the end of 1801 'a new Polytheist, meeting Lords many, & Gods many'): 'If I were to live in London another half year,' he replies, 'I should be dried up wholly.' The true writer *'must* have silence and a *retired study'.*[48]

The 'Pitt' profile, often singled out for praise by modern critics,[49] implicitly plays out this argument about the sort of writing life Coleridge should lead. Pitt is attacked for unfeeling detachment and abstraction. Famously, 'he was cast, rather than

---

[46] Samuel Taylor Coleridge to Robert Southey, 11 Dec. 1794, in *CL*, ed. Griggs, iii. 137.

[47] Samuel Taylor Coleridge to William Sotheby, 19 July 1802, in *CL*, ed. Griggs, ii. 814.

[48] Poole's remark is quoted from Coleridge's reply of 31 Mar. 1800, in *CL*, ed. Griggs, ii. 584. For the concurring views of Lamb and Wedgwood see Holmes, *Early Visions*, 260. Coleridge's remark about being 'a new Polytheist' comes in a letter to William Godwin, 19 Nov. 1801, in *CL*, ed. Griggs, ii. 775.

[49] John Colmer calls it Coleridge's 'greatest single triumph in journalism', in *Coleridge: Critic of Society*, 62. Erdman calls it 'more than usually stately and judicious', in the Introduction to *Essays on His Times*, i, p. xcvi. Holmes calls it a 'masterpiece' in *Early Visions*, 263.

grew'[50] (just the sort of sentence Coleridge's more 'genial' prose, with its uniform complexity, could do with); which is to say, 'he was always full-grown: he had neither the promise nor the awkwardness of a growing intellect' (p. 220). A little 'revelry and debauchery' at university would have done him good: 'they would have given him a closer communion with realities, they would have induced a greater presentness to present objects' (p. 220), a phrase, from Coleridge's viewpoint, both journalistic, in its simplicity or straightforwardness, and elevated, in its abstraction. Pitt is a man whose 'sincerity had no living root of affection', whose heart was 'solitary', whose imagination 'unpopulous' (pp. 220–1). Hence the eerily uninstanced character of his discourse. 'Press him to specify an individual fact of advantage to be derived from a war, and he answers, security! Call upon him to particularize a crime, and he exclaims Jacobinism! Abstractions defined by abstractions! Generalities defined by generalities!' (p. 223). Pitt's case for national prosperity is 'unenforced by one *single image*, one *single fact* of real national amelioration, of any one comfort enjoyed where it was not before enjoyed, or any one class of society become healthier, or wiser, or happier. These are things, these are realities' (p. 224).

It is tempting to relate this criticism to Coleridge's immediate circumstances: up to his elbows in the 'local and temporal'; 'a pure Scribbler' at work from nine to midnight on 'present realities'; if not quite debauched (he was working too hard) then full of high spirits, 'a continuous feast', according to Lamb, with whom he was living at the time.[51] But coldness and abstraction were only in part Pitt's problem. His fluency was also singled out for censure: 'a premature and unnatural dexterity in the combination of words, which must of necessity have diverted his attention from present objects, obscured his impressions, and deadened his genuine feelings' (p. 219). This dexterity, continues Coleridge, invoking a familiar distinction, 'though inauspicious for his real being, was favourable to his fame. He heaped

---

[50] Samuel Taylor Coleridge, 'Pitt and Bonaparte. Pitt', originally printed on 19 Mar. 1800 in the *Morning Post*, is reprinted in *Essays on His Times*, ed. Erdman, i. 219–27. The remark about being 'cast' occurs on i. 219. Subsequent references cited by page numbers in the text.

[51] Quoted in Holmes, *Early Visions*, 262.

period on period; persuaded himself and the nation that extemporaneous arrangement of sentences was eloquence, and that eloquence implied wisdom' (pp. 221–2).

The autobiographical implications here are obvious. Coleridge consistently associated journalism with 'present realities', a realm of experience imagined as wholly alien to Pitt (despite his career as a professional politician), which is part of what's wrong with Pitt. But he also saw journalism as shallow, eliciting and rewarding mere dexterity, Pitt-like fluency. Coleridge makes this point about fluency in a sentence that smacks of Wordsworth, always the anti-journalistic standard: 'The mere man of talent hears [Pitt] with admiration, the mere man of genius with contempt—the philosopher neither admires nor contemns, but listens to him with a deep and solemn interest, tracing in the effects of his eloquence the power of words and phrases, and that peculiar constitution of human affairs in their present state which so eminently favours this power' (p. 225). Coleridge wrote this sentence at full journalistic throttle, yet its air of deliberation suggests 'silence and a *retired study*'. Such sentences, like the parentheses Coleridge always defended, 'are the *drama* of reason, and present the thought growing, instead of a mere *Hortus siccus*'.[52] The profile's overall success, in contrast, depends upon virtues of a more modest or worldly character—soundness, straightforwardness. Though Pitt's weaknesses offer Coleridge an occasion for pondering his own situation, he remains 'on task', resists *entortillage*, what Hazlitt maliciously called a too 'willing homage to the Illustrious Obscure'.[53] Fluency and abstraction may exert opposing pulls in Coleridge's own life, but in Pitt's life they combine; this combination remains Coleridge's focus, for it is the key to Pitt's character. Because 'pressed'—by the journalistic format—he neither 'wanders' nor 'loses himself', as he might in non-journalistic contexts, or in his own ill-fated periodicals.

The best of Coleridge's early political pieces in the *Morning Post* transform the tensions between abstraction and fluency

[52] Samuel Taylor Coleridge to Thomas Poole, 28 Jan. 1810, in *CL*, ed. Griggs, iii. 282.

[53] William Hazlitt, from a review of *The Statesman's Manual* published in the *Examiner*, reprinted in *The Collected Works of William Hazlitt*, ed. P. P. Howe (21 vols.; London, 1930–4), vii. 116.

into an enabling partnership, as Coleridge himself came to realize in the *Biographia* and elsewhere (for instance, in a note at the end of the second issue of the *Friend*, on 8 July 1809, in which he informs subscribers of his intention to gather his journalism into a book, 'Essays from the *Morning Post*'). Though he continues reflexively to stress their ephemeral character, quoting unnamed friends (Wordsworth?) to the effect that journalism 'wasted the prime and manhood of my intellect',[54] he also attributes a larger public benefit to these pieces. 'I do derive a gratification from the knowledge, that my essays contributed to introduce the practice of placing the questions and the events of the day in a moral point of view; in giving a dignity to particular measures by tracing their policy or impolicy to permanent principles, and an interest to principles by the application of them to individual measures.'[55] These benefits seem to have been welcome and effective. Coleridge's claim, in the first edition of *Table Talk*, to have 'raised the sale of the *Morning Post* from an inconsiderable number to 7000 per day in the course of one year' is exaggerated, but he certainly increased circulation.[56] In 1795, when Stuart bought the paper (for a mere £600), it was selling only 350 copies a day. By 1803, when he sold it, its circulation had risen to 4,500. Though much of this increase derived from a shrewd programme of mergers, the paper's evolving editorial 'impartiality' also played its part. Coleridge was instrumental in establishing this impartiality, what the hostile new historicist critic, Alan Liu, calls 'a neutral and/or adversarial stance "opposed" equally to Government and Opposition'. It was a stance the public wanted; in Liu's summary: 'recantation [of Jacobin or anti-war sentiment], quite simply, sold newspapers'.[57]

Coleridgean impartiality figures also in a *Morning Post* article of 21 October 1802 entitled 'Once a Jacobin Always a Jacobin'. This article, full of careful and perceptive distinctions, sees Jacobinism, which it calls 'an error in speculative politics', as both misguided, an evil, and the expression of a larger virtue,

---

[54] *BL*, ed. Engell and Bate, i. 215.   [55] Ibid. i. 217.

[56] Erdman's Introduction to *Essays on His Times*, i, p. lxiii. The 'inconsiderable number' was 900 (see Samuel Taylor Coleridge, *Table Talk*, ed. Carl Woodring (2 vols.; Princeton, 1990), i. 160).

[57] Liu, *Wordsworth*, 413, 420.

since it appeals not only to the young and ignorant, but to 'those who, judging of men in general, from their own uncorrupted hearts, judge erroneously, and expect unwisely'.[58] To persecute radicals with the zeal of the present government (the 'particular measure' or 'question of the day' which is the article's occasion) is, in the light of this wider 'moral point of view', 'impolicy'.

Such a conclusion, it might be argued, derives from the harmonious interplay of study and newsroom (or Ivory Tower and Grub Street)—as figured in a style both deliberative and plain.[59] 'If we have been prolix,' apologizes Coleridge, after detailing an eight-point 'Jacobin's Creed', as well as the gradations between 'complete Jacobin', 'Semi-Jacobin', and Jacobin 'shadings', 'let the importance of the subject induce our readers to consider it as a venial fault. Concerning a term, which nine-tenths of the nation have been in the habit of using, either as a name of glory, or a name of reproach and abhorrence, it is not only our advantage but even our duty to have clear, correct, and definite conceptions.'[60] That this sort of carefulness ('slipperiness' to detractors like Liu[61]) elevates public discourse is more important to Coleridge than the effect individual articles have on 'particular measures' (though Coleridge is also convinced of such an effect[62]). Also important are the personal functions performed by essays like 'Once a Jacobin Always a Jacobin': not only do they excuse Coleridge's own youthful radicalism, but they put the lie to the charge 'of having dreamt away my life to no purpose'. Looking back on his career as a writer Coleridge

---

[58] Samuel Taylor Coleridge, 'Once a Jacobin Always a Jacobin', originally printed in the *Morning Post*, 21 Oct. 1802, reprinted in *Essays on His Times*, i. 373, 372.

[59] It also derives from the fact that, as Colmer puts it, Coleridge 'had not yet formulated any fully consistent set of political principles' (*Coleridge: Critic of Society*, 77).

[60] 'Once a Jacobin Always a Jacobin', in *Essays on His Times*, ed. Erdman, i. 370.

[61] See Liu, *Wordsworth*, 416–17: 'What sells was what was right: a paper should hold aloof from party connection and represent only the normative or bipartisan view—a respectable *median* view that on particular issues could jump back and forth between established party views. . . . Traditionally venal and opportunistic, the *Post* was uniquely situated to begin the task of selling out to the new public and improvising the ideology of impartiality. . . . To reform opportunism as impartiality, the slippery Stuart needed an even more philosophically slippery propagandist. He found his man in our missing link: Coleridge, the master amphibian of test-the-waters politics.'

[62] He thought his articles instrumental in rupturing the Peace at Amiens; he also thought that Napoleon had ordered his arrest (see *BL*, ed. Engell and Bate, i. 216).

concludes that, though 'I may perhaps have had sufficient reason to lament my deficiency in self-control, and the neglect of concentring my powers to the realization of some permanent work', such a charge applies 'to verse rather than prose'.[63] It is journalism, ironically, with its liberating constraints and contingencies, which allows him to make such a claim.

[63] *BL*, ed. Engell and Bate, i. 221.

3

De Quincey and the Edinburgh and Glasgow University Circles

GREVEL LINDOP

De Quincey's relationship with the world of scholarship was always a problematic one. The most brilliant and independent-minded of students, he fled from Oxford in 1808 half-way through degree examinations which had augured outstanding success, just as six years earlier, an admired and privileged senior boy, he had absconded from Manchester Grammar School. It is somehow characteristic that the world of Scottish academia, which was to prove so fruitful and supportive for his later literary career, should first be mentioned in his work only to receive a contemptuous dismissal.

In his autobiographical *Confessions of an English Opium-Eater* (1821)—subtitled 'Being an Extract from the Life of a Scholar'—De Quincey is eloquent in defending his right to the title of 'philosopher', one whose 'dreams (waking or sleeping, day-dreams or night-dreams)' are of general interest because of his wide human sympathies. For, says De Quincey, the essential qualifications for sustaining 'any claim to the title of philosopher' include 'not merely the possession of a superb intellect in its *analytic* functions' (and he offers Coleridge and Ricardo as instances of such '*subtle thinker*[s]'), but also,

such a constitution of the *moral* faculties, as shall give him an inner eye and power of intuition for the vision and the mysteries of our human nature: *that* constitution of faculties, in short, which (amongst all generations of men that from the beginning of time have deployed into

I am grateful to Dr Barry Symonds for information and suggestions which contributed much to this paper; and to the British Academy for a research grant which made Dr Symonds's assistance possible.

life, as it were, upon this planet) our English poets have possessed in the highest degree—and Scottish Professors in the lowest.[1]

These are strong words: in the whole history of the world, we are being told, English poets (Shakespeare? Milton? Wordsworth?) have possessed the greatest insight into human nature; and Scottish professors the least. Since Coleridge has already been named amongst the *'analytic'* thinkers, it would seem that the English poets are winning hands down.

Looking at De Quincey's hyperbole in a wider context, one is likely to have two reactions. One is a question: who precisely are these Scottish professors, and why are they being so aggressively opposed to the English poets? The other is the reflection that in later life De Quincey was in fact to spend much of his time in the company of Scottish professors. Indeed, they provided a social and intellectual milieu for De Quincey then in very much the same way as certain English poets—most notably Wordsworth and Coleridge—had done in his youth. And whilst his friends at Edinburgh and Glasgow Universities may not have influenced De Quincey as profoundly as the poets, they were, on the whole, both more consistently friendly to him and more helpful to the development of his future reputation. De Quincey is a writer who stands intriguingly on the thresholds between English and Scottish culture, between the scholarly and the poetic. And as a writer of periodical essays working from this viewpoint he stands also on the threshold between literary scholarship and literary journalism.

The passage quoted above shows De Quincey at his most disingenuous. For he immediately adds a footnote: 'I disclaim any allusion to existing professors, of whom indeed I know only one.' This hardly seems to make the 'allusion' more tactful. If he is *not* referring to 'existing' professors, the passage is gratuitous; and it more or less annihilates in passing the one he *does* happen to know. (In any case, how many professors is one supposed to 'know' in order to make such a judgement? We normally assess poets and professors by their published work, not by personal acquaintance.)

The one professor whom De Quincey *did* 'know' in 1821 was,

[1] Thomas De Quincey, *Confessions of an English Opium-Eater and Other Writings*, ed. Grevel Lindop (Oxford, 1985), 5.

in fact, John Wilson (1785–54), famous as 'Christopher North' of *Blackwood's Magazine*, and from 1820 Professor of Moral Philosophy in the University of Edinburgh. We shall return to him. But (and this is a further element of prevarication in De Quincey's attack) it is likely that De Quincey's disclaimer itself was false: for in conversation with Keats's friend Richard Woodhouse, shortly after writing the *Confessions*, De Quincey was eloquent in his contempt for Dugald Stewart, Wilson's predecessor in the Edinburgh chair and still much the most famous living Scottish (or indeed British) philosopher. 'He thinks', recorded Woodhouse, 'very meanly of Dugald Stewart, who has no originality or grasp of mind in him, who constantly misunderstands and misquotes writers from taking their opinions at second-hand from others . . . All Dugald Stewart's disquisitions are little, and the subject of them of no moment, even if true.'[2]

No doubt Dugald Stewart was not the only intended victim of De Quincey's shaft. Advertising himself as a Kantian—one who 'read Kant . . . and . . . understood him, or fancied that I did',[3] and who hoped to write *Prolegomena to all Future Systems of Political Economy*[4] (whose very title advertises its Kantian allegiance), De Quincey would naturally have shared Kant's contempt for the well-known Scottish 'Common Sense' school of philosophy, expressed in a famous passage of Kant's own *Prolegomena to Any Future Metaphysics*, which poured scorn on 'Reid, Oswald, Beattie'—prominent Scottish philosophers who had completely 'missed the point' of Hume's work.[5]

This storm in a metaphysical teacup may seem far removed from De Quincey's day-to-day life as a writer for the magazines; but in reality the two matters are intricately connected. John Wilson, as a member of the hard-pressed editorial team of the

---

[2] James Hogg, *De Quincey and His Friends: Personal Recollections, Souvenirs and Anecdotes of Thomas De Quincey, his Friends and Associates* (London, 1895), 75–6.

[3] *Confessions*, 53.

[4] Ibid. 66.

[5] Cited in Manfred Kuehn, *Scottish Common Sense in Germany, 1768–1800: A Contribution to the History of Critical Philosophy* (Kingston and Montreal, 1987), 4. No doubt De Quincey was also aware of Coleridge's sneer at Thomas Brown in *Biographia Literaria*, a work which in some respects provided a model for *Confessions*: see Robert Morrison, ' "Reviewers and Frenchmen" in Coleridge's *Biographia Literaria*', *Notes and Queries* 240 (NS 42), no. 2, June 1995, 180.

recently founded *Blackwood's Edinburgh Magazine*, had started in 1819 to beg De Quincey to contribute articles. De Quincey had recently lost his editorship of the *Westmorland Gazette*, and was, in theory, available; and Wilson was in no doubt about De Quincey's journalistic talents. 'Whatever and whenever you send,' he had urged De Quincey, 'it shall be inserted, and nothing can ever come wrong.'[6] In early 1820 Wilson had actually held back the printing of one issue of *Blackwood's* in the expectation of an article from De Quincey which had failed to arrive. And then, in July of the same year, Wilson had been elected by the Edinburgh town council to the Chair of Moral Philosophy at Edinburgh University. The election was largely a political gesture: like the council, Wilson was a Tory, whereas his rival, Sir William Hamilton, had Whig sympathies.

Wilson's philosophical knowledge left much to be desired, and he turned to the far more erudite De Quincey for help and advice. The desperation of his position as a newly elected professor, who would have to give 120 lectures in the next six months on a subject about which he understood next to nothing, is evident from a letter of August 1820:

I am quite at a stand respecting my lectures, but have been reading some books, some of which even I understand. What is good in Clark's *Light of Nature*? He is an insufferable *beast* as to style, and seems to me to have no drift but to leewards. If you think otherwise, give me notice of those parts of his book that you think worth reading. As I have to lecture on Moral Philosophy, I should merely give such general views of the intellectual part of our nature as are essential to an understanding of Man as a Moral Being:—and first of the physical nature of Man. What should I treat of in the Senses—Appetites and bodily powers? It seems to me—perhaps I said it before—that I should have a lecture on 'The Origin of Knowledge' when treating of the Senses. What are the books? and what theory is the true one? And your objections to Locke.

. . . I forget if I mentioned to you that I intend giving half a dozen lectures on the Greek Philosophers, Socrates, Plato, Aristotle, etc. Have you any books about them and their systems; or can you write me some long letters about either, or their philosophy?

[6] *De Quincey Memorials*, ed. H. A. Japp (London, 1890), ii. 42–3.

. . . What does, in your belief, constitute moral obligation?—and what ought to be my own doctrine on that subject? Are there good essays on the Stoic and Epicurean Philosophy, and where?[7]

At the same time, from under his editorial hat, Wilson continued to press De Quincey for *Blackwood's* articles. Whether or not De Quincey wrote any lectures for Wilson (most of whose material was eventually furnished by his long-suffering friend Alexander Blair),[8] De Quincey allowed himself to be recruited as a *Blackwood's* contributor and in December 1820 left his home in Grasmere, travelled to Edinburgh and began work for the magazine. Among other things, he promised an article on opium—the first hint of what we now know as the *Confessions*. 'Opium', he told the magazine's proprietor William Blackwood, 'has reduced me for the last six years to one general discourtesy of utter silence. But this I shall think of with not so much pain, if this same opium enables me (as I think it will) to send you an article.'[9] And the next day he told Blackwood that he was working on an 'Opium article'.

Within a month, however, De Quincey had quarrelled with William Blackwood, and was back at Grasmere, having published only a single item (a translation from Schiller) in the magazine. After a few more months he travelled south to London, and in September 1821 the first episode of *Confessions of an English Opium-Eater* appeared in the pages of *Blackwood's* deadly rival, the *London Magazine*.

This crowded sketch, showing Wilson as Edinburgh editor and professor, De Quincey as magazine contributor and potential ghost-writer of lectures, indicates how fluid the frontier between the academic and the journalistic worlds could be, at least in Scotland; it also shows how sharp-edged was De Quincey's swipe at 'Scottish Professors', at least for those in the know. The *Confessions*, after all, might have appeared in Professor Wilson's magazine had he and his proprietor played their

[7] Elsie Swann, *Christopher North (John Wilson)* (Edinburgh, 1934), 151; see also *De Quincey Memorials*, ed. ii. Japp, 44.

[8] Swann, *North*, 127–59 *passim*.

[9] Horace A. Eaton, *Thomas De Quincey: A Biography* (London, 1936), 262. For general information about De Quincey's biographical context, see Eaton, together with Grevel Lindop, *The Opium-Eater: A Life of Thomas De Quincey*, revised edn. (London, 1993).

cards better. Such are the personal (almost, one has to say, the petty) matters which can be unpacked from De Quincey's phrase. Yet there are wider perspectives opening out from the passage—perspectives which can tell us a good deal about the orientation of the *Confessions* and about the future course of De Quincey's life.

In 1821, as *Confessions* was written, a crisis was approaching for the Scottish universities and their intellectual world. The crisis centred upon philosophy. The Scottish university system at that time differed greatly from the English, in that Scottish students went to university early—at the age of 15 or 16—and that the study of philosophy, throughout a four-year general course which also included mathematics, science and classics, was compulsory. Philosophy was thus the keystone of the Scottish academic edifice, and one direct result of this was that virtually all significant British philosophy had for generations emanated from Scotland. On the other hand, the Scottish system was vulnerable to a number of serious objections and in 1826 (five years after the writing of *Confessions*) a Universities Commission was established which attempted to 'reform' the Scottish universities on the English plan. These objections included the charge that Scottish youth went to university too early; the universities, it was argued, were thus wasting their resources by standing in for grammar schools. Secondly, the centrality of philosophy—an aspect of the curriculum which in Scotland had descended directly from the medieval system—was questioned. Metaphysics, it was argued, was not a suitable study for everyone; it wasted time better devoted to other things; and the very integration of the curriculum meant that professors of classics or mathematics spent far too much time on the general, philosophical foundations of their subjects. The result of all this, in the English view, was the production of a race of immature metaphysicians, ready in argument but lamentably elementary in their knowledge of Greek verse or calculus.[10]

Much might be, and of course was, said on both sides. But more damaging, because they drove a wedge into the very centre of the Scottish system, were arguments that the Scottish philoso-

---

[10] For a full account of the controversy and its context, see George Elder Davie, *The Democratic Intellect: Scotland and her Universities in the Nineteenth Century* (Edinburgh, 1961).

phy itself was inadequate. Really the onslaught was not so much a wedge as a pincer-movement. From one side, Oxford men— academics and their former pupils amongst the governing classes—trained in classical philosophy, Aristotle in particular, claimed that Scottish classical knowledge lacked sophistication. Ill informed in linguistic and literary terms, it left Scottish metaphysics without an adequate foundation in the Greek origins of Western thought. Meanwhile, on the other wing, a more modern school claimed that the great advances in thought had been made in Germany. Kant's reproof of the Scots was damning.

It is striking that De Quincey had allegiances—which he prominently advertises in *Confessions*—to both these move-ments. Throughout *Confessions* he repeatedly 'boasteth himself to be a philosopher'[11] (a claim which has been insufficiently investigated by critics); and he energetically displays both his acquaintance with the Kantian philosophy and his extensive scholarship in the field of Greek literature. Indeed, one might argue that whilst many of the aesthetic and psychological reflec-tions in the *Confessions* are Kantian in flavour, the frequent discussions of happiness, pleasure and pain represent an implicit ongoing debate with Aristotle's *Ethics*. Without arguing that the *Confessions* is a kind of *roman à clef* attacking Scottish philoso-phy, it is tempting to suspect that it may be mined with more than one private joke aimed at Wilson, and coloured by the Oxonian Germanophile De Quincey's recent contact with Edin-burgh intellectual life.

That contact was destined to become increasingly close. Having turned to the *London Magazine* after the failure of his relationship with *Blackwood's*—a period through which his friendship with Wilson persisted, though at times uneasily—De Quincey returned to *Blackwood's* in the autumn of 1826, ini-tially with items about, or translated from, German literature, and then with a steady stream of articles on all kinds of topics from 'Murder, Considered as One of the Fine Arts' to current politics. He moved permanently to Edinburgh in 1830, and besides continuing *Blackwood's* work, wrote for—and briefly edited—the Edinburgh *Evening Post* newspaper in 1827–9.

[11] *Confessions*, 5.

From 1833 he did extensive work for *Tait's Edinburgh Maga-zine* and (from 1850) for *Hogg's Instructor* and *Titan*. De Quincey thus became essentially an Edinburgh writer. After 1846, when *Tait's* was bought by the Glasgow *North British Daily Mail*, he also spent a good deal of time in Glasgow, writing perhaps for the *Mail* (though if so none of this work has yet been identified) as well as for *Tait's*.[12]

In both Edinburgh and Glasgow, De Quincey's friends were drawn, chiefly, from the intellectual circles surrounding the universities. This was natural enough, in view of the fact that his original contact with Scots literary life had been made through Wilson; but it also reflects the very close interpenetration which then existed between the academic, journalistic and literary worlds in Scotland. To trace De Quincey's movements through the mazes of Scottish intellectual society between 1830 and 1859 would almost involve compiling a new biographical encyclopaedia of nineteenth-century Scotland. Merely to offer a selective listing, De Quincey's close friends at one time or another included: Adam Black, publisher of the *Encyclopaedia Britannica* and brother-in-law of William Tait of *Tait's Maga-zine*; Tait himself, a former student at Edinburgh University, who was a Radical intellectual and something of a scholar in his own right, publishing such items as Bentham's *Collected Works* and Professor Thomas Brown's *Philosophy of Mind*; John Hill Burton, a graduate of Aberdeen University, who was a profes-sional journalist—editing *The Scotsman* in the 1840s, as well as writing for the *Westminster* and *Edinburgh Review*s and contributing extensively to *Blackwood's* from the 1850s until 1880—but also the biographer of Hume and the leading Scot-tish historian of his time; Robert Chambers, editor and propri-etor of *Chambers's Journal* and a prolific author on history, biography and folklore, prominent in scientific and theological circles for his proto-Darwinian *Vestiges of the Natural History of Creation* (1844); Sir William Hamilton, among the most prominent philosophers of his day, who had studied (as a contemporary and friend of J. G. Lockhart) at Balliol College, Oxford and, having lost the 1820 contest for the Edinburgh

---

[12] Colin Rae-Brown, *Universal Review*, 5, 13 Nov. 1889, 399.

Chair of Moral Philosophy to Wilson (with whom he remained friends), became Professor of Civil History the following year, moving to the Chair of Logic and Metaphysics in 1836 after making his philosophical reputation with a series of articles in the *Edinburgh Review*; J. F. Ferrier (the nephew *and* son-in-law of John Wilson), who after studying at Oxford and Heidelberg, contributed essays on philosophy (as well as a translation of Tieck and an early review of Elizabeth Barrett's poetry) to *Blackwood's* and became Professor of Civil History at Edinburgh, later moving to the Chair of Moral Philosophy at St Andrews; E. L. Lushington, Professor of Greek at the University of Glasgow; John Pringle Nichol, a lifelong friend of John Stuart Mill and Professor of Astronomy at Glasgow; and—not so much a close friend as an admiring young acquaintance—David Masson, son of an Aberdeen stone-cutter, who after graduating from Aberdeen University and studying divinity for three years at Edinburgh edited the *Aberdeen Banner*, wrote popular histories for Chambers, contributed prolifically to *Fraser's Magazine*, the *Quarterly*, the *Westminster*, the *Leader* and the *North British Review*, and became Professor of English at University College London in 1853—a commitment which did not hinder him from establishing, as its first editor, *Macmillan's Magazine* in 1859.

Masson met De Quincey some time in the latter's last years, apparently introduced by older Edinburgh literati, and retained a lasting impression of his brilliant conversation, his courtesy and his prodigious memory. Masson made his own name as a scholar with his six-volume documentary biography of Milton; but he is now remembered chiefly as the editor of the fourteen-volume *De Quincey's Writings* (1889–90), produced in the years immediately following his retirement from the Chair of Rhetoric and English Literature at Edinburgh University, to which he had moved from London. It is thus striking that the form in which De Quincey's works have been transmitted through the twentieth century was determined by his contact with the Edinburgh academic world. It is hard to believe that Masson would have undertaken his extensive collected edition had he not known of De Quincey as an almost legendary figure in the Scottish academic world which had seen the start, and the culmination, of his own career—a legend which had been amply confirmed by a tantalizingly brief meeting with the great essayist in his last years.

The sketch offered in the last two paragraphs—largely, and unashamedly, drawn from entries in the *Dictionary of National Biography* (that most stylishly written of reference works, itself poised nicely between scholarship and journalism)—shows how closely intertwined were the worlds of the periodicals and the universities in nineteenth-century Edinburgh. It is clear that authors, editors, publishers and professors changed roles with the greatest of ease, and that moves could be made in any direction. To highlight some specific examples, we have already seen De Quincey as a former newspaper editor helping to write lectures for Wilson, a philosophy professor who was simultaneously a magazine editor in need of his friend's journalistic services. Hamilton provides us with the example of an academic gaining a chair on the basis of a series of articles in a literary periodical. Ferrier wrote both philosophy and *belles-lettres* for *Blackwood's*, and when he applied (unsuccessfully) for the Chair of Moral Philosophy at Edinburgh in 1852, the journalist De Quincey wrote him an eloquent, persuasive and fairly technical testimonial. (Amusingly, an editorial in the London *Athenaeum* on 24 December 1828 had recommended De Quincey himself as a candidate for the Chair of Logic at the new London University on the strength of his essays in *Blackwood's*, noting as the only real alternative among the 'older men' Coleridge, 'who, probably, would be scouted by the Council as a writer of poetry and a dreamer'[13]—charges from which the English Opium-Eater was apparently exempt.) Both Chambers and Burton furnish examples of freelance scholars of great reputation who were also periodical editors, Chambers combining this with the running of a publishing company and Burton having for a time edited a national newspaper. Masson, much of whose career falls after De Quincey's death, provides in some ways the most striking instance, that of a man who moves from newspaper editing through the world of literary journalism into two university chairs and subsequently establishes himself as a literary scholar.

[13] 'Mr De Quincey and the London University', *Athenaeum*, 24 Dec. 1824, 969.

If there seems, incidentally, to be an improbable profusion of professors in the catalogue of De Quincey's academic friends, this is largely owing to the lack of 'other ranks' in the Scottish universities at this time. The pyramid was, as it were, all apex: there was no broad base of lecturers or fellows, and professors acted as both lecturers and tutors. John Wilson, for example, who cannot have been—or at any rate cannot long have continued to be—quite the philosophical duffer he appeared at the beginning of his professorship, gave several lectures each week, and also spent a three-hour session on Saturday afternoons going over students' essays in public debate with a class which may have numbered some 200 students.[14]

It is interesting that of De Quincey's closest academic friends, nearly all (the notable exception being Nichol, the astronomer) had English educational allegiances: Hamilton, Wilson and Ferrier were all Oxford products; Lushington was a Cambridge 'Apostle' and the friend of Tennyson and Thackeray. One wonders if De Quincey chose his friends mainly from those academics sympathetic to the 'English' reforming of the Scottish system. Later on, at any rate, De Quincey was certainly inclined to take the English view of the Scottish universities; in 'Professor Wilson', an essay of 1850, he explains in passing that 'It is the Scottish custom, through the want of great public schools for the higher branches of education, that universities, to their own great injury, are called upon to undertake the function of schools. It follows from this that mere schoolboys are in Scotland sent to college . . .'[15] And his 1852 testimonial for Ferrier stresses—as if aiming at the acknowledged weaknesses of the Scottish system—that Ferrier has received, at Oxford, 'the basis of a classic education, combined with a training rigorously scholastic' followed by 'a sudden leap . . . into the ocean of German philosophy and literature' and that

now—at this crisis— . . . at the opening of a new era, when railroads will bring to universities critical auditors of a new class—countrymen of Kant, Schelling, and Hegel—the supreme chair of Philosophy should be filled by one who has such a mastery of the Continental philosophies as at once qualifies him for appropriating their uses, and for the task

[14] Davie, *Democratic Intellect*, 19.
[15] 'Professor Wilson', *Collected Writings of Thomas De Quincey*, ed. David Masson (London, 1889–90), v. 292.

(now becoming even more important) of disarming their evil tendencies.[16]

In any case, it is clear that if we think of literary journalism and literary scholarship as two worlds which come together for some form of *rapprochement*, we are (at least with regard to Victorian Scotland) looking at the process from the wrong end. Literary journalism and scholarship were not two things but one—or rather, they formed the ends of a spectrum. People, publishers and periodicals could move to and fro along this spectrum, sometimes appearing more scholarly and sometimes more journalistic, but the two ends had not yet moved so far apart that the middle segment had snapped.

Just occasionally, indeed, we can put our finger on the exact point where breakage is imminent. Such a point is indicated in the *DNB*'s account of Hamilton's career, in the episode where (in 1829) MacVey Napier takes over editorship of the *Edinburgh Review* and invites Hamilton to supply essays on philosophy. His articles on 'The Philosophy of Perception' (1830) and 'Logic' (1833) made Hamilton's reputation not only in Britain but also in America; translated, they soon made him a respected figure in France and Germany. But the *Edinburgh*'s former editor Francis Jeffrey was forthright in his condemnation, describing the first paper as 'sheer nonsense' and, more significantly, as 'the most unreadable thing that ever appeared in the review'. Obviously these were the kind of papers which would nowadays appear in a learned journal. (*Blackwood's* published a number of fairly technical philosophical articles over the years, including some by Wilson; but then, with the professor himself as its *de facto* editor and resident humorist, *Blackwood's* was a special case.) In 1830 it was still thought possible that an educated general public might make sense of such things; but the strain was showing, and the combined forces of increasing academic specialism and of the economic pressure on magazines to woo the largest possible audience, were beginning to destroy the old inclusiveness. By the end of the century classical scholarship, history, political economy, mathematics, metaphysics, natural science and the countless new applied and social sciences would

---

[16] W. E. A. Axon, 'De Quincey and J. F. Ferrier', *Manchester Quarterly*, 17 (1895), 272–3.

all have their own sheaves of journals—organs not of the old 'Literary and Philosophical' societies but of learned organizations, professional institutes, and, increasingly, university departments; whilst for better or worse the general periodicals would carry only simplified summaries and overviews. Still, De Quincey was happy enough to live in that prelapsarian age when metaphysics, astronomy, classical studies and reviews of the latest poetry could sit side by side in a magazine aimed at all educated readers.

What effect did the Scottish academic milieu have on his work? Fuller answers to this question may emerge once a complete and chronologically structured edition of De Quincey is available. In the mean time a few guesses may be made. In all probability what his academic friends supplied to De Quincey (apart from general society, free dinners, help with finding accommodation, the occasional loan of money or clothing and the other multifarious services which a generous and civilized circle of friends will naturally offer an impecunious man of genius in any age) was, in no particular order: general 'copy', ideas for articles, and books.

By 'copy', I mean that in their company De Quincey as a matter of course saw things, heard things, had experiences and acquired anecdotes which, one way or another, could be worked up into material for articles. They might be as trivial as excursions to the seaside with Wilson to discover if every tenth wave were really bigger; or as richly suggestive as his visits to the Glasgow Observatory during J. P. Nichol's tenure of the Chair of Astronomy there.

Nichol had arranged for the observatory to be resited from the Glasgow College grounds to Dowanhill and in 1840 visited Munich to purchase the latest optical equipment. De Quincey, who had met Nichol at an Edinburgh dinner party, had received a standing invitation to visit him at the observatory and arrived in March 1841, apparently to take refuge from creditors.[17] He stayed until the German telescopes arrived and displaced him, at which point he exchanged astronomy for Greek and went to stay with Professor Lushington nearby. Contact with Nichol, who was investigating the nature of nebulae, led to De

[17] Charles Mackay, *Through the Long Day: Memorials of a Literary Life During Half a Century* (2 vols.; London, 1887), i. 75.

Quincey's composition, in 1846, of 'The System of the Heavens as Revealed by Lord Rosse's Telescopes', where he explores the symbolism of the relationship between observatory and city:

How tarnished with eternal canopies of smoke, and of sorrow, how dark with agitations of many orders, is the mighty town below! How serene, how quiet, how lifted above the confusion, and the roar, and the strifes of earth, is the solemn observatory that crowns the heights overhead! And duly, at night, just when the toil of overwrought Glasgow is mercifully relaxing, then comes the summons to the labouring astronomer![18]

The reflector telescope, which Nichol demonstrated to De Quincey, worked its way even more deeply into *Suspiria De Profundis*, the elaborate series of meditations on time, memory and suffering which De Quincey contributed to *Blackwood's*, in four instalments, during 1845. Here the apparatus forms a hidden metaphor in the magnificent opening passage on dreams:

The machinery for dreaming planted in the human brain was not planted for nothing. That faculty, in alliance with the mystery of darkness, is the one great tube through which man communicates with the shadowy. And the dreaming organ, in connexion with the heart, the eye, and the ear, compose the magnificent apparatus which forces the infinite into the chambers of the human brain, and throws dark reflections from eternities below all life upon the mirrors of the sleeping mind.[19]

The observatory and its telescope—although never explicitly mentioned—have become the human mind itself, and its capacity to dream. The 'machinery', the 'tube', the 'apparatus', the 'mirrors' were all, literally, what De Quincey had seen under Nichol's tutelage.

Many other examples could be cited of the manner in which social contact with academics may have supplied De Quincey with material for poetic development. One especially interesting possibility is that Lushington too may have contributed significantly to the development of *Suspiria*. After the move from Nichol's observatory to Lushington's house in 1841, Lushington became one of De Quincey's closest friends. De Quincey trusted the professor so fully that during 1844 he wrote

---

[18] *Collected Writings of De Quincey*, ed. Masson, viii. 27–8.
[19] *Confessions*, 88.

him a series of letters apparently revealing more details about his health, his mental states and his opium addiction than he offered in writing to anyone else. At this time De Quincey was also drafting *Suspiria* and when it was published he wrote to Lushington, gratefully associating him and Nichol with the work almost in terms of dedication: 'Whatever pleasure you may at this time have found in the original *Confessions*, to which, in part, I fancy myself indebted for the great kindness shown to me in Glasgow by yourself and Professor Nichol, will probably be trebled in this second series. I, if at all I can pretend to judge in such cases, find them very greatly superior to the first.'[20] (The reference to a 'second series' points to the fact that *Suspiria de Profundis* was billed in *Blackwood's* as 'A Sequel to the *Confessions of an English Opium-Eater*'.) Given De Quincey's intimacy with Lushington at this time, one wonders if the most famous section of *Suspiria*, 'The Palimpsest of the Human Brain', which compares human memory to a Greek vellum whose text is scraped off and repeatedly overwritten, yet can be recovered by chemical means, owes something to Lushington's knowledge of classical manuscripts. The essay seems to be based on up-to-date knowledge of Greek palaeography and the chemistry which could be applied to its problems. Lushington is certainly the most likely source for such information. Yet surprisingly little is known about him, and the possibility that he contributed to De Quincey's theory of the mind, and hence to the nineteenth-century thinking about memory and the unconscious which led up to Freud's work, has never been investigated.

With regard to ideas for articles, an anecdote from Charles Mackay—however unreliable in detail—offers a plausible enough model for the kind of thing that must often have occurred. Mackay, editor of the Glasgow *Argus*, recalls dining with De Quincey and Nichol (again at the observatory)—a neat demonstration, incidentally, of the interplay between academic and journalistic worlds—when debate about the ultimate relativity of the terms 'up' and 'down' led to a proposal for an article:

[20] John Mack, 'De Quincey and Two Glasgow Professors: II. De Quincey and Lushington', *The College Courant: Journal of the Glasgow University Graduate Association* (Martinmas 1952), 30.

'I have often thought,' said I, 'of writing an article to be called "Quarrels with Words". Take the word "morality" for instance; that also is a relative not a positive word; in fact, a word that is modified or wholly changed in its meanings by geography, or by lapse of time . . .'

'Write the article,' said De Quincey, 'or let me do it.' . . .

'I wish you would write the article,' I said to Mr. De Quincey. 'I resign all my copyright in the idea to you, and shall look out for it in *Maga*.'[21]

The article, says Mackay, never appeared, 'though I expected it for many months.' No doubt De Quincey rarely wrote the articles other people thought he should write. None the less, that suggestions for worthwhile subjects should have developed out of his university friends' conversation is altogether likely. When one reflects that the university libraries, and the professors' personal bookshelves, must have supplied many of the books used by the debt-ridden De Quincey, one begins to wonder how far the choice of subjects in his later work reflects Scottish academic preoccupations of the time. Though there is no obvious preponderance of subjects, and articles on politics, English literature and autobiographical episodes are frequent at most periods, it is noticeable that from 1840 onwards there is a steady stream of essays on classical topics, often with an emphasis on ancient history or the solving of textual problems; several papers touching on astronomy; and a number of pieces on philosophy, on logic and on individual philosophers. The availability of books, and of men who were authorities on these subjects, cannot have been irrelevant to De Quincey's choice of topic. They produced some of his least-read essays, but also some of his most splendid.

To sum up, it seems likely that De Quincey's contact with academic Scotland was more important for the nature of his work than has generally been recognized. He was lucky in being able to take advantage of the particular conditions that prevailed in nineteenth-century Scotland, where the worlds of what we would now classify as science, scholarship, literature and journalism thoroughly interpenetrated each other and movement between them was easy. It is unlikely that an impecunious writer for the magazines, however brilliant, would have found any advantage in hanging, so to speak, on to the coat-tails of

[21] Charles Mackay, *Forty Years' Recollections* (London, 1877), 321–3.

Oxford or Cambridge, or even of the new London University. Yet in Edinburgh and Glasgow De Quincey was able to do just this, and everyone benefited.

Both De Quincey himself and his most prominent outlet, the *Blackwood's Magazine* of Wilson's time, drew their strength precisely from occupying, and harvesting, the debatable land between the poles of journalism and scholarship. If there is a moral for contemporary culture, it is that we should be very wary of letting these poles draw too far apart. In our own time it has been periodicals such as *The Times Literary Supplement*, the *London Review of Books* and *PN Review*, together with literate scientific popularizers such as the excellent *Scientific American*, that have maintained some sense of a common and fruitful intellectual community. In the long run it may well be that the contents of these periodicals are both more influential, and of more lasting value, than nine-tenths of what appears in the scholarly journals.

4

Journalism, Scholarship, and the University College London English Department

John Sutherland

Grevel Lindop has written about the nourishment which journalism can get from contact with universities and university people (specifically in the literary world around the great Scottish universities in the early nineteenth century).[1] I shall approach the same topic from the other side: the stimulus which universities—specifically their English departments—can derive from contact with the world of journalism. I shall do this by sketching the life history of a single English department, that of University College London. As it happens, it is, at 167 years, the oldest such department in England (some would say the world).

My chair at UCL was endowed by a newspaper magnate, Lord Northcliffe, whose name is synonymous with twentieth-century lower journalism. Calling it the 'Dirty *Daily Mail* Chair of Modern English Literature' might make the source of the endowment clearer. Delving beyond its aggrandizement by the Harmsworth family, the headship of UCL's English department reaches to the Adamic figure of the Revd Thomas Dale (1797–1870), the first to hold the appointment in 1828 (although English did not yet have full departmental status, and UCL was then the University of London).

Dale survives in the educational record only because he was the first of his kind. References to him, on those few occasions on which they crop up, are invariably derisive. The promise with which he concluded his inaugural lecture, that he would 'labour in all things to inculcate virtue by his teaching of literature', has

---

[1] See above, Chapter 3.

been much quoted against him.[2] The unmemorability of Dale might be ascribed to the fact that, unlike Edinburgh's pioneers Hugh Blair and Adam Smith, Dale left no lasting books. Nevertheless, as Franklin E. Court has recently established in *The Social and Historical Significance of the First Literature Professorship in England* (1988), there is an interesting story and some familiar skulduggery behind Dale's appointment.

Dale was chosen with some care, out of a strong field, as the candidate of one of the founders of University College, Lord Brougham. His main qualification was his reputation as a good classroom teacher ('I am', Brougham said, 'a little sick of professors who cannot teach or who will not devote themselves to it'). Dale was also felt to be the safest candidate to establish a new and somewhat dubious subject. His respectable dullness, his dog collar and even the fact of his intellectual nonentity were assets.

Dale's inaugural lecture was a prospectus of his curriculum. The subject would be divided into language and literature— 'bridged' by 'rhetoric' and the study of 'style'. On the literary, or belletristic, side Dale gave prominence to Anglo-Saxon poetry, Chaucer, Shakespeare and Spenser. In philology, Dale was wholly ignorant of the advances recently made by the Germans and Danes. This was a serious shortcoming. But he successfully set up that biped, 'lang and lit', which has proved a durable long-term structure for English departments. Dale also established a junior/senior class system which defined English as a subject with progressively more complex levels or grades—a degree-worthy subject, in other words.

Dale resigned after two years, in 1830, not because of his intellectual inadequacy (as is often suggested) but because of quarrels about resourcing—a prophetic event at UCL. In the first century of UCL's existence there were eleven professors of English. Three who succeeded each other dominated over a continuous seventy-year span. The first of this great trio was David Masson (1822–1907), who took over in 1853 on the

---

[2] My sources include the University College London archive; Bryan Bennett, 'Meet Henry Morley', *UCL USA Centenary News* (1990), 17–26; Franklin E. Court, *The Social and Historical Significance of the First Literature Professorship in England* (New York, 1988) and *Institutionalizing English Literature: The Culture and Politics of Literary Study, 1750–1900* (Stanford, Calif., 1992); Negley Harte, *The University of London, 1836–1896* (London, 1986) and D. J. Palmer, *The Rise of English Studies* (London, 1965).

sudden, unexpected retirement of Arthur Hugh Clough (better
known as a poet than a professor of English). Masson assumed
his chair at the age of 31. He was a Scot (as have been a
disproportionate number of professors in the English Department at UCL). More significantly, Masson was a magazine
journalist, and an outstandingly good one. Like other Scots,
David Masson had come to London (in 1847) looking for bigger
worlds—specifically a more lucrative market for his pen. In
London he found employment in higher journalism, made
friends with literary people like Thackeray and became something of a disciple of Carlyle's.

According to D. J. Palmer in *The Rise of English Studies*
(1965), Masson's significant achievement was to redirect the
essentially belletristic curriculum at UCL towards literary history. His great work, a biography of Milton (begun at UCL)
massively contextualizes Milton's poetry in the poet's life and
times. The examination papers Masson devised for his pupils
were obsessed with periods, genres and dates. It was his quaint
(but not illogical) practice to set the same first question every
year. And I would argue that Masson's pedagogic achievement
was more complex than Palmer allows. He was, in 1852, a
journalist who had established himself as an authoritative com-
mentator on modern literature—more particularly, on contemporary fiction and poetry. His 1851 essay in the *North British
Review*, comparing Thackeray and Dickens, stands up extraordinarily well. In his first year as departmental head, Masson
introduced Wordsworth into his course. Nor were his examination questions on the laureate dry or pedantic. In 1853, the final
question for senior class was: 'State Wordsworth's theory of
Verse as connected with Poetry; criticise that theory; and suggest
another.' It is the instruction to 'suggest another' which catches
the eye and stirs the mind. Wordsworth, we should recall, was
just two years dead in 1853.

By 1856, a main feature of Masson's senior class syllabus was
'literature of the last seventy years'. 'Moderns' such as Scott,
Byron, Coleridge and even the still-living Ruskin figured in the
annual class exams. Masson also threw in some wonderfully
zany questions for his pupils. The senior class in 1857, for
example, was instructed to 'write a short description of University College, as if to a person who had never seen it'.

Masson was congratulated in 1856 and 1857 by the Council for increasing the size of the English class. As a mark of their dour pleasure, the college authorities endowed a £5 prize, on the subject of 'Druids and Druidism'. The year 1859 was to be the high point of Masson's tenure at UCL. In it he produced a critical monograph, which was well ahead of its time, *English Novelists and their Styles*. The same year saw the first volume of the Milton biography (the great work was not concluded until 1880). And in 1859 Masson assumed the editorship of *Macmillan's Magazine*. Doubtless there was the usual common-room grumbling at the idea of a professor of English dabbling in mere journalism. He remained editor of the magazine until 1867. In 1865 Masson went to Edinburgh as professor of English where he served thirty years. He has the honour of a memorial chair of English in that department.

Masson was succeeded in 1865 by Henry Morley (1822–94)—an academic remembered less as a scholar than as a heroic popularizer of English Studies. Morley gave the department its first distinctive 'character'. Fifteen candidates were shortlisted for the vacancy left by Masson. The appointment committee stated their priority with utilitarian bluntness: 'We must bear in mind, and our Professor must bear in mind, that the practical end of our English class is to teach our Students to use their own language well both in speaking and writing.' They were defining what today we would call the 'service function' of English studies. In their profile of the candidates, the committee began by noting that 'Mr Henry Morley . . . has achieved a reputation as a journalist.' This was an understatement. Morley had been associated with Charles Dickens for fifteen years as sub-editor on *Household Words* and *All the Year Round*. Since 1860 he had been editor-in-chief of the *Examiner*, another weekly with strong Dickensian connections. Dickens was Morley's god. And he inherited from the Great Inimitable a sense of the larger British public—a public which was hungry not just for comic fiction, but for higher education.

Morley had begun professional life as a country surgeon. From earliest youth, he had been consumed with a love of Spenser's *Faerie Queene* and yearned for the literary life. In 1848, the year of revolutions, young Henry Morley gave up his career in medicine for schoolmastering and journalism in London. These were the 'hungry forties', and the experience of the capital's suffering in this period formed what was to be a lifelong mission of philanthropy and a dedication to practical good. As Charles Dickens's right-hand man, Morley wrote useful articles on such matters as public health and sanitation. He did not, however, let his pedagogic ambitions lapse. From 1857, he served as a voluntary (unpaid) teacher at King's College London, building up the class enrolment from twelve pupils to 115.

Morley loved 'extension' teaching—instruction which was a practical expression of what Brougham had called the 'diffusion of useful knowledge'. His biographer reproduces some of Morley's diary entries, recording his trips all over the country— lecturing in Birmingham one night on Spenser, the next in Bristol on Fielding. Morley was evidently a driven man, but his mania had a purpose. It was his principal article of faith that the spread of literary knowledge would—like the spread of Christianity in Africa, or drinkable water in Shoreditch—exercise a civilizing influence.

The shadow of the working man's college lay heavily on UCL's English faculty in Morley's years of power there. He lectured indefatigably, inside the college and outside. But he was a publishing, as well as a teaching, lecturer. As the appointment committee of 1865 noted: 'he has proposed to himself as the labour of his life a complete review of English Literature from the very origin of the nation and language to the present day'. This was the 'English Writers' project, scheduled for twenty titles covering the national literature from start to finish. A panorama, or map, of the subject.

Morley's main opponent in the run-off in 1865 was a young Cambridge don called Hales. Morley got the election, on the strength of his manifest teaching skills, and the 'English Writers' project. With hindsight, it was the right choice. Morley was the kind of pioneer the department needed: a man with little sensibility and no doubts, sustained by the conviction that the one needful thing was 'more'—more students, more classes, more books, more learning, above all more time. Morley's prime years coincide with the great reform of the 1870 Universal Education Act. And he shared W. E. Forster's vision of a wholly literate nation, combining it with the huge constituency of Dickens's reading public.

A main requisite for the evolution of English literature, in Morley's view, was accessible reading matter. He resurrected into print scores of classic authors, ranging from Aristotle to Shakespeare. He has over a hundred books to his credit in the British Library catalogue. If one adds the sixty-three titles in Morley's 'Universal Library' and the 214 items which he edited for Cassell's 'National Library', one is in *Guinness Book of Records* territory. These editions were accompanied by wide-ranging tables of dates and periods, sketches, samplers, and histories of English literature. Given that Morley's *First Sketch of English Literature* runs to 1,104 pages in its twelfth edition, the mind trembles at what he would have come up with had the College allowed him a sabbatical.

All that mattered to Morley was coverage. He taught everything in the department, from Anglo-Saxon and Icelandic sagas to Browning. He built up the lecture course from four to twenty hours a week. He was able to recruit, by his own energetic example, volunteer helpers, such as the selfless F. J. Furnivall, Gregory Foster and the philologist, R. G. Latham. Morley was equally energetic in pastoral matters. He took a keen interest in the establishment of a Student Union, the expansion of college premises, the setting up of halls of residence. He was in the forefront in getting women admitted at UCL (a year before Somerville College, Oxford was founded). His argument in favour of admitting women was characteristic. It would be, as he said in a letter of 1872, 'a most substantial addition to our usefulness'. The word usefulness sums up the man.

Morley's was a regime marked by access for all-comers. There were over 200 pupils studying English at the highpoint of his tenure—virtually the same number as today, when a staff eight times larger collectively produces barely as much as Morley's personal publication list. UCL's example inspired the setting up of a colonial network of English departments in provincial colleges, using the mechanism of the central University Administration. Even the Oxford English School, founded in 1894, owes much to Morley. The first professor of English at Oxford, Walter Raleigh, was a graduate of Morley's class.

Morley's was a success story but not one that needed to be continued beyond his time. For one thing, the new university colleges, combined with diminished resistance in the old seats of learning, siphoned off the student intake, which by the late 1880s had declined to a student body of around 100—twice what it had been when Morley took over but only half what it was at his zenith. It was also time for new thinking on the subject. At its worst, Morley's universal educative theory produced a kind of robotic learning. An 1866 question to the senior class, for example, requires them to 'Analyze the Spenserian stanza, paying particular attention as to why its last line is an Alexandrine.' It is extraordinary that the man who saw the first chapters of *Hard Times* through the press could not see the Gradgrindism of such questions. (For those who are curious, the answer is on p. 449 of Morley's *First Sketch*: 'the Alexandrine destroys expectation of continuance'.) Morley's great strengths were those of the journalist-cum-extension lecturer. He was a one-man diffusion machine. His weakness was that he could not see beyond, or rise above, that role. His were the simple virtues of journalistic energy and single-mindedness.

The next election to the chair (now endowed in Frederick Quain's name) was in 1889, Morley having held the position for twenty-four years. It was a crucial appointment. The *proxime accessit* was Edward Arber, a 53-year-old Morley clone who ran the Birmingham English department single-handed and had 153 publications to his credit. In their wisdom, the UCL committee chose instead a young 34-year-old Scot, W. P. Ker (1855–1923). Ker had taken a traditional upward route for clever young Scots: a Snell Exhibition at Glasgow University followed by a second (abbreviated) undergraduate course at Balliol College, Oxford. Here he was strongly influenced by Benjamin Jowett, architect of the modern humanities tutorial teaching system.

Ker's career was deformed when Oxford awarded him an astonishing second (astonishing, that is, to his friends and instructors) which debarred him from the automatic Oxford career in philosophy which he had fondly expected. None the less, in 1879, he was made a fellow of All Souls, a position which he retained for forty-four years, until his death. In 1883, aged 28, he was one of a crop of six new professors appointed at University College, Cardiff (a London-administered institution). He was to spend five years there before taking up his post at UCL.

Ker was the most intellectual of the professors of English hitherto appointed at UCL. He cannot have interviewed well.

All commentators note his introverted style; 'William the Silent' was his nickname as a student. A. C. Bradley, in his confidential reference to the College, recalled that 'Ker's failing, when I knew him at Oxford, was costiveness.' Partly this reticence was the affectation of late Victorian manliness. Ker's was the silence not of nervousness, nor of stupidity, but of muscular intellectuality. He was a rowing man as a student and an enthusiastic Alpinist in later life, indeed 'he idealized mountains' and died walking in the Italian Alps.

If 'diffusion' had been Morley's battle-cry, 'concentration' was Ker's. His friend McCunn recalls that 'he reminded one sometimes of an oxygen cylinder'. Ker's inaugural lecture in October 1889, was an extraordinarily assured performance. After perfunctory compliments to Masson's *Milton* and Morley's *English Writers*, the bulk of the lecture was a devastating critique of journalistic superficiality, and the quixotic historical comprehensiveness of his predecessors. Ker wholly disavowed Morley's totalism—what he sarcastically called 'the historical malady'. 'The student of English Lit unless he is careful,' Ker declared, 'will find himself a student of the *omne scribile*, a vagrant on the confines of things in general.'

It was not where Ker intended to be found. 'One has to limit oneself, in order to get accurate knowledge,' he told his audience. 'Accurate knowledge' (a term which he passed on to his friend A. E. Housman, who joined the College four years later) was to be distinguished from 'index learning'. He repudiated utterly the journalistic academic style. The examination paraphernalia of dates, facts, names, and literary periods and that rote learning about the architecture of the Spenserian stanza must go.

Ker made 'research' a departmental priority. He wanted the discovery of more Grimm's Laws. There must be no more of what he termed the 'passive tourism' of the literary history syllabus: exploration was the needful thing. Above all, Ker was concerned with the pre-literary origins of literature. Even in his inaugural lecture, he explores the socio-racial beginnings of literary form, in Teutonic Epic and French Romance. He was to lead his subject into an awe-inspiring prehistorical mist. 'The earliest beginning we can make is already late and old', he declared. Ker was ceaselessly in search of an archetypal wholeness in the literary fragments which have descended to posterity.

Ker regarded exams not as memory tests, but as 'a game to be tried between the examiners and examinees'. Questions under his regime became subtle traps for the unwary. Unlike the herring-like 'journalist', Morley, who spawned books in batches of twenty, W. P. Ker was very slow to publish. His first significant publication, *Epic and Romance*, appeared when he was 42. He was indeed, as Bradley said, costive by nature. Partly, the slowness was a function of the learning he needed to amass. A comparatist *avant la lettre*, he taught himself 'the tongues and the literatures of all lands in Europe to the borders of the Slavs'. Ker founded the Department of Scandinavian Studies at UCL and directing it remained his longest connection with the College.

Morley had left the English department at UCL with a highly developed service function—a kind of freshman English programme, with all the brash certainty that such programmes need. Morley was by nature social and familial. He regarded students as his children, and he treated their minor ailments, drawing on his early medical training. Ker, by contrast, 'raised' the department intellectually, forming it by the 1890s into an honours school. Under him, the department was a place for degree students and for research. An aloof master–disciple relationship ruled, not pastoral care. (Women undergraduates were routinely reduced to tears by caustic male lecturers.)

The level to which Ker aspired to bring UCL was that of the place from which he felt exiled, Oxford. He occupied a house at 95 Gower Street, 'virtually over the shop', but 'at the end of each week', it is recorded, 'he was always to be found at Oxford', in his rooms at All Souls. Apparently, some of his companions at High Table wondered where William got to during the week. Since the weekdays in town invariably meant twelve lectures, a batch of tutorials and much committee work, one cannot be too critical of his physical and spiritual absenteeism. There is, however, no question that, for all his loyal years of labour in Gower Street, Ker's heart was elsewhere. 'Oxford was the centre of his life', a friend recorded: 'his feeling for Oxford was less that of a son to his mother than of a subject to his queen'.

When he was appointed to the Oxford Chair of Poetry in 1920, Ker regarded it as the 'greatest distinction of his life'. Had he not been so attached to Oxford (then battling to create its English School) it is likely that Ker would not have had a mark to which to raise the UCL English Department. Elevation was the recreation as well as the work of his life.

In 1928, six years after Ker's retirement, Viscount Rothermere and Cecil Harmsworth, with an endowment of £30,000 (a vast sum, in the currency of the day) created a chair and an annual lectureship in the name of their recently dead brother, Lord Northcliffe—founder of the *Daily Mail* and proprietor of *The Times*. It was made a condition of the donation that the chair should go to 'an eminent man of letters'. The endowment institutionalized a double character in the department. The Quain Professor of English Language and Literature (a university appointment) became the custodian of the department's philological/philosophical heritage. The Lord Northcliffe Chair of Modern English Literature (a Privy Council appointment) embodied the department's journalistic/belletristic tendency—the tradition of David Masson and the young Henry Morley. As it happened, this duality was not to be fulfilled for sixty years.

With Ker's successor, R. W. Chambers, the department entered what is, for me, its least congenial era. Chambers, who graduated from UCL in 1894 and was fired by Ker's new vision, was a lifelong disciple (even down to Ker's monastic way of life). But Chambers was a disciple with nowhere to go. In his inaugural lecture, Chambers outlined a series of dead ends facing his department. Over the last couple of years, along with Ker, he had fiercely resisted the reforms of the 1921 Board of Education Report on English which had proposed that the subject redefine itself into what Classics had once been—the central humanities discipline. One of Ker's last papers, for the English Association, was written against this spurious 'Humanities Ideal' and its 'watering down' tendency.

Chambers made his inaugural lecture a lofty retort to the report, with its criticisms of compulsory Anglo-Saxon and medieval English. This willed traditionalism was to cut UCL off from the great revolution in English teaching which took place at Cambridge under Richards, Leavis and Willey. Nor were there any attractive alternatives to fall back on at UCL. Chambers specifically disowned the totalism of Morley—his mission to 'tell the story of the British mind' through the whole cycle of the national literature, 'Freshman English' writ large and long. At the same time, Ker's pan-Europeanism had been cut off at the root, destroyed by the First World War. Ker's *Epic and Romance*, the bible of the department for thirty years, enshrined a cultish reverence for Teutonic heroism as the epic base of European literature. Many of the young men Ker and Chambers had imbued with that belief died in the trenches, victims of Prussian beastliness.

In 1923, Chambers presided over a shattered subject, unable to move forward, disconnected from its own past. 'All that most of us can aspire to do,' he declared 'is to make isolated contributions by editing an author, or writing a biography or a number of scattered essays.' UCL duly became the home of isolated contributions. Following Ker, UCL also became the home of authoritarian professorship. Chambers was a UCL product, man and boy (he was appointed to the Quain Chair from his post as College Librarian). The appointment of another internal candidate, C. J. Sisson as the first Lord Northcliffe professor was indicative of an inward-turned department. Sisson was a very civilized professor but possessed no eminence as a scholar. His main publication, on his appointment, was an account of Shakespeare in India.

The heads of UCL's English department, over the next thirty years, were evidently too powerful for the good of the department. One can see how it came about. In the days of Morley, the English Department was a one-man-band. The head of department was monarch of all he surveyed, but he didn't survey very much. As the departmental structure grew, with the honours school, degree courses, endowed chairs, the powers of the governing professor were not constitutionally curtailed. This phase—the era of the autocratic head of department and the department as professorial fiefdom—has received satiric immortalization in David Lodge's *The British Museum is Falling Down* (1981), where Holles and Bane are caricatured as Tweedledum Northcliffe and Tweedledee Quain tyrants.

I want at this point to leap forward over the regimes of James Sutherland and A. H. Smith to the period I know at first hand—

that associated with Frank Kermode, Randolph Quirk, Stephen Spender and Karl Miller. The UCL English Department was reformed yet again in late 1967–8 by the energetic new professoriate of Quirk (Quain), Kermode (Northcliffe) and Spender. There were close links between these men. Quirk and Kermode had been childhood friends at school on the Isle of Man. Kermode and Spender had been co-editors of *Encounter* before jointly resigning after the CIA-funding revelation in 1963.

Two crucial constitutional innovations were brought in. First, a new comprehensive syllabus which emulated the ambitiousness of Morley's coverage and Ker's devotion to depth. Second, a departmental Board of Studies was appointed to control the syllabus. The head of department, although he or she is a voting member, may not chair this board, but sits to one side on a kind of stool of humility. Above all, the new leadership introduced a new journalistic alertness and breadth of vision. Spender and Kermode were both card-carrying higher journalists. Spender, particularly, represented the London literary world incarnate, for the Leavisite faction. Kermode, since his early days at Manchester, had been a *Guardian* reviewer. Like Ker, he loved the gamesomeness of literary criticism: his early reviews were collected under the title *Puzzles and Epiphanies* (1962). Kermode was also instrumental in the dissemination of theory through his graduate seminars of the late 1960s and early 1970s. He set up the department's first courses in American literature. While conducting the department, he was a regular reviewer for the *Listener* and the *New York Review of Books*, and following Barthes's example he wrote over a hundred essays of a literary and cultural kind for the *Daily Telegraph*.

Kermode's regime represented a brilliant recapitulation of all that had preceded him in the department and achieved a fusion of its scholarly and journalistic traditions. His five years' tenure was hugely transformative without being in any sense a rupture with the past.

His successor in 1974 was Karl Miller. To anyone with historical hindsight, Miller was Masson *redux*. There were, however, rumblings at the departmental level—dire threats in the xerox room. George Steiner was quoted as being offended by the thought of a man who had been literary editor of the *Spectator* and the *New Statesman* and editor of the *Listener* becoming the Northcliffe Professor of English at UCL. Miller had no doctoral degree (nor for that matter, had Kermode or Spender). He had embarked on research at Harvard but came to distrust it (one of his first acts at UCL was to purge the postgraduate community—much to the department's eventual intellectual health). Miller had to his name a mass of brilliant writing and scholarly publication, but none of it was in 'learned' journals, merely journals. He was, in the highest sense, a journalist.

There was, as I say, resistance—as there had been to Masson and Morley. But the then Provost of UCL, Noel Annan, was himself a humane man of letters (and a reviewer who had often appeared in journals edited by Miller). Generally, the appointment was welcomed. And as it was to turn out, the years of Miller's rule at UCL, 1974–92, were to be a departmental highpoint—only equalled, in my view, by the 1870s, under Morley. Building on the new syllabus devised by Kermode and Quirk, Miller strengthened the creative writing element in the department, which now had among its number Spender, A. S. Byatt and Dan Jacobson (all of them distinguished literary journalists, as well as critics and creative writers). One can trace all sorts of apostolic lines reaching out from Miller's years in the world of higher London journalism. Jeremy Treglown, later editor of the *TLS*, was a Miller appointment as a lecturer. Blake Morrison was a Ph.D. student under his direction. Others, such as Mark Lawson and Lynne Truss, graduated from the department in these years. Later, Miller took an interest in the creation of the *London Quarterly*.

Momentously, it was during his years at UCL—in the cultural vacuum created by the industrial strike which closed *The Times* and its supplements for a year—that Karl Miller founded the *London Review of Books*, which he was to edit and co-edit from 1979 to 1992. He was joined by a journalist who had worked with him earlier, Mary Kay Wilmers (currently editor of the *LRB*), and by other journalistic colleagues such as Ian Hamilton. In his role as professor of English, Miller also now had a new range of academic contacts. The *LRB*, under Miller, quickly broke away from its 'marsupial' character as a supplement to the *New York Review of Books* to create a new style and voice in British higher journalism, a blend of the academic and the traditionally journalistic. As those with a historical perspective noted, Miller had imported the *Edinburgh Review* into the present day, and into literary London. The tone of the paper mixed the Leavisite serious note with something quite sprightly and metropolitan. It combined British and American cultural concern. And it had at least part of its root-work in the UCL English department. The department has much to be proud of over the last 170 years or so, but its connection with the *LRB*, more particularly the link between scholarship and London journalism which it represents, is one of its greatest achievements.

5

Darke Conceits: Churton Collins, Edmund Gosse, and the Professions of Criticism

VALENTINE CUNNINGHAM

Among the Christmas presents John Churton Collins received in 1889 was a tribute from a student who was attending one of his many University Extension courses. It was a set of verses called 'Christmas 1889', and the kind of knowing fan-letter any teacher of literature might relish:

> Who never *snubs* a questioner?
> Who never says, 'Your papers, sir,
> Are far too long; *short* I prefer'?
> Our teacher.

> Who well deserves his Christmas feast
> And six weeks holiday at least
> Lecture and paper-work all ceased?
> Our teacher.

There's much more in the same vein and, clearly, the pupil has not read his Browning for nothing. But it's the poem's sixth verse that really attracts because of its claim for the teacher's scholarly-critical mastery:

> Who guides us through the 'Fairie Queene'
> And beauty shows, before unseen,
> And what the 'darke conceit' doth mean?
> Our teacher.[1]

'Darke conceit': it was the phrase Edmund Spenser used in his famous letter to Sir Walter Raleigh for the 'continued Allegory'

---

[1] L. C. Collins, *Life and Memoirs of John Churton Collins* (London, 1912), 71–2.

of *The Fairie Queene*. If anybody could crack the allegorical codes of Spenser's epic it would, of course, be John Churton Collins. He was the master, we might say, of literature's dark conceits wherever they occurred. He was, simply, formidably learned—in the classical texts, in English literature, in literary history. He was educated as a classicist at Balliol College, Oxford, but as many a classicist was—F. W. Bateson is a later case in point—he'd been drawn into the burgeoning world of the professional study of English literature in the University Extension movement and in university colleges spreading across Victorian London and the great provincial cities, and he had recycled himself as an expert in English literature. So committed in fact did Collins become to his new subject that his published polemics helped immensely in establishing an idea of what the professionalized university study of English in England might be like. He began as a mere man of letters who'd fallen more or less accidentally into teaching, but he turned himself into what we can recognize as the first self-conscious and fully professional scholar-critic in England. It took time for his talents to be fully endorsed. The hard-worked peripatetic and extra-mural teacher failed, as none of his enemies forgot to remind the world, to gain the professorial appointments he wanted in Oxford and London. It was only in 1905 that he was given the Chair of English at Birmingham. But belated though the appointment was, it can be seen as a recognition by the academy—to be sure, the provincial academy, but still the academy—that Collins's style of literary learning and critical investigation was the coming thing.

Collins's career covered the period when the subject of English literature was being invented for study in universities. It was a slow birth, involving a sequence of awkward battles against the suspicions of Cambridge and Oxford, of compromises with belletrism and philology and classical studies and antiquarianism, a coming to terms with the vernacular reading interests of dissenting academicians and working-class autodidacts, of provincial vicars and the daughters of the bourgeoisie, a regrouping of the critical forces powerfully represented by the Victorian journals, those assorted mouthpieces of novelists and poets, of Nonconformist pastors, Anglican vicars, gentlemen of leisured reading interests, cultivated industrialists, of aesthetic civil servants with time on their hands for books and of the seething Victorian army of men and of course women (one thinks of the young George Eliot and of Margaret Oliphant in particular) contriving a living by their pens. It involved an inevitable professionalization, a distinct move away from the freelance milieu, a hardening up of the part-time world in which, say, the minister of Cross Street Unitarian Chapel Manchester, the Revd William Gaskell, would serve also as a teacher of English literature at Owens College Manchester, or the Revd Charles Kingsley could also function as Professor of English at the Queen's College for Women in London. It was the creation of a class of literary players who would be paid a full-time salary for reading and teaching and writing about English literature. John Churton Collins was one of its chief members. The new professionals' arguments with the old world they emerged from would of course go on well into the twentieth century—as the polemics of F. R. Leavis and the *Scrutiny* group at Cambridge and of F. W. Bateson at Oxford clearly show.[2] But it can be argued that we owe it in a massive way to Collins that the criticism of vernacular texts was hauled out of the mixed and murky world of Victorian literary criticism, in particular from the world of the long magazine article fired by seriousness but still infected by amateurish enthusiasm, by the *parti pris* of poets and novelists and the snobberies of classicists, as well as by the circulation of leisurely opinion in gentlemen's clubs and the common rooms of Oxford and Cambridge, and made to be the business of a critical world that we can recognize as very like our own, the modern critical world in fact, where what American academics designate as 'scholarship' (we're all 'scholars' in the academy) has become fundamental and where 'research' into texts and contexts and intertexts, into how texts arise, and what they 'really' mean, and how such hermeneutical activity is theorized, is the recognized basis of opinion and teaching, and where, all added together, these things constitute, for much of the literary world, reading itself.

Collins knew his own worth. His polemics for his new profession are justifiably conceited. But what I want to suggest is that Collins's immense conceit—not just about local dark conceits,

---

[2] See Valentine Cunningham, 'F. W. Bateson: Scholar, Critic, and Scholar-Critic', *Essays in Criticism*, 29 (Apr. 1979), 139–55.

but about what constituted good and scholarly literary criticism—could be just as much a darkening of counsel as what he loudly deplored in the world of mere opinionatedness, of hasty coming to journalistic judgement and of the more or less scanty scholarship in the great Victorian periodical reviewing machine. I would also argue that the opponents and antagonists of Collins, the hacks and dunces he set himself to wrestle with in what he thought of as the unprofessional arm of the literary enterprise, in particular his famous target Edmund Gosse, were by no means as disregardable in their critical work, were not such rubbishy literary-critical labourers as Collins stridently alleged. And in suggesting that what Collins and Gosse were variously about bore likenesses as well as dissimilarities, I offer the story of Collins at war with Gosse as a kind of allegory, a parable no less, of what I suggest (*mutatis mutandis*) is the false dichotomy which would sharply divide 'literary scholarship' (the real business of criticism, as those professionals labelling themselves 'scholars' of literature believe) from what the mere reviewer, the journalist, the media critic, gets up to. This is that crude modern dividing off of the 'scholar' in the university literary faculty from the critic out there on the street; the distinction variously announced as the professor versus the *feuilletoniste* (the version of this opposition most commonly heard in Germany); the true professional versus the amateur, the belletrist, the mere man of letters; the thoughtful, careful, disinterested, unpartisan (not least because in some tenured sinecure), unworldly servant of long-term views and wide, learned perspectives, as against the shoddy worker, the hack, the short-termist, the ignorant, the careless, the tyro—those 'whipper-snappers' of *The Times Literary Supplement*, as the late F. W. Bateson once called them in an indignant riposte to that journal, refusing to be airily dismissed by what he thought of as unread boys.[3]

It's a distinction with a certain puritan pride in it. The scholar's word is incorruptible, the hack is for sale—his views infected because he's opinionated at a price, never wholly

---

[3] 'At my age I am not prepared to have one of your whipper-snappers call me "engagingly dotty" . . . just because I argue that, though Addison was a trivial thinker, his prose style is excellent. . . . Your reviewer, if he can spare the time, should read the *Spectator* . . .', *TLS* (10 Dec. 1971), 1553.

disinterested, likely to be in some editor's or proprietor's pocket. And, of course, I would press my allegation that this is too extreme a polarization because of the larger truth it seems to me to register—namely that there is, simply, no one business of criticism which reigns supreme at the expense of all others, that no one particular critical activity is the sole proprietor of all truth, with a right to dismiss all the others, and especially the humble activity of reviewing, of literary journalism, as axiomatically second-rate, disregardable, unserious, nigh on worthless.

It is clear which side Churton Collins stood on and for, which side he thought university literature departments should be on, where he wanted the study of English literature to be, and where he thought the proper function of criticism was not being maintained. The weekly reviews, he said, were an 'irresponsible tribunal'.[4] Their contributors were log-rollers, mutual admiration societies, charlatans encouraging charlatans.[5] These were the sort of charges that would become quite standard in later years. In Collins's indignant accusations you can hear the hostility of the Leavises towards the clique-puffery and flank-rubbing of literary London in the 1930s, or of Hugh Kenner at his most scathing about the old-boy networks of the same metropolitan literary culture in the 1970s and 1980s in which the Oxford Boys scratch each others backs, Craig propping up Julian as he puts in a useful word or two for Martin, and the like.[6]

The upshot of this surrender of judgement to the chummy veniality of the club, the useful acquaintance, and the shrewd calculation of personal advantage is that for Collins (as later for the Leavises and for Kenner) reviewing is a mockery, at best a sort of empty shadow boxing. The irresponsibility of the reviewing machine is a main grouse of the articles collected in the *Ephemera Critica* volume. Reviewers' bad habits are a symptom of the general malaise of literary discussion and education in

[4] John Churton Collins, *Studies in Poetry and Criticism* (London, 1905), 245.

[5] J. C. Collins, 'Log-Rolling and Education', *Ephemera Critica, or Plain Truths About Current Literature* (London, 1901), 133 ff.

[6] F. R. Leavis, 'The Literary Racket', *Scrutiny*, 1 (1932); Q. D. Leavis, 'The Background of Twentieth Century Letters', *Scrutiny*, 8 (1939): both in F. R. Leavis, ed., *A Selection from Scrutiny*, i (Cambridge, 1968), 160 ff. Hugh Kenner, *A Sinking Island: The Modern English Writers* (London, 1988), 254 ff.

England. 'It is time for some one to speak out', roared Collins's Preface:

It is the fate of the serious book to be 'reviewed', in the course of a few days, by the same man for three or four, or it may be for five or six, daily and weekly journals, and their fortune in the market made or unmade by a censor who has probably done no more than glance at their half-cut pages, and who, if he had studied them from end to end, would have been no more competent to take their measure than he would have been to write them. This leads, it is needless to say, to every kind of abuse: to works which deserve to be authorities on the subjects of which they treat dropping at once into oblivion, to works which every scholar knows to be below contempt usurping their places; to the deprivation of all stimulus to honourable exertion on the part of authors of ability and industry; to the encouragement of charlatans and fribbles; to gross impositions on the public.[7]

Exaggerated charges? Satirical exuberance? Maybe. But the vision of some desperate hack reviewing the same book for many papers is an exact description of the fate of Edward Thomas, churning out endless reviews, several a day, some of them separate reviews of the same book for different papers, in order to keep himself going as a writer—a ghastly grind which brought immense disgust and self-loathing ('Another huge parcel . . . to gulp and vomit and return to the vomit'[8]). As for the charge that reviewers did no more than glance at a book's half-cut pages, Wyndham Lewis, for one, thought he'd detected that going on, as shown by his marvellous satire in *The Roaring Queen* on Arnold Bennett's weekly declarations of the best books. (In this 1930s novel, too libellous to appear in Lewis's lifetime, Sammy Shodbutt, egged on by his wife Joanie, is driven to keep, so to say, upping the ante as to how much of a book he needs to read before he can decide it's the best book of the week. They eventually agree Shodbutt could tell from the title alone. Flaubert, Shodbutt excitedly alleges, could of course do it even if the book had never been written. And 'so could you' Joanie chirps.[9]) Collins's disgust at all this shoddiness is highly principled—his is the moral high ground of criticism. From it he fired his most famous critical salvoes, the notorious attack in the

[7] J. C. Collins, 'The Present Functions of Criticism', *Ephemera Critica*, 3, 13–14.

[8] John Moore, *The Life and Letters of Edward Thomas* (London, 1939), 148.

[9] Wyndham Lewis, *The Roaring Queen*, ed. Walter Allen (London, 1973), ch. 6.

Quarterly Review (1886) on Edmund Gosse's Clark Lectures, given in the University of Cambridge and published by the Cambridge University Press in 1885 as *From Shakespeare to Pope: an Inquiry into the Causes and Phenomena of the Rise of Classical Poetry in England.*

It's a long piece (forty pages, 20,000 words or so), full of *schadenfreude*, joyously relishing the chance to put to shame a rival for academic honours. But its target is ambitiously wider than the mere occasion of the polemic. Gosse is not just offered as sacrificial lamb; he's presented as a symptom. Collins's large claim is that he's analysing what's currently up with the whole state of modern literary teaching in the universities, and what dire consequences await universities if the likes of Gosse are given the podium and the salaries (the title of Collins's piece is 'English Literature at the Universities'). Collins is determined to demonstrate, and he does it almost to excess, how this rot starts in the reviewing business and how, by contrast, a reviewer should behave. He is calling attention to the corrupting spread of Gosse the reviewer's habitually shoddy critical tricks, out from the pages of the journals and into the lecture halls of a great university. A large aim, then, is to expose the infectious complicity of the great world of the academy, and of creative writing, with the worthless inhabitant of Grub Street. So Collins's own refusal to allow personal considerations to affect the tone and content of this blow for scholarly standards is much to the point. Gosse is an old acquaintance, but friendships must not hold you back from telling the truth about books. The dirt must be dished, even on a friend. This critic is no log-roller. Allowing interestedness to sway judgement is just what's wrong with the reviewing world. Not endorsing such complicities was just one more of the things Gosse could not understand.

Gosse and his book were, of course, sitting ducks. It was very easy to convict the Clark Lecturer of many a 'gross chronological blunder', of 'habitual inaccuracy with respect to dates', 'slovenliness' about history, inaccurate transcription ('incapable of transcribing a date correctly, even when it must have been before his very eyes'), 'ignorance' ('of the simplest facts of Literature and History', 'of the commonest facts of history and biography'), and, gravest offence, 'simulating familiarity with works which he knows only at second hand, or of which he knows nothing more than the title'.[10]

All these were, manifestly, a hack's faults. Gosse privately admitted he was guilty of being 'cocky and careless',[11] and those traits were, of course, exemplified in the journeyman reviewer's readiness to tackle any literary task that paid, to come up with a view by some near deadline, in other words to read fast and fudge up at speed authoritative sounding responses. How Gosse performed when he was asked to do a piece on the novelist Henrik Conscience in September 1883, just a couple of years before the Clark Lectures were published, well illustrates his own customary *modus operandi*. It shows the reviewer's normal hubris in full flight, as well as nicely indicating the Grub Streeter's daily plight:

At 1.30 Harwood wrote to me by hand asking for an article for this Saturday on the Flemish novelist Conscience, who has just died. I had never read one of Conscience's books, and I felt very much inclined to say no, but I did not like to do so, and assented. At 4 I went up to the B. M. and took notes for an hour, then to Kolckmann, from whom I borrowed four of Conscience's books and bought 2 more. I read in the omnibus, in the train, walking home, all through dinner till 9, when I turned to and wrote my article, finishing it and posting it on the stroke of 12. I don't think it is a bad article either. You must not think I am any the worse for it, on the contrary the excitement gave me a pleasant fillip: I am better today than I have been for days.

Gosse's biographer Ann Thwaite believes this a 'vivid instance of how he could not turn down a commission, and how conscientious he was'.[12] It is hardly the latter. This is not how a very serious critical conscientiousness works. Gosse ought to have had a bad conscience about Conscience, but he did not. Ann Thwaite is certainly right, though, to see here the hack's habit of never turning down a commission if it's at all manageable. Financial need, financial desire, drive. And Gosse's career is in numerous respects a paradigm case of the reviewer's normal

[10] J. C. Collins, 'English Literature at the Universities', *Quarterly Review*, 163 (1886), 289–329.

[11] To John Addington Symonds. Quoted in Ann Thwaite, *Edmund Gosse: A Literary Landscape 1849–1928* (London, 1984), 232.

[12] Ibid. 232.

pressures and anxieties. Is the piece going in? What will the fee be? (The *Cornhill* 'pays splendidly'.) What about a rise? (An American magazine is offering him £100 an article, he tells the *Sunday Times* late on in his career, and 'Arnold Bennett receives £50 each time for the tosh he contributes to the *Evening Standard*', so 'Don't you think Sir William Berry could afford to pay me even more?') Even for a reviewer so ubiquitous and eminent as Gosse there was always the fear of the sack and the subsequent slide in income. In March 1919 the *Daily Chronicle* 'dismissed me without a day's warning': 'I leave you to think how pleasant it is at my age to be treated like this.'[13] Indeed so. And reading Gosse's life is to be plunged into the atmosphere of the money worries of a freelance man of letters as vividly telling as in any set of Grub Street memoirs—Brian Aldiss's memoir, *Bury My Heart at W. H. Smith's*, it might be, with its recollections of John Betjeman being done down over yet another vanload of review copies brought in to Sanders' shop in Oxford's High Street from his home out Wantage way ('A fiver, John?'), an encounter very near the knuckle for any more recent hack who has ever clustered with his plastic bags of nearly new tomes in the porches of Gaston's, the London review-copy merchants.[14]

The errors Collins was convicting Gosse of were the results of the literary hack's normal drivenness, which commonly precludes slow and close reading, and leaves little time for checking and rechecking. Those were scholarly habits Gosse never allowed himself to acquire. Where Collins was now expanding with bitter invective and satirical gloating, Edward Dowden had already sounded a warning note—Gosse's collection of English Odes, published in 1881, contained several howlers in the texts of well-known poems as well as inaccuracies in the notes[15]—and Collins would be able to repeat his hatchet job later on when Gosse's *Short History of Modern English Literature* came out in 1898 (an attack included in *Ephemera Critica*). Gosse would not, perhaps could not, learn. Speedy through-put of articles and reviews and books was the game he was playing. He was

---

[13] *A Literary Landscape 1849–1928* (London, 1984), 109, 130, 483–4.
[14] Brian Aldiss, *Bury My Heart at W. H. Smith's* (London, 1990), 30. For Gaston's, see Paul Theroux, 'Lady Max', *Granta*, 40 (Summer 1992), 85 ff.
[15] Thwaite, *Edmund Gosse*, 232.

always hastening forwards, forever moving on to what he hoped would be yet more prominent and well-lit ground—more *coups*, more fresh talents, more boastable finds. It was a tendency which made him ready prey, of course, to the likes of the notorious forger T. J. Wise, who could easily palm off on him new-minted stories, say, of what Browning allegedly said about the alleged first edition of Elizabeth Barrett's *Sonnets from the Portuguese* which Wise had just cobbled up for sale. Gosse was a sucker for the latest find, a long-standing gull of the crooked Wise. And there's more than a whiff of conjuring trick and charlatanry about Gosse's intrepid craze for being first with the newest literary thing. It was the showman and ringmaster in him that kept him pushing forward, on, on, slamming down his thoughts, getting the pieces out, speeding on to the next book, the next reputation, the next payment.

People in Cambridge, of course, rallied to Gosse as he came under Collins's withering fire, and so did the great and good in the literary world—Rider Haggard, Henry James, Browning, Tennyson, and the 'men in clubs', as Virginia Woolf scathingly labelled the males of the Establishment in *Jacob's Room* (1922)—even though almost everyone, even Gosse's friends, seems to have recognized the gentleman scholar's habitual slap-dash way with detail, facts, quotations, dates. No one who had supported Gosse's candidature for the Clark Lectureship and for the Fellowship at Trinity College which went with it, was going to admit too loudly to having backed a shallow historian or the literary equivalent of a card sharper. But even when the literary editors sided with Collins—and it was easy to see how the practices Collins associated with Gosse brought the literary business into disrepute and had distinct disadvantages for all readers and all reading—they found it hard to do much about the malaise of reviewing as deplored by Collins. Collins's *Life* cites the editor of a 'Leading Review' who wrote on 16 October 1902:

I feel with you that the great mass of modern criticism, so-called, is shamelessly inadequate, ignorant, injudicious, and often, indirectly at all events, corrupt. Even when it is none of these, it is far too often mealy-mouthed and afraid to speak out; and I think you have done a great service to literature in exposing humbugs and blind guides, and in maintaining a high standard of knowledge and judgement in your own literary estimates. Whether you do not sometimes overleap your mark in excessive severity I am not sure; but at all events it is, in the critic nowadays, a fault on the right side.

As to the . . . . , one difficulty is that our space is so limited, that one cannot afford to waste it often on the small fry, or on the literary scum of the day. It seems better if one has to choose, to praise a good book than to abuse a bad one—to call attention to something great or at least important, than to give additional notoriety to a mean production . . .[16]

Collins was, in other words, on his own. It was being left up to him—at least this was his view of the matter—to set a counter-example, to show in practice as well as by precept how a different kind of critical work might be conducted. It was a mission he took to with relish, even fanaticism.

Take, for example, Collins's *Studies in Poetry and Criticism* (1905). It's offered proudly as the work of the new Professor of English Literature in the University of Birmingham. Collins has at last got the position from which he can demonstrate how the proper business of criticism might be performed in the new context of the university study of English. The book's Preface is characteristically tough-mouthed. Criticism is not 'a loose record of personal impressions'. Critics must be scholars. Criticism is worthless unless it's the outgrowth of sound scholarship and knowledge. And the studies in the book show how this combination is to work. Especially fine, and an example of Collins at his best, is the long essay on 'Longinus and Greek Criticism'. It attempts precisely 'to recall criticism to its old sources and traditions, and thus to illustrate how, if it is to be what it is of power to be, it must rest on far more solid foundations than undisciplined and uninstructed susceptibility,—on the foundations, that is to say, laid by its classical masters'. Collins's argument and the critical exercise he's mounting run together in an exemplary, as it were self-reflexive, metatextual way. Both are typical of Collins. The case is for English literature's being read in the context of classical literature, and for modern criticism's being based in the practice of the ancients. The thrust is aggressively traditional and canonical—the critic can only function adequately if he has been as well educated in traditional reading and theory, in the great Western canon of

---

[16] L. C. Collins, *Life and Memoirs*, 157.

writings, and of thinking about literature, as Collins has been (the implied sneer at the well-intentioned amateur of the Gosse kind is starkly obvious). And Collins's resultant critical-scholarly practice is no doubt dazzlingly assured, a masterly illustration of how to do historical criticism which, it is implied, the others, especially in the newly accumulating faculties of English in Liverpool and Manchester and Leeds and Notting-ham and the rest, but above all in Oxford, will ignore to their detriment. The publishing history of Longinus' essay on the Sublime is given in loving scholarly detail. This is how to do a textual, bibliographical job of work. Longinus' essay is read with canny power. This is how a careful reading acquires authority. Evidently, Collins is showing off, strutting his stuff, demonstrating to all his contemporaries just how to use an old text both for the information it might contain and for the critical guidance it might offer: this is a model of how a truly scholarly criticism might proceed. And it's done, too, at exemplarily great length. There's no obvious reviewer's rush here: the engagement with Longinus' text takes fifty-eight pages. It was worked up, we learn from the *Life* of Collins, over several weeks of intensive labour.[17]

The Longinus work is all of a piece, to take another example of Collins' magisterial procedures, with his series of long and extremely impressive articles on Tennyson in the *Cornhill*, 'A New Study of Tennyson' (1880–1), essays which were the basis for his book *Illustrations of Tennyson* (1891) and his edition of *In Memoriam, the Princess and Maud* (1902). These articles read now as quite staggeringly modern in their force and tone, and in their serious engagement with questions of theory as well as in their careful exegetical practice. They propound a theory of influence. There are certain poets, the likes of Virgil and Tennyson, who work by imitating other poets rather than work-ing from nature. The pieces offer a theory of cultural derivation. Classic English literature must be seen within a family relation with the classics of the southern European past, and of Greece and Rome in particular. What's more, these essays announce a programme of research: Tennyson must be read, as Virgil has been read, by scholars who are equipped to take in his enormous

---

[17] L. C. Collins, *Life and Memoirs*, 154. J. C. Collins, 'Longinus and Greek Criticism', *Studies in Poetry and Criticism*, 204–62.

range of classical allusions, imitations, analogies, adaptations and 'simple transferencies'. And, of course, for this is ever Collins's way, the articles offer themselves as 'inaugurating' this 'branch of Tennysonian research', by looking at *In Memoriam* in particular for its classical bases, especially Virgilian ones, and inspecting the Tennysonian epic *Idylls of the King* for its borrowed, indeed stolen, substance.[18]

So much, you are intended to think, for the 'fribbles and criticasters',[19] the mere 'scribblers' who deal with great literature, indeed with any literature, 'not with any honest desire to contribute to [its] elucidation, but simply with the hope of scrambling cheaply into notoriety', as Collins put it of certain crass amenders of Shakespeare's text.[20] This was to be a QED for proper, scholarly, dignified, deep reading, as against the quick shallowness of the *feuilleton*. Here was how to do business in great literary-critical waters. Let Gosse and his kind be left, as the Victorian by-word had it, to make Gosses of themselves, to potter on in the papers as unsound critics, even though sympathetic ones, doing what Collins described as gossiping 'pleasantly and plausibly' in their own way, but leaving the serious ground to the serious men in the serious faculties of English—especially in Collins's Birmingham.[21]

But, of course, this was a contrast—good scholarly practices as against mediocre journalistic ones, serious criticism against scarcely serious opinionatedness—that was far too extreme. It was too extreme in practice then; it is too extreme now; it's certainly too extreme in the allegory of reading which I'm offering. Clearly, what even Collins allows as the decent prerogatives of the reviewer's mode—sympathetic talk, plausible gossip, second-hand scholarship (what Gosse described in his book *Gossip in a Library* as 'a little criticism, a little anecdote, a little biography'; what Gosse intended by the Kit-Kat, the pleasant half-portrait)—had, and have, their critical force and their critical legitimacy.[22] Some of Gosse's 'ten-minute sermons' (as he

---

[18] 'A New Study of Tennyson', *Cornhill Magazine*, 41 (1880), 36–50; 42 (1880), 36–50; 44 (1881), 87–106.

[19] 'Longinus', 216.

[20] 'Text and Prosody of Shakespeare', *Studies in Shakespeare* (London, 1904), 312–13.

[21] 'Our Literary Guides', *Ephemera Critica*, 110ff.

[22] *Gossip in a Library* (London, 1891; new edn., 1913), 7.

called them) in the *Sunday Times* [23]—for instance his piece
'Yorick and His Eliza'[24]—are brilliant vignettes in the sharpest
fashion of Virginia Woolf or V. S. Pritchett. They are, if you
like, impressionistic critical-biographical short stories, and, in
their way, in their lively engagement with the real biographical
and social matrix out of which fictions come, they are as legiti-
mate a branch of insightful critical work as an original and
learned study of Tennyson's Virgilian obligations or an examination of Longinus as critical model.

What's more, they serve an important function, not always
attended to in works of academic literary criticism, and, indeed,
specifically repudiated by some academic critics, of making
reading seem a humanistic activity which involves the fictive
imagination, and gives access to thought by means of this pleasurable aesthetic engagement. The very liveliness, the linguistic
verve, the phrase-making, the speculation, the stylish buzz
which are precisely what Collins disliked in Gosse—all of them,
of course, part of the burden or duty imposed on reviewers to be
interesting, to amuse and thus to help make journals and newspapers attractive—are of considerable value in the enticing of
readers to read. And if, as many recent critics have suggested,
criticism is a story of reading, it does help if it has some of the
charm and imaginative vigour, the verbal punch and push of the
better kind of stories. There is, to be sure, a great deal of critical
tosh and tushery and mere padding in, say, Gosse's *A History of
Eighteenth Century Literature* : 'Whether we read' *Gulliver's
Travels* 'as children do, for the story, or as historians, for the
political allusions, or as men of the world, for the satire and
philosophy, we have to acknowledge that it is one of the wonderful and unique books of the world's literature'.[25] But again
and again Gosse's phrase-making—that knack of summary
which makes him such an efficient narrator of a literary life and
which would help make his autobiography-cum-biography
Father and Son so memorable—does hit some critical nail neatly
on the head in the manner of old-fashioned examination questions. 'The style of Addison is superior to his matter, and holds

[23] *Books on the Table* (London, 1921), vii.
[24] Reprinted in *More Books on the Table* (London, 1923), 77 ff.
[25] *A History of Eighteenth Century Literature (1660–1780)* (London, 1909),
192.

a good many flies in its exquisite amber'.[26] (Discuss!) Reading Gosse you can see where pointed critical-historical phrase-makers as diverse as George Saintsbury, G. K. Chesterton, G. M. Young or C. S. Lewis are coming from. It's not necessarily great criticism, but it's not utterly despicable either. And it is possessed of a sheer readability—frequently purchased, to be sure, at a cost of slight and slighting summations, of fat texts being skimmed rapidly for some slick *mot*, of compressed histories, rubbishy paraphrases and traducing biography—a blessed readability which is the reason why, I'd guess, *From Shakespeare to Pope* was simply read to bits in the reading room of Oxford's Radcliffe Camera (so that it had to be withdrawn to the stacks), and why Gosse's *Gray*, his *History of Eighteenth Century Literature* and his *Studies in the Literature of Northern Europe* are still on the open shelves of that undergraduate library. As for Gosse the over-reacher, the eager novelty-seizer, trying to grab notoriety by being first with the name-making names, by that very token Gosse was the trail-blazer for Ibsen in England, the only real public advocate of minor Danish literature we've ever had, the pioneer of American Studies, the early advocate of Gide, and so on.

Frank Swinnerton's tribute to Gosse in *The Georgian Literary Scene* (1938) was rather to be expected, for he was himself a hack on Gosse lines, as the 'Author Note' to that volume makes clear: 'Office boy to Hay Nisbet, newspaper publishers, March 1899; clerk to J. M. Dent & Co., 1901–7; reader to Chatto & Windus, 1909–26. Sole book reviewer to the London *Evening News*, 1929–32. Principal novel reviewer to the *Observer* since April 1937.' But the tribute is aptly pointed in its forceful recognition of the mingled virtues and defects of the reviewing type—as well as displaying, naturally enough, for its own part, the good reviewer's perennial touch for the briskly telling phrase (and for the concomitantly thinning summary):

Gosse—pilloried at the beginning of the twentieth century by Churton Collins for writing about eighteenth century literature without taking the trouble to read the whole of it, and by Duncan Tovey for reprinting a corrupt text of Gray's letters while boasting that he had collated

[26] *A History of Eighteenth Century Literature (1660–1780)* (London, 1909), 193.

every word with the originals, still in 1934 being pilloried by Carter and Pollard for accepting as genuine several glaring modern literary forgeries, and in fact ridiculed or lambasted by almost all who have seriously tilled the ground he lightly scratched—contributed much to English knowledge of French and Scandinavian literature and wrote a book about his father which, when it was published in 1907, caused every scholarly sin to be forgiven him by the non-pedantic. To the end of his life he hobnobbed with writers, old and young. He had in his temperament both malice and vanity, and perhaps he was a snob (which means that he preferred the literary *ton*, and liked to stand well with the fashion); but he had taste, a pen, and a tender feeling for letters.[27]

But what of Churton Collins and his clamantly advertised brand of scholarly criticism? Not everyone was as impressed by the critical results of his scholarly proclivities and researches as he might have hoped. Tennyson's description of Collins as 'a louse upon the locks of literature' may well be apocryphal, but it certainly captures the feeling of the indignant marginal notes Tennyson scribbled on Collins's *Cornhill* articles about his intertextual affinities: 'No', '!!!', 'Not known to me', '!!!Non-sense', 'Nonsense' and so on.[28] And nor was Collins himself free from the rushed judgement and the need for the hasty critical decision. (Like most, I suspect, of his successors, however scholarly they are.) Certainly, though Collins might spend long, able, scholarly weeks on Longinus, he was never able to relax into a life of perpetually slow and considered reading, research and writing. Lengthy polemics about Oxford English, endless skirmishing with Gosse and his sort, devoted politicking for jobs and for projects like the founding of the Oxford Passmore Edwards Scholarship in English and Classics, his thousands of lectures up and down the country, especially for the University Extension Movement, the numerous syllabuses he had to prepare, and, of course, his persistent grubbing and hacking for the very journals whose principles he criticized (he had, after all, eight children to feed), did leave him as perpetually exhausted as

---

[27] *The Georgian Literary Scene* (London, 1938), 173.
[28] See Tennyson's notes on *In Memoriam*, reported by Christopher Ricks, ed., *The Poems of Tennyson* (London, 1969), footnotes on 862, 878, 885, 893, 908, 921, 925, 944.

he was commonly rushed. In that very month or so in Oxford
when he prepared the Longinus piece he also wrote three articles
for the *Saturday Review* ('What is Poetry?', 'Romanticism and
Classicism', and 'In Honour of Chaucer'):

also I have carefully revised the proofs of my 'Ephemera Critica';
making also important additions; and I have also carefully revised and
settled the texts of Greene's 'Friar Bacon and Friar Bungay' and 'Looking Glasse' for my edition of Greene. I often worked thirteen hours a
day and never less than eleven, seldom going to bed before 2.30, often
at 3, rising at 9.[29]

His was a life of continuous 'also'. He had, he said, the
'instincts of the bee'. But—we might say—he had the instincts of
the hack as well. It comes as no surprise to discover that one of
his earliest professorial efforts at Birmingham University was
to establish the very first university School of Journalism in
England. (Nor is it any surprise to learn that news journalists
complained its syllabuses were too concerned with turning out
'leader-writers, note-makers, reviewers, critics', rather than reporters.) Collins was by no means immune from making a Gosse
of himself. It is one of those large ironies which literary history loves to arrange—though again no surprise—that when
Collins's edition of the *Plays and Poems of Robert Greene*
appeared from the Clarendon Press in 1905, the young turk of
textual criticism W. W. Greg stepped forward in the second
number of the newly founded *Modern Languages Review* (April
1906)—the *MLR* being precisely, of course, one of the new
scholarly organs Collins's polemics had, as it were, anticipated
and that the newly professionalized, or Collinsized, university
departments of English needed as outlets for their Collinsized
researches—to devote thirteen whole pages to savaging Collins's
editorial inaccuracies, for all the world as if Collins himself were
one of the old-school critical bounders the *MLR* and the burgeoning professoriate and the new university departments of
English had been set up to counter and put out of business: 'It is
high time that it should be understood that so long as we entrust
our old authors to arm-chair editors who are content with
second-hand knowledge of textual sources, so long will English
scholarship in England afford undesirable amusement to the

[29] *Life and Memoirs*, 154.

learned world.'[30] And so on. But of course the implied vision of scholarly-critical work which does not contain inaccuracies or shaky readings, or critical judgements the rational reader can disagree with, would prove a chimera, as the new world inhabited by Greg was quickly to find out. It was finding it out, in fact, already, in this magisterial uncovering of Collins's own feet of clay. And time has indeed shown—if time were needed to show what must have been obvious from the start—that no amount of time, long or short, spent on critical thinking is any guarantee of the quality of critical judgement, that scholars are as capable of silliness and error as any reviewer, just as, conversely, coming to speedy judgement does not necessarily or inevitably lead to mistaken readings. You can be a critically canny fast reader just as you can be a bad slow one. Again and again, critical suggestions bred and germinated in the brooding atmosphere of the Ivory Tower have proved silly and daft, or just plain feeble or even unscholarly, by contrast with the criticism thrown up in the rush of the market-place, or hammered out, Walter Benjamin-style, at the table next to the orchestra in the café. The reading by Greg himself of the Dumb Show in *Hamlet* has long been a classic source of anger and amusement over how the sharpest and wisest textual critic can get a reading abominably skewed.[31]

Still, who, after Greg's attack, would want to imagine there was any kind of strict border between a Gosse and a Collins, and between what each of these men of letters represents? Not me. Nor Collins either, I fancy—he who, within two years of Greg's hard words, was found dead, drowned in mysterious circumstances in a dyke near Lowestoft, presumably an act of suicide by a man overwhelmed by some despair, it's easy to guess, at the difficulties of doing criticism well and of living the critical life to his own high standards and not just, as some supposed, over repeated rebuffs from Oxford. The Professor had found it hard to take, I surmise, that he might merely be in a different compartment of the same boat as the Reviewer, rather than, as he would wish, in some different vessel

[30] *Modern Languages Review*, 1/2 (Apr. 1906), 238–51.
[31] For discussion of W. W. Greg on the Dumbshow, see e.g. Terence Hawkes, 'Telmah', *That Shakespeherean Rag: Essays on a Critical Process* (London, 1986), 92–119.

altogether. My case is that the Professor and the Reviewer always were in the same boat, that they still are, and that the Collins-Gosse affair is as nice an allegory of this proximity as you'll find anywhere.[32]

[32] Phyllis Grosskurth is unsympathetic to Collins, all the way to his sad end: 'Churton Collins: Scourge of the Late Victorians', *University of Toronto Quarterly*, 34 (1964–5), 254–68.

6

Literature, Propaganda, and the First World War: The Case of *Blackwood's Magazine*

David Finkelstein

Former editors of *Blackwood's Magazine* (or *Maga* as it was universally known) cherished the following anecdote of a near-death experience. It is February 1918, and in a dugout on the Arras line in France, a soldier sits reading his favourite monthly journal. The call to arms is sounded and, slipping the issue into a pocket of his trenchcoat, the soldier prepares for duty. A shell explodes nearby, sending shrapnel spinning through the trenches. A fragment finding its way to him is stopped by the thick pages of the magazine nestling in his breast pocket. The chewed-up pages of the journal are subsequently sent to Edinburgh as proof that *Blackwood's Magazine* possesses miraculous powers. The relic is still preserved in the archives of the National Library of Scotland.

Among the questions which come to mind regarding this incident are some related to literary journalism, to readership, to material production, to cultural contexts and to the connections between literature and literary production during the First World War. What was *Blackwood's Magazine* doing at the front, and how did it get into the hands of this soldier? What was in its pages to appeal to, and be read by, such a reader? Who were the journal's targeted and actual reading audiences? Finally, what can the answers to such questions tell us about the role of literary

I would like to thank Dr Tom Barron of the University of Edinburgh, Dr Douglas Mark Peers of the University of Calgary and members of my department at Napier University for their constructive comments during the preparation of this piece. I would also like to thank the National Library of Scotland for permission to quote from the Blackwood publishing archives.

journalism in forming and reinforcing cultural and literary values during periods of political and social upheaval?

Behind these issues lies another matter, namely how, in particular circumstances, literary journalism and literary journals can become subject to the political concerns of the state. *Blackwood's Magazine* proves an apposite case for investigation, especially when viewed as part of a specifically political product, developed to shape and mould public opinion and views between 1914 and 1918. It was one of many media sources through which British public perceptions were consciously manipulated by the government during the war. By collaborating in this effort, *Blackwood's Magazine* also ensured its own economic viability and success, vastly increasing its sales and advertising revenue.

Much critical attention has focused on the role of the Edinburgh publishing firm William Blackwood & Sons and *Blackwood's Magazine* in nineteenth-century cultural and literary history; little has been written on the journal's role in the twentieth century. This neglect has to do with its move away from a dominant position in the nineteenth century, when it championed George Eliot, Anthony Trollope and Joseph Conrad, among others, towards a dull existence as the favoured journal of a predominantly military and colonial service audience. Founded in 1817 as a more nimble Tory alternative to the severe *Edinburgh Review*, its early issues featured the barbed commentary of John Wilson ('Christopher North'), James Hogg ('The Ettrick Shepherd') and Thomas DeQuincey, among others. Under the editorship of John Blackwood (1845–79), it slowed in pace but rose in literary influence, perfectly reflecting mid-century literary tastes and values. It also cultivated a reputation as the periodical of empire, read by officers and administrators in their clubs and meeting rooms. But as the empire faded, *Blackwood's Magazine* was left behind to rely increasingly on tales of hunting, shooting and fishing to fill its pages, as well as on serialized works of 'popular' authors such as Neil Munro, Ian Hay, John Buchan and Winifred Fortescue. The reasons for this had less to do with aesthetic considerations than with economic patterns and editorial policies that derived from a particular agenda pursued after the retirement of its literary adviser David S. Meldrum in 1910, and the death of its fourth editor William Blackwood III in 1912. More specifically, this agenda shaped the subsequent success of the journal during the First World War.

George Orwell suggested in 1941 that *Blackwood's Magazine* in the twentieth century had become identified with all that was anathema to disillusioned, post-war middle-class intellectuals, who equated it with an anti-intellectual, pro-imperialist mentality: 'If you were a patriot you read *Blackwood's Magazine* and publicly thanked God that you were "not brainy".'[1] But this generalization overlooks an important aspect of the magazine's contents. The literature published in the journal's pages was 'popular': collections of adventure tales, thrillers, comic novels and quiet reflections of middle-class, middle-brow tastes and views. These were not works pushing at the edges of contemporary literary mores; rather they were 'thumping good reads', solidly crafted with no expectations other than to amuse or catch the reader's interest. Such a journal could be said to have been more influential in its day precisely because it reflected the static, diffuse nature of contemporary Edwardian literary and cultural tastes. That its pages remained cocooned in wartime literary conventions had much to do with its unofficial yet economically successful role as a participant in state-controlled literary propaganda.

At the start of the war in August 1914, British government bodies quickly recognized that official mechanisms needed to be established not only to control information being published concerning the war, but also to mobilize public support at home and influence opinion abroad. From the outset, as one source suggests, 'censorship and propaganda became the twin pillars upon which the British government waged its war of words against the Central powers'.[2] In 1914, the British government had no official department dedicated to propaganda and censorship. By 1918, it had developed a highly sophisticated system which was to prove the model upon which other governments and foreign powers based their own propaganda machinery.[3]

---

[1] George Orwell, *The Lion and the Unicorn* (Harmondsworth, 1982), 64–5.

[2] P. M. Taylor, *The Projection of Britain* (London, 1981), 12, quoted in Stephen Koss, *The Rise and Fall of the Political Press in Britain* (London, 1990), 678.

[3] M. L. Sanders and Philip M. Taylor, *British Propaganda during the First World War, 1914–18* (London and Basingstoke, 1982), 1.

Shortly after war broke out, an official press censorship office, the Press Bureau, was established to monitor and censor press material published in Great Britain. (Media wags promptly renamed it the 'Suppress Bureau'.[4]) The Bureau worked closely with the Admiralty and War Office, and was advised by establishment figures and academics such as Professor Gilbert Murray and Sir Charles Oman, Chichele Professor of Modern History at Oxford. Strict control was maintained over printed material sent to the front, and a secret list drawn up of books and periodicals which were prohibited for export.[5] Until May 1915, the Bureau allowed only one 'Official Eyewitness', E. D. Swinton, to do all the reporting of conditions on the British battlefront. Swinton and Oman were not only frequent contributors to *Blackwood's Magazine*, but formed part of the journal's unofficial network of contacts with government and military departments throughout the war.

Initially, articles were submitted prior to publication for censoring by the Press Bureau. While this process was not compulsory, it was in the interests of all parties to comply, particularly in light of the 1914 Defence of the Realm Act, which made it an offence, punishable by military and civil court prosecution, to publish information 'of such a nature as is calculated to be or might be directly or indirectly useful to the enemy'.[6] As the war dragged on, the censoring activities of the Press Bureau increased. By 1917, all material initially passed by the censors for publication in periodical form had to undergo a second round of inspection if reprinted in book form. For example, when the Blackwood firm proposed reprinting 'Airman's Outings', Alan Bott's accounts from the front first serialized in *Blackwood's Magazine*, the director of the Press Bureau wrote back outlining the hurdles now facing such proposals:

We must point out that the articles which you now propose to publish in book form were passed separately as magazine articles. If you now propose to publish these—and others which we have not seen in book form, we must ask you to submit two copies of the book as

---

[4] Sanders and Taylor, *British Propaganda*, 19.
[5] Stanley Unwin mentions this list in connection with the censoring of several books and journals published by his firm in 1914–18. See Unwin, *The Truth About a Publisher* (London, 1960), 140–1.
[6] Sanders and Taylor, *British Propaganda*, 9.

you propose to issue it and it will then be dealt with in the ordinary way.[7]

In other words, not only had the firm and the author to comply with initial censoring demands and permissions for article publications, but subsequent reprints had to be fully rearranged and produced in print before the War Office and the Press Bureau would consider approving them. Such tactics could cause havoc in publishing schedules should previously approved material suddenly fall foul of the censor. In practice, while material in this category was usually given immediate approval, the layers of interference greatly slowed down periodical deadlines.

The system depended not only on censorship but on active propaganda at home and abroad. In September 1914, a War Propaganda Bureau was set up under the direction of Charles Masterman, based at Wellington House in London, which held secret meetings with authors and representatives of the press.[8] On 2 September, twenty-five representatives of the literary, academic and media establishments, all male and middle or upper-middle class, gathered to debate how literary journalism could be put to the service of the war effort. They included William Archer, J. M. Barrie, Arnold Bennett, A. C. Benson, Sir Arthur Conan Doyle, John Galsworthy, W. J. Locke, Henry Newbolt, Thomas Hardy, Gilbert Murray and H. G. Wells. Also invited, but unable to attend, were Sir Arthur Quiller-Couch and Rudyard Kipling, who sent messages of support.[9] The participants resolved to aid in the production and dissemination of material and views liable to promote the war effort. One of their first acts was to enlist fifty-four established authors, including well-known women writers such as Flora Annie Steel and Mrs Humphry Ward, in producing an 'Authors' Manifesto' in support of the war. This was published in mid-September 1914, as a full-page spread in the *New York Herald*.

Material produced under the jurisdiction of the Bureau was to

---

[7] 10 Aug. 1917, Frank Swettenham to George W. Blackwood, National Library of Scotland, Blackwood Papers, MS 30179.

[8] Gary S. Messinger, *British Propaganda and the State in the First World War* (Manchester, 1992), 35.

[9] Ibid. That such writers were present is not surprising, for they represented an influential core of British literary society, 'men of letters' whose writings were widely read and whose opinions were respected.

include books, pamphlets, translations of foreign material, re-
cruitment posters, photographic material and films. A. S. Watt,
one of the directors of the literary agency A. P. Watt and Sons,
was recruited to help place material. Acting as the major link
between authors and the mass media, Watt also organized the
publication of pamphlets, books and other propaganda with
British and American publishers. Private publishing houses, as
opposed to official government sources such as the HMSO, were
used for this purpose, to create the impression that such material
was the independent product of concerned private citizens,
rather than part of a directed government campaign. Publishers
used by Wellington House included Hodder & Stoughton,
Methuen, John Murray and William Blackwood & Sons.[10]

The concerted use in propaganda campaigns of a secret core
group of 'men of letters' (for very few women were officially
part of this programme) continued after the reorganization of
the Bureau in the spring of 1916. Additions to the staff included
John Buchan and the poet Alfred Noyes, both contributors to
Blackwood's Magazine. Lecture tours and radio broadcasts
organised by the Bureau intensified during this period, partly to
counter German propaganda efforts in the US.[11] In early 1917,
further reorganization established Buchan as the director of a
new Department of Information, set up to focus its energies
solely on the development of texts and printed material for
publication at home and abroad.

The themes and images promoted by British propagandists
centred on German aggression and 'Prussian militarism'. Germany was depicted as a society based on militarist principles,
whose soldiers, the implacable Huns or Boches, had no moral
compunction about violating women, mutilating babies and
desecrating and looting churches.[12] Such images were not new:
many originated in the period after German unification under
Bismarck in the 1860s, and in particular after the Franco-
Prussian war of 1870–1, when German military power and

---

[10] Peter Buitenhuis, *The Great War of Words: Literature as Propaganda 1914–18 and After* (London, 1989), 16.

[11] Details of the British propaganda campaign in the US can be found in Stewart Halsey Ross, *Propaganda for War: How the United States was Conditioned to Fight the Great War of 1914–1918* (Durham, NC, 1996), 27–90.

[12] Sanders and Taylor, *British Propaganda*, 137. For a full discussion of the content of wartime British propaganda, see ibid. 137–63.

superior organization overwhelmed a French army which had been considered until then to be the best organized force in continental Europe. *Blackwood's Magazine* could claim some responsibility for imprinting such views of German militarism and behaviour upon late nineteenth-century British middle-class popular culture, through its publication of George T. Chesney's *The Battle of Dorking* (1871), an immensely successful, panic-inducing tale of a German invasion of Britain. *The Battle of Dorking* has been widely cited as establishing the pattern of propagandistic fiction in which 'the whole aim was either to terrify the reader by a clear and merciless demonstration of the consequences to be expected from a nation's shortcomings, or to prove the rightness of national policy by describing the course of a victorious war in the near future'.[13]

First World War propaganda used familiar images of an inherited, Teutonic national militarism and lust for conquest to provide a focus for effective textual attacks against the enemy. Stories of war atrocities were frequently used to paint a vision at the outset of a brutal German army invading peaceful neighbours, in this case Belgium and France, leaving behind a trail of blood, terror, murder and rapine.[14] Early press releases issued by British sources featured unsubstantiated reports of mass executions of civilians, crucifixions of Allied soldiers, and mutilations of women and children. These and other stories were later detailed in the 30,000-word Bryce Commission report, devastatingly effective at the time though subsequently discredited, published in early 1915 by a distinguished investigatory committee headed by Viscount Bryce.[15] The report, coming shortly after the German sinking of the ocean liner *Lusitania*, did much to turn US public opinion against the Central Powers.

In contrast, the Allied nations were portrayed in press reports as reluctant warriors forced into action: the French, sophisticated and urbane, defending themselves from enslavement and seeking to avenge their humiliating defeat of forty years before; the British army, joining in this defence of French sovereignty and Belgian neutrality, filled with plucky, loyal, cheerful and

---

[13] I. F. Clarke, *Voices Prophesying War*, 2nd edn. (Oxford, 1992), 33.
[14] Buitenhuis, *Great War of Words*, p. xvi.
[15] See Halsey Ross, *Propaganda for War*, 50–60.

patriotic volunteers, drawn from all parts of the British Empire, and led by incisive and efficient generals.[16] From pamphlets to recruiting posters, periodical fiction to journalistic reportage, the war effort was promoted along clearly defined lines. There was little room for alternative views. Indeed, those who reported on matters seen as embarrassing or damaging to the war effort often faced censure, as was the case with the London evening paper *The Globe*, closed down for two weeks in November 1915 after it provoked a government crisis by reporting the imminent resignation of Lord Kitchener, then Secretary of State for War.[17]

Blackwood's Magazine, however, had little trouble with the censors, as it participated actively in the promotion of the war effort. From the outbreak of the conflict, the editor fully and unequivocally supported the Allied cause. 'No one here had the slightest intention of interfering with Germany or any other continental nation,' wrote George Blackwood to General Robert Oliver in September 1914, 'but now that we have been wantonly assailed through the violation of the neutrality of Belgium, we shall not lay down the sword until the German military power is rendered harmless to its neighbours.'[18] The result was the insertion of articles and stories reiterating standard perceptions of German wartime behaviour. 'He had not then taken the Moloch form that he wears today', one piece typically announced in February 1915 regarding the pre-war German, 'The Moloch who suggests the bombardment of his own most beautiful temples, and inspires the massacre of women, children, and unarmed men, and the employment of dum-dum bullets and jigsaw bayonets.'[19] Two and a half years later, *Maga*'s contributions had not changed in tone. 'We refuse to condone the thousand brutalities of which they are guilty', remarked one contributor in September 1917, adding, 'We have not made war in the spirit of the burglar and the murderer. We

---

[16] Buitenhuis, *Great War of Words*, p. xvi.

[17] For further discussion of this incident, see Nicholas Hiley, ' "Lord Kitchener Resigns": The Suppression of the *Globe* in 1915', *Journal of Newspaper and Periodical History*, 8/2 (1992), 27–41.

[18] George W. Blackwood to General Robert Oliver, 17 Sept. 1914, National Library of Scotland, Blackwood Papers, MS 30401, 773.

[19] 'The Old Junker: A Souvenir', *Blackwood's Magazine* (Feb. 1915), 157.

have not butchered women, and robbed houses and burnt churches.'[20]

By contrast, articles and fiction in *Maga* which focused on the Allied forces emphasized a sense of honour and unity at the front, and highlighted the good work being done by individuals at home on behalf of the war effort. Likewise, militarist tropes and conventions suitable for maintaining morale at home and at the front were promoted. Contributions emphasizing patriotism, honour, duty and heroic action had always featured in *Blackwood's Magazine* before 1914, usually in the context of the British imperial mission abroad. Whether building bridges in India, fighting rebels on the Afghan border or boarhunting in Africa, the activities of the British soldier and colonialist, as reflected in the magazine's pages, were part of a popular culture that one revisionist social history has suggested was a British 'world view embracing unique imperial status, cultural and racial superiority, and a common ground of national conceit on which all could agree'.[21]

Imperialist metaphors and tropes were commonplace in turn-of-the-century, upper-middle-class British culture.[22] *Blackwood's Magazine* increasingly participated in the dissemination of such codes under the editorship of William Blackwood III between 1879 and 1912. What his successors did between 1914 and 1918, however, was to incorporate them into the war material produced for the magazine's pages. At its basic level, whether in articles, stories or novels, the journal offered a version of the war as an uneven moral struggle between two empires, weighted towards the ethical superiority of the British. 'The importance of moral qualities for success in war can scarcely be overestimated', thundered C. A. L. Yate, a frequent contributor to *Blackwood's*, in the opening article of the September 1914 issue, establishing the theme which frequently recurred in subsequent issues.[23]

---

[20] Charles Whibley, 'Musings without Methods', *Blackwood's Magazine* (Sept. 1917), 422.

[21] John MacKenzie, *Imperialism and Popular Culture* (Manchester, 1986), 9.

[22] Ibid. 9 n. 2; Robert H. Macdonald, 'A Poetics of War: Militarist Discourse in the British Empire, 1880–1918', *Mosaic*, 23/3 (Summer 1990), 17–35.

[23] C. A. L. Yate, 'Moral Qualities in War', *Blackwood's Magazine* (Sept. 1914), 287.

One example of such material in *Blackwood's Magazine*
was John Hay Beith's *The First Hundred Thousand*, a popular
series of sketches published monthly under the pseudonym of
Ian Hay between November 1914 and November 1915. In this
work, Beith, a former public-school master turned writer, gave
an idealized portrayal of the training and subsequent battle
experiences of a fictional Scottish regiment, representative of
'Kitchener's army', so named after the men who in 1914 responded to the newly appointed Secretary of State for War's
appeal for army volunteers. *The First Hundred Thousand*, and
its sequel *'Carry On!'*, serialized between January 1916 and
October 1917, employed many of the commonplace sentiments
and assumptions about the British warrior and his enemy encouraged by government censors and propagandists. Farcical in
manner yet mindful of the task all have volunteered for, Beith's
soldiers begin army life as a ragged bunch of individualists, an
'awkward, shy, self-conscious mob'.[24] Training progresses and
the mob becomes a cohesive unit, bound together by common
public-school codes of fair play, self-sacrifice and team spirit.
The unifying codes and values of war as sport are crucial to the
successful moulding of this motley collection of shopkeepers,
trade unionists and civil servants.

'Playing the game' and Beith's other masculine tropes of war-
ring sport, or even sporting war, are present in much of *Maga*'s
material from September 1914, when Charles Whibley pro-
claimed that 'when the vast armies of today stand face to face in
conflict, they are playing a "game" which may be discerned only
in corners'.[25] While Beith does not go so far as to quote the
notorious lines from Henry Newbolt's 'Vitai Lampada', 'The
river of death has brimmed his banks / and England's far, and
Honour a name / but the voice of a schoolboy rallies the ranks:
/ "Play up! Play up! And play the game!"', the sentiment is the
same, indivisibly fusing sports and war into one honourable
course of action.[26] Beith evokes the supposedly selfless conduct
of team games and suggests that in similar fashion, war demanded that participants, in the words of one critic, 'behave as

[24] *Blackwood's Magazine* (Nov. 1914), 707.
[25] Charles Whibley, 'Musings without Method', *Blackwood's Magazine* (Sept. 1914), 397.
[26] Henry Newbolt, *The Island Race*, 5th edn. (London, 1902), 82.

though the battlefield were an extension of the playing field, requiring the same attitudes and spirit'.[27] At times the text strains extraordinarily hard in its attempt to press home these points, as in the case of 'Wee Pe'er', who dies in basic training from pneumonia due to over-eager attention to duty. Caught coughing by an officer while on sentry duty, he is commended for not reporting to sick bay. ' "Good boy!" said the officer to Peter. "I wish we had more like you." '[28] Later, in contrast to several fellow soldiers who report ill suffering from minor foot sores, Peter refuses to shirk his duty when night operations take place in a downpour:

Wee Peter, who in the course of last night's operations had stumbled into an old trench half-filled with ice-cold water, and whose temperature to-day, had he known it, was a hundred and two, paraded with his company at the appointed time. The company, he reflected, would get a bad name if too many men reported sick at once.[29]

Peter's actions, although ultimately fatal, are intended as an object lesson in duty and self-sacrifice. His loyalty is rewarded, with an overblown burial with full military honours, 'leaving Wee Pe'er—the first name on our Roll of Honour—alone in his glory beneath the Hampshire pines'.[30] The irony of such honour being accorded to this young soldier, felled not in battle but in training camp by a pedestrian case of pneumonia due in large part to neglect by his commanding officers, is overlooked in this homage to the principles of self-sacrifice.

In time, shirkers are weeded out and a sense of destiny is instilled in the now fully trained recruits. The result is a change 'from a fortuitous concourse of atoms to a cohesive unit of fighting men . . . and the future beckons to us with both hands to step down at last into the arena, and try our fortune amid the uncertain but illimitable chances of the greatest game in the world'.[31] This view of war extends throughout the ranks, with the commanding officer becoming the ideal team captain, 'an upright, gallant figure, saying little, exhorting not at all, but instilling confidence and cheerfulness by his very presence'.[32]

[27] Macdonald, 'Poetics of War', 19.
[28] *Blackwood's Magazine* (Apr. 1915), 454.
[29] Ibid. 455.
[30] Ibid. 456.
[31] Ibid. 450. [32] *Blackwood's Magazine* (Nov. 1915), 713.

At the heart of the text is a belief in the justness of the cause to which these soldiers now bend their efforts:

Despite the rawness of our material and the novelty of our surroundings, in the face of difficulties which are now happily growing dim in our memory, the various ranks have never quite given up trying, never altogether lost faith, never entirely forgotten the Cause which has brought us together. And the result—the joint result—of it all is a real live regiment, with a *morale* and soul of its own.[33]

There is no room to doubt the sense of mission behind these men's preparations. The socialists, trade unionists and obstinate individualists present at the beginning of basic training are eventually disciplined and absorbed into the massed ranks of 'Kitchener's army', while shirkers and drunkards are eliminated. In the end, Beith's volunteer army possesses all the moral and intellectual codes necessary to fight successfully on behalf of the 'Cause'. Indeed, as Peter Buitenhuis suggests, it is through these tropes that *The First Hundred Thousand* and *Blackwood's Magazine* establish the myth of the volunteer soldier, a man offhandedly brave, carelessly efficient and incurably philistine, for both home-front and active-service audiences.[34]

The value of Beith's work was quickly recognized by advisers to the Propaganda Bureau. In his capacity as commissioning editor for the publishers Thomas Nelson & Sons, John Buchan made a bid to include it as part of Nelson's Continental Library series, an offer rejected by Blackwood for fear that sales of their own hardcover edition would suffer from the competition.[35] At the same time, unknown to the editor, well-placed contacts in the government acted to ensure its swift approval by the Press Bureau. Sir Charles Oman, one of the Bureau's top advisers, personally took charge of the work's clearance. 'I happen to be the Censor who has passed it month by month', he later wrote to George Blackwood on its publication in hardcover, adding, 'I don't think that I cut out ten sentences from first to last—which is not generally the case with War-Stuff.'[36]

[33] *Blackwood's Magazine* (May 1915), 630.
[34] Buitenhuis, *Great War of Words*, 113.
[35] John Buchan to George W. Blackwood, 25 Nov. 1915, Blackwood Papers, National Library of Scotland, MS 30170; George W. Blackwood to J. H. Beith, 23 Dec. 1915, Blackwood Papers, National Library of Scotland, MS 30402, 447.
[36] Sir Charles Oman to George W. Blackwood, 12 Nov. 1915, Blackwood Papers, National Library of Scotland, MS 30172.

For these readers, part of the work's appeal lay in its potential use in army training. 'Its instructional value for young officers would be so great that I would strongly recommend its publication if possible', noted a Brigadier-General in charge of home defences at the time. He continued, 'It puts matters in a way that would appeal to young officers infinitely more than any of the recognised text-books.'[37] In confirmation of this aspect of the book's value, George Blackwood frequently passed on reports of its unofficial use as a military handbook to J. H. Beith. The artist responsible for the frontispiece noted, for example, 'A few days ago in a lecture on Military matters we were recommended to read "The First Hundred Thousand" as being *the* book—so it has become a Corps handbook—and the ordinary textbooks on "Field Service", "King's Regulations", etc., are out of date.'[38] Within a year of its publication in book form in December 1915, *The First Hundred Thousand* had sold over 115,000 copies in Britain and its colonies. Sales in the United States subsequently topped 350,000 copies, the highest figure for a work of war fiction in 1917.[39]

Soon *The First Hundred Thousand* was being used as a model propagandistic *Maga* piece. Sylvia Townsend Warner's only contribution to *Blackwood's Magazine*, for example, an article on her experiences in a war munitions factory (submitted in November 1915 through her father, George Townsend Warner, himself a prolific contributor to the journal), was accepted only after she heeded suggestions that it be recast, as George Blackwood put it, 'more on the lines of "The First Hundred Thousand" and "The Wards in War Time" so as to bring out more of the personal side of the workers and incidentally introduce the nature of their work'.[40] What Sylvia Townsend Warner thought of these suggestions is not recorded, but the request illustrates how even *Maga*'s non-fiction narratives were being editorially shaped to conform to the literary mould established by Beith's work. The war had to be humanized and made

[37] Brigadier-General B. F. Edwards to George W. Blackwood, 18 Feb. 1915, Blackwood Papers, National Library of Scotland, MS 30170.

[38] Stanley Cursiter to George W. Blackwood, 23 Jan. 1916, Blackwood Papers, National Library of Scotland, MS 30173.

[39] Alice Payne Hackett, *Sixty Years of Best Sellers 1895–1955* (New York, 1956), 122–3.

[40] George W. Blackwood to George Townsend Warner, 6 Nov. 1915, Blackwood Papers, National Library of Scotland, MS 30402, 391.

relevant to readers. The result was an article in which Warner describes the lives of the men and women making shell casings for gun emplacements, and more specifically her personal impressions of the sights, sounds and daily banter of the workshops. The backchat and camaraderie of these industrial workers—' "Oo, dearie, ain't it caowld," said the girl beside me, wriggling her thin bones against me in an effort to get past'—is used to foreground the vital work being performed in the factory. In the end, Warner formulates a paean to the war workers, the mechanics who are 'priests of a new rite', standing

before a thousand clattering altars. Unswerving from the most exacting of standards, they set the knives which must be true to a hair's-breadth, and rigid as steel and muscle can clinch them: and going from one machine to another, always watching, always setting to rights, they flirt with all the workgirls—flirtations that are algebraic in their detachment and universality.[41]

Warner's article, once suitably revised, was published in February 1916 under the by-line 'a Lady Worker'.

Due to the success of *The First Hundred Thousand*, John Beith was recalled from the front in late 1916 to work under the direction of Arthur Willett, the Washington correspondent of the London *Times*, who spearheaded British propaganda efforts in the US. 'I have got the establishment of a publicity bureau in my hands', Willett wrote in December 1916 to Geoffrey Dawson, editor of *The Times*.[42] Members of this unofficial and highly secret group included Beith, the head of British Intelligence Sir William Wiseman and the playwright Harley Granville-Barker. Beith's tasks included undertaking lecture tours of Canada and the US to promote *The First Hundred Thousand*, to reinforce the concerted British campaign countering German propaganda, and to persuade the neutral elements in North America to side with the Allies. 'I was yanked off to this country a few weeks ago,' he wrote jokingly to George Blackwood from New York in October 1916, 'and here I am, lecturing on the war and interviewing reporters, and generally countermining Boche propaganda.'[43] Between October 1916

[41] *Blackwood's Magazine* (Feb. 1916), 200, 202.
[42] Halsey Ross, *Propaganda for War*, 79.
[43] J. H. Beith to George W. Blackwood, 31 Oct. 1916, Blackwood Papers, National Library of Scotland, MS 30173.

and May 1918, Beith gave over 330 lectures in North America, and in 1918 was awarded the CBE for his services.[44]

During Beith's tour of the US, and at the request of the War Propaganda office, he produced a short text aimed at British and American audiences, entitled 'Getting Together'. The piece was subsequently offered to the Blackwood firm for publication in the magazine. The story of its production, as reconstructed from documents in the Blackwood archives, illustrates very clearly the links forged during the war over propagandist periodical literature between authors, literary agents, government agencies and literary journals.

Beith began work on 'Getting Together' in November 1916. It was to be 'a plea for better relations between our Country and America', Beith wrote to George Blackwood,

> suitable for both sides of the Atlantic, pointing out to this Country that we are fighting her battles for her and that she must not be peevish about the blockade; and to our people that the *real* America is strongly pro-Ally; is bitterly ashamed of Wilson; but resents outside criticism of the 'too proud to fight' type.[45]

Promoted as a work in which 'the average American and the average Briton "get together" in an open-minded discussion of the Questions which most vitally concern each', its objective was to counter negative public opinion generated by Allied blockades of Atlantic shipping routes, by Allied censoring and monitoring of mail sent to and from the US, and by British press reports antagonistic to the US maintenance of neutrality.[46] In the opening section, Beith set out a series of rhetorical questions the average Briton might face visiting Yankee shores, and provided justifications for British actions, combining anti-German propaganda with appeals to American patriotism and moral values. 'How about that blockade? What are you opening our mails for—eh?' enquires the American participating in this imagined dialogue. The answer is that such minor inconveniences are justified because 'we, on our side, are engaged in a life and death

---

[44] Facts noted in the introduction to *A Welcome to All American Soldiers and Sailors* (London, 1918), a pamphlet Beith wrote for the American Expeditionary Forces Young Men Christian's Association based in Russell Square, London.

[45] J. H. Beith to George W. Blackwood, 11 Nov. 1916, 12 Nov. 1916, Blackwood Papers, National Library of Scotland, MS 30173.

[46] Dust-jacket cover, *Getting Together* (London, 1917).

struggle for the freedom of the world'.[47] This provides Beith with an opportunity to castigate Americans for their lack of support in this great struggle, at the same time reinforcing the anti-German stance: 'We know that you are not against us; still, considering the sacredness of our cause, and the monstrous means by which the Boche is seeking to further his, we feel that you have not stood for us so out and out as you might'.[48] The puzzled American patriot of the text responds by listing the good works done by US patrons on behalf of the Allied cause and, promising that underneath it all Americans are really pro-Ally and pro-British, concludes, 'Why can't you Britishers be a bit kinder in your attitude towards us?'[49]

Having completed the text, Beith tried placing it in appropriate British publications. He offered George Blackwood the piece for *Blackwood's Magazine*, explaining that it would be syndicated across the US and then published in pamphlet form. In so doing, Beith made clear that the piece was not entirely under his control, but rather in the hands of the Propaganda Bureau. Blackwood had to go through A. S. Watt for formal clearance and approval from Wellington House. 'If you would like it for Maga first,' Beith wrote, 'it would perhaps be as well to find out about this from Watt, who is in close touch with Wellington House.'[50]

What emerges from these and subsequent comments is the extent to which the government encouraged such material to be circulated in as many ways as possible. More interestingly, it illustrates the manner in which such literary journalism was harnessed to economic production. Publishing the work in as many forms as possible increased the revenue potential of government-sponsored material. While Beith produced the work, the American publisher Frank Doubleday, of Doubleday and Co., set about arranging for its serialization in the US, to coincide with publication in pamphlet form. It was issued as a 50-cent, 85-page booklet and reprinted in *The Outlook*. A. S. Watt, acting as intermediary, then arranged for simultaneous publication in Britain by Hodder & Stoughton. Blackwood's enquiry as to its availability for his March 1917 number brought

---

[47] *Getting Together*, 12.   [48] Ibid. 39.   [49] Ibid. 12.
[50] J. H. Beith to George W. Blackwood, 12 Dec. 1916, Blackwood Papers, National Library of Scotland, MS 30173.

an instant, approving response. 'So far as the Wellington House people are concerned,' A. S. Watt wrote, 'they would be glad to see "Getting Together" published serially in the March number of *Blackwood's Magazine* and afterwards in shilling book form by Messrs. Hodder & Stoughton.'[51] George Blackwood, however, never an Americophile, subsequently changed his mind, unconvinced of the merits of Beith's arguments and piqued by what he perceived to be a lack of support for the British cause in the US. 'I am afraid it is not the point of view which appeals to me, or is likely to appeal to the ordinary Britisher,' he wrote to Beith. In rejecting the piece, Blackwood reflected the opinions Beith's text had been written to change.[52] John Buchan, in his capacity as Director of the reorganized Department of Information, brought pressure to bear on Blackwood to publish the work, aware of the value of reaching the audience represented by *Blackwood's Magazine*. 'I am very anxious that the book should be published as soon as possible in this country with a view to future happenings', he hinted to George Blackwood. He added, in an indirect attempt to force Blackwood to change his mind, 'Do you think, from the same point of view, you could expedite its appearance as much as you conveniently can?'[53] Blackwood remained unmoved. 'Candidly,' he wrote, 'I don't agree with the sentiments expressed. The Yankee proper may be pro-Ally, but he is not, seemingly never will be, pro-British!'[54] Beith, Watt and the Department of Information were left to find another British periodical outlet for the piece.

Buchan's interest in placing the Beith piece in *Blackwood's* arose out of his own knowledge of the journal. As a frequent contributor to its pages, he well understood the market and audience represented by the magazine. He also shared the senti- ments of his contemporary Joseph Conrad, who wrote that 'one was in decent company there and had a good sort of public. There isn't a single club and messroom and man-of-war in the

[51] A. S. Watt to G. W. Blackwood, 31 Jan. 1917, Blackwood Papers, National Library of Scotland, MS 30179.

[52] George W. Blackwood to J. H. Beith, 3 Mar. 1917, Blackwood Papers, National Library of Scotland, MS 30403, 99.

[53] John Buchan to George W. Blackwood, 14 Mar. 1917, Blackwood Papers, National Library of Scotland, MS 30176.

[54] George W. Blackwood to John Buchan, 16 Mar. 1917, Blackwood Papers, National Library of Scotland, MS 30403, 114.

British Seas and Dominions which hasn't its copy of Maga.'[55] While such statements reflect only a partial view of *Maga*'s market, they do suggest a general perception of audiences shared by most of its contributors, and more importantly, promulgated by the editor. 'You should point out', George Blackwood told Watt when initially justifying his interest in Beith's 'Getting Together',

that if the article is to appear in my Magazine, it will have a very wide circulation all through the British Empire, and particularly on the various Fronts where there are many officers who subscribe regularly for [sic] my magazine, and also to a certain extent in neutral countries.[56]

George Blackwood's understanding of *Maga*'s audience was based on long-standing editorial policies that targeted British colonial service interests and readers. Once war had started, he took steps to build on this core group of readers, supplying free copies of the magazine for distribution to British naval messrooms under the Newspapers for the fleet scheme, administered by the London Chamber of Commerce.[57] At the same time, the increasing use of propagandist war stories coincided with a staggering increase in sales and readership both at home and at the front. Between April 1914 and April 1917, Edinburgh sales more than tripled from 4,900 to 18,500 copies a month. Likewise, the London office recorded a jump in monthly sales from 4,200 to 13,700 copies a month.[58] For George Blackwood, the success of the magazine was clearly linked to the firm's military connections, the role these connections played in producing and gathering the war material featured in its pages, and the journal's long life as a reflector of mainstream, conservative literary values. In short, *Maga* had gained renewed vigour from maintaining the literary status quo. 'The old lady is very flourishing indeed from the point of view of sales', Blackwood wrote towards the end of 1915, 'and we have certainly been most

---

[55] *The Collected Letters of Joseph Conrad,* iv. *1908–1911*, ed. Frederick Karl and Laurence Davies (Cambridge, 1990), 130.

[56] George W. Blackwood to A. S. Watt, 26 Jan. 1917, Blackwood Papers, National Library of Scotland, MS 30403, 47.

[57] Southerwell Piper to George W. Blackwood, 22 Aug. 1914, Blackwood Papers, National Library of Scotland, MS 30168.

[58] Blackwood Papers, National Library of Scotland, MS 30866, MS 30680.

successful in the war articles which have come to us. Come, I may say, without any attempt to get them, and due undoubtedly to the connection which my Uncle took such care to establish with both the Services. He would rejoice in Maga's success.'[59]

With *Maga* benefiting from its contacts in securing, censoring and passing appropriate war material for consumption by its readers, it is not surprising that the magazine's circulation began to rise so dramatically among armed forces subscribers. *Blackwood's Magazine* provided appropriately optimistic reading material for soldiers at the front. More importantly, it provided it in suitably small, easily digestible chunks. As Geoffrey Gathorne-Hardy wrote from French trenches after reading John Buchan's *The Thirty-Nine Steps*, first serialized in *Maga* between July and September 1915: 'It is just the kind of fiction for here. Long novels I cannot manage in the trenches. One wants something to engross the attention without tiring the mind, in doses not too large to be assimilated in very brief intervals of spare time.'[60] Other works serialized in suitably readable chunks during this period included Arthur Quiller-Couch's *Nicky Nan, Reservist* and J. H. Beith's '*Carry On!*'

Further information about the general identity of *Blackwood's Magazine*'s readers can be found in the advertisement pages. *Maga*'s advertisements between 1914 and 1918 reveal a subtle change in assumptions about its readership, or rather an overlapping and overlaying of advertisers and advertising messages seeking to address a more complex mix of readers.

Initially, only minor changes are evident in *Maga*'s advertisements. Such is the case with the August 1914 issue, for example, the inside front cover of which features a plain announcement of a new edition of Edward Hamley's *The Operations of War*, first published in 1866 and a set text for military schools in Britain and the US until superseded in the 1890s. Likewise, an advertisement for the fourth edition of a manual on nursing, *Practical Nursing*, set deep in the supplements on the eleventh page, is

---

[59] George W. Blackwood to Herbert Cowell, 30 Dec. 1915, Blackwood Papers, National Library of Scotland, MS 30402.

[60] John Buchan to George W. Blackwood, 4 Nov. 1915, Blackwood Papers, National Library of Scotland, MS 30170. *Blackwood's Magazine* featured Buchan in similar fashion during the Second World War, serializing his last novel *Sick Heart River* between Oct. 1940 and Apr. 1941.

headlined as a work which 'SHOULD BE IN EVERY HOME'. By September, however, adjustments have been made to reflect Britain's new wartime priorities. The same ad for *Practical Nursing* is now given pride of place on the inside cover, replacing Hamley, with an extra, underlined caption announcing 'The Red Cross Nurse will find this volume invaluable at the present time'. Similarly, the ad for Hamley's work becomes part of a reorganized grouping of Blackwood publications, collected under the bold banner of 'BLACKWOOD'S WAR BOOKS'.

Such remodelling initially served to give old products a new currency. As the war continued and Maga's audience increased, its advertisements begin reflecting an awareness of a wider wartime audience. Alongside adverts for *Country Life*, insurance policies and P&O excursions, there now appear ones targeted at nurses, service personnel and their families. Blackwood's publications also begin to be promoted in the context of their appropriateness to war themes and frontline readers: *The Green Curve*, by 'Ole Luk-Oie', for example, baldly advertised in September 1914 as a collection of strikingly realistic stories, is transformed by October 1915 into something quite different. 'This is MODERN WAR from WITHIN', the reader is now informed, ignoring the fact that these stories first appeared in *Blackwood's Magazine* in early 1912. More importantly, the collection acquires a new advertising hook: it is written not by an anonymous source, but by a privileged military observer, in this case E. D. Swinton, the official government eye-witness at the front. Promoted as a work by a soldier primarily for soldiers, and secondarily for the public, the collection becomes transformed from a mundane series of stories into 'A REAL BOOK ABOUT REAL WAR'. While such tactics were primarily ways of giving old goods a new sales spin, they suggest an awareness of the magazine's changing readership. This is reinforced by their placement next to advertisements for trenchcoats, trench periscopes, portable disinfectors that 'safeguard the health of those who are fighting for their country', and appeals for donations to War Relief funds and frontline volunteer services such as the Red Cross.

As Beith himself wrote, 'We read . . . [the newspapers] . . . right through, beginning at the advertisements and not skipping even the leading articles. Then, when we have finished, we frequently read them right through again . . . They give us information as to how the war is progressing—we get none here, the rank and file, that is, and they afford us topics for conversation.[61] Both troops and home audiences, isolated and with only partial access to news of the front, depended on publications such as *Maga*, censored though they were, to entertain them and provide general overviews of the war. Under such circumstances, journals like *Blackwood's Magazine* acted as an important conduit for an influential propaganda campaign against the German forces, and helped sustain the myth of British military superiority and superior moral values in the face of adversity. The manner in which much of the literary journalism of the period was subsumed to the interests of the state provides us with a salutary lesson in media control. It also illustrates how the distinctions between artistic individualism and social responsibility, the aesthetic ideals and economic realities of literary publishing, can be deliberately blurred in times of war and political instability. Such willing conformity of literary establishments to a cause, and the role they then play in reinforcing the myths and values of a dominant political and cultural agenda, are not unique to Britain and the first World War.

[61] 'The First Hundred Thousand', *Blackwood's Magazine* (Oct. 1915), 441.

7

'Crimes of Criticism': Virginia Woolf and Literary Journalism

HERMIONE LEE

'Crimes of criticism' is a phrase used in an unsigned essay by Virginia Woolf, published in *The Times Literary Supplement* in 1923 and called 'How it Strikes a Contemporary', on the difficulties of contemporary criticism.[1] What guidance is there, the essay asks, for the modern reader? Contemporary criticism is suffering from a loss of authority. There used to be rules which controlled 'the great republic of readers', critics of authority like Dryden or Keats, Flaubert or Coleridge. Now it's an age of fragments and interruptions and telephone calls. There has been a shift in the class structure. We are cut off from our predecessors. Modern work is 'noted under pressure', producing irritation as well as pleasure. Contemporary critics can no longer generalize. We have plenty of policemen, but no judges. No one knows, for instance, what to say about *The Waste Land*: is it just 'waste paper'?[2]

Critics, she says, will tell you that this has always been the case: writing about the present has always been a problem for reviewers, and people have always made mistakes about living writers: 'From the store of their experience they [the critics] proceed to bring forth terrible examples of past blunders; crimes of criticism which, if they had been committed against the dead and not against the living, would have lost them their jobs and imperilled their reputations.' But it seems to her that things are much more difficult than before, and that contemporary critics

---

[1] 'How it Strikes a Contemporary', *TLS*, 5 Apr. 1923, (henceforth in *The Essays of Virginia Woolf*, 6 vols., ed. Andrew McNeillie (London, 1986– *Essays*)), iii. 353–60.

[2] Footnote in *Virginia Woolf: Collected Essays*, 4 vols., ed. Leonard Woolf (London, 1966–7 (henceforth, *CE*)), ii. 155; not reprinted in *Essays*, iii.

are now more likely to commit crimes. She feels some longing for the 'enviable certainty' which allowed writers in the past 'to believe that your impressions hold good for others—to be released from personality'.[3] There is a painful difference between reading contemporaries and reading 'old books'.

So what is the critic to do today? Retreat into writing only about the dead? No. The critic in response to this situation should be 'generous' to contemporaries, but wary. 'He' (as she always calls him or her) should think of the present not only in relation to the past but also 'in relation to the future'. He should think of new books as transitional. As for readers, she can only advise them not to submit to the control of any critic or reviewer alive, but to respect their own instincts and 'check them by reading and reading again the masterpieces of the past'.

The essay suggests the complicated and often contradictory feelings Virginia Woolf had towards committing her own 'crimes of criticism'. There are several things going on here. She makes a distinction between writing about the past and writing about the present, a distinction which often takes the form of a contrast between 'essays' and 'reviewing' or 'journalism'. But at the same time she recommends that the writing of the present should be judged in the context of a rereading of the past. She is anxious about her judgement of contemporaries, aware that contemporary writing may require new forms of criticism, and half-nostalgic for some kind of lost authority or certainty of judgement. So there is a close connection between what she says in the 1920s about the difficult fragmentariness of modern fiction and what she says about the difficulties for the modern literary critic.

The same mixed feelings about contemporary criticism appear again in 1931 in an essay on the fierce early nineteenth-century criticism by John Lockhart in *Blackwood's Magazine*.

It is plain, as we turn over the pages of Lockhart's resurrected reviews, that to write about a new book the moment it comes out is a very different matter from writing about it fifty years afterwards. A new book is attached to life by a thousand minute filaments. Life goes on and the filaments break and disappear. But at the moment they ring and resound and set up all kinds of irrelevant responses. Keats was an

---

[3] 'How it Strikes A Contemporary', *Essays*, iii. 357.

apothecary and lived in Hampstead, and consorted with Leigh Hunt and the Cockneys; Shelley was an atheist and had irregular views upon marriage; the author of Jane Eyre might be a woman, and, if so, was a very coarse one. It is easy to say that these were ephemeral accidents and that Lockhart should have brushed them aside; but they rang loud in his ears, and he could no more have disregarded them and the prejudices of his readers than he could have flung aside his blue dressing gown and marched down Albemarle Street in a tweed cap and plus fours. But even so, Lockhart was not so far out as might be expected. [Also] there is a virtue in familiarity. We lose something when we have ceased to be able to talk naturally of Johnny Keats. . . . A little of the irreverence with which Lockhart treated the living would do no harm to our more sober estimates of the dead.[4]

We can do for Virginia Woolf what she says should be done for 'Johnny' Keats: reread her as if she were a contemporary and see how the 'crimes of criticism'—the compromises and obstructions of her literary market-place—affect her writing and her reputation. Such readings of Virginia Woolf[5] have only recently become fully possible with the fine (and ongoing) editing of her essays by Andrew McNeillie. Before the publication of this annotated edition, Virginia Woolf's criticism had been more often read as an accessory to or a source of commentary on her fiction (or even, in some cases, as a means of denigrating the fiction by praising her as an essayist). I would prefer to read her fiction and non-fiction as overlapping and connecting genres. Indeed, one of the most remarkable things about Virginia Woolf's writing is its interconnectedness. For all the bold changes and contrasts she goes through, for all her prolific variety, it's possible to read her entire work as one continuing, connected plot. And one of the deepest connecting threads—perhaps even more than for most writers—is the story of her reading and what she does with her reading.

All through her life, Virginia Woolf's fiction takes shape in the context of a discussion with herself on the processes of writing and reading. A great deal of her writing—and this is beginning to be seen more clearly now that the work unpublished in her

---

[4] 'Lockhart's Criticism' [review of *Lockhart's Literary Criticism*, ed. M. C. Hildyard, 1931], *Blackwood's Magazine*, 23 Apr. 1931, *CE* i. 183.
[5] e.g. in an unpublished thesis on Virginia Woolf's essays and journalism by Leila Brosnan, University of Edinburgh, 1994, and in *Virginia Woolf and the Essay*, ed. Beth Carole Rosenberg and Jeanne Dubino (New York, 1997).

lifetime is taking its settled place in the Woolf canon—is a meta-narrative about the evolution of fiction: the way it comes into being, the way its 'phases' develop historically, its confrontation with social pressures, its alteration through reader reception. Virginia Woolf was making her own 'history of the book', in the diary and the letters, in the two volumes of *The Common Reader*, in 'Phases of Fiction' (which was intended as a whole book about fiction but which appeared, after a great deal of work, only as a long essay), in 'How Should One Read a Book?', in *A Room of One's Own*, and finally in the unfinished book she was writing in the last year of her life, *Reading at Random*.

A selective chronology would show how closely the writings on reading and the writing of fiction were interlinked. A year after 'An Unwritten Novel', in May 1921, she started to talk to herself about a book called 'Reading', which would make her 'read like an expert' and shape her reading of 'literature in bulk'.[6] In the autumn she promised herself again she would start her 'Reading' book.[7] Early in 1922, while she was revising *Jacob's Room* and beginning to make up stories about Mrs Dalloway, she wrote 'Byron & Mr Briggs', which was meant as the introduction to the 'Reading' book, and which raised the question of the relation to literature of 'the common reader', partly in the form of a conversation between some of the characters from her novels.

Throughout 1922, she was taking extensive reading notes, and writing her 'Reading' book in alternation with *Mrs Dalloway* (she called this 'rotating my crops').[8] She published an essay called 'On Re-reading Novels' in July 1922 where, in response to her reading of Percy Lubbock's *The Craft of Fiction*, she analysed her readings of James and Flaubert. In the autumn of 1922, when *Jacob's Room* was published, she wrote 'Modern Essays', on the changing reading public and the relation between literature and journalism.

In the spring of 1923, when the 'Mrs Dalloway' stories had started to turn into a book called *The Hours*, and she was reading for the book which was going to be *The Common Reader*, she published 'How it Strikes a Contemporary'. In the

---

[6] *The Diary of Virginia Woolf*, 5 vols., ed. Anne Olivier Bell (London, 1977–84), 23 May 1921, ii. 120.

[7] *Diary*, 15 Nov. 1921, ii. 142.   [8] *Diary*, 3 Sept. 1922, ii. 198.

autumn of 1923 she wrote a 'conversation' about Conrad which reused the critical method of 'Byron & Mr Briggs', and wrote a short essay called 'Mr Bennett and Mrs Brown',[9] in response to an attack by Arnold Bennett on the lack of characterization in *Jacob's Room*. The piece reworked the ideas in 'Modern Novels'. Between June 1923 and December 1924, while she was writing *Mrs Dalloway*, she wrote three memoirs which she would publish together in *The Common Reader* as 'Lives of the Obscure', about the virtues of reading bad as well as good books. In 1924 she wrote 'The Patron and the Crocus', an essay on the modern writer's audience, a light piece called 'Indiscretions', on personal prejudices in reading, and a lecture called 'Character in Fiction'. This fused together 'Modern Novels' and 'An Unwritten Novel' (and bits of *Jacob's Room*, too) and extended the theme of 'Mr Bennett and Mrs Brown' into an imagined encounter on a train, as a way of describing the difference between the 'Edwardian' and the 'Georgian' novelists.[10]

In the spring of 1925 she published *Mrs Dalloway* and *The Common Reader*, which had some new general pieces, including the introduction, and a revised and extended version of 'Modern Novels', called 'Modern Fiction'. In the late summer she wrote a number of stories (just as she had between *Night and Day* and *Jacob's Room* and again between *Jacob's Room* and *Mrs Dalloway*) which moved her on from *Mrs Dalloway* towards *To the Lighthouse*. In the autumn, she gave the lecture 'How Should One Read a Book?' By the end of 1925 she was thinking about (and taking notes for) a book 'for the H.P. . . . about fiction'.[11] For most of 1926 she wrote *To the Lighthouse* instead, but in the autumn of 1926 she started to plan the 'book on literature' again, and worked on it throughout 1927, while publishing essays on reading and writing called 'Poetry, Fiction and the Future' (revised as 'The Narrow Bridge of Art'), 'An Essay in Criticism' and 'Is Fiction an Art?' (revised as 'The Art of Fiction'). She worked at the fiction book, 'Phases of Fiction',

[9] 'Mr Bennett and Mrs Brown', 1923, *Essays*, iii. 388.

[10] The lecture (*Essays*, iii. 501) was then reworked again (twice), first as an essay for *The Criterion* called 'Character in Fiction', published in July 1924 (*Essays*, iii. 420–38), and then, finally, as a Hogarth Press pamphlet called 'Mr Bennett and Mrs Brown', published in Oct. 1924 (*CE*, 319–38).

[11] *Diary*, Dec. 7 1925, iii. 50.

while she was writing *Orlando* in 1928 and *A Room of One's Own* in 1929. It became very burdensome to her, and was eventually published not as a book but as three long essays in the *Bookman* in the early summer of 1929. These essays on the history of literature and on reading were closely connected to *Orlando* and *A Room of One's Own*.

In the 1930s this pattern of interconnection between essays and fiction continued. *The Waves* kept pace with the reading for the second *Common Reader*, *The Years* and *Three Guineas* with much writing on the relation between art and politics, *Roger Fry* with an essay on 'The Art of Biography' and with her own memoir-writing, and *Between the Acts* with *Reading at Random*, a third projected book on the history of reading and of English literature, with the emphasis on anonymity and communality.[12]

In this lifelong non-fiction writing, she continually explored the relations between the market, the audience, the patron, and the writer. Like her father Leslie Stephen, she was always closely involved in the market-place. It is clear from her diary that she is always intensely conscious of how much she is earning.[13] All the more so, because it took a long time for her earnings to become substantial. Leonard Woolf calculated that from 1909 to 1921 she earned only £205 from her books. In 1923 she was reporting furiously in her diary on having been 'snubbed' by J. C. Squire, the editor of the *London Mercury*, who had offered her £13 for an article, had refused to agree when she asked for £15, and had ended up making her accept £13 after all.[14] Only after the publication of *Mrs Dalloway* and *The Common Reader* in 1925 did her earnings from her books go over the magic figure of '£500 a year'; only then was she earning more than her husband; only then could she start turning down some

---

[12] This survey of her essays leaves out the many pieces on individual authors (e.g. the long 1928 essay on Hardy, product of many years of rereading), the enormous range of her readings and rereadings in memoirs, fiction, history, poetry and science shown in the *Collected Essays*, and the many uncategorizable pieces which hovered between fiction and fact, autobiography and history, e.g. 'Thunder at Wembley' (1924), 'Street Haunting' (1927), or 'The Sun and the Fish' (1928).

[13] Paul Delaney (who is writing on the finances of 20th-cent. writers) suggests in 'A Little Capital' (*Charleston Magazine*, Summer/Autumn 1993) that LW was the materialistic one and VW was 'quite unworldly' about money; I disagree.

[14] *Diary*, 17 Mar. 1923, ii. 239: 'Yet I dont much mind, & only think that poverty & the shifts it puts one to is unbecoming.'

of the books she was offered for review.[15] In the late 1920s and 1930s she earned much bigger sums from American editors, and was always particularly pleased when she could be paid twice for the same piece: '£60 in America for the Times's £10', for instance, for a piece on Forster in 1927.[16]

Until 1925 literary journalism was her main source of income and her main job. And her professional life was part of the world of small magazines, journals, and publishing presses. John Middleton Murry at the *Athenaeum* (which merged with the *Nation* in 1921); Eliot at the *Criterion* from 1923; Desmond MacCarthy in the *New Statesman*, and Leonard Woolf as editor of the *Nation* from 1924 to 1930: such figures all had a close bearing on her work. Her connection, through friendship and family, to the literary magazines, and her central position in the publishing of new writing through the Hogarth Press, raises one of the most problematic areas in her writer's life, that of what *Scrutiny* in the 1930s would call 'clique-puffery'.[17]

Once Leonard Woolf became a magazine editor, beginning on *War and Peace* in 1916 and taking on the literary editorship of the *Nation* in 1923—by which time Virginia Woolf was a major reviewer and well-known author—they were at the centre of the literary power-structures, and had plenty of opportunities for 'clique-puffery'.[18] Others of their friends reviewed each other,

---

[15] For VW's earnings, see Leonard Woolf, *Downhill All the Way* (London, 1970), 142; John Mepham, *Virginia Woolf: A Literary Life* (London, 1991), 130–1; J. H. Willis, *Leonard and Virginia Woolf as Publishers* (Charlottesville, Va., 1992), appendix B.

[16] *Diary*, 23 July 1927, iii. 149.

[17] Reviewing one's friends was common practice in the 1920s and 1930s. See Selina Hastings, *Evelyn Waugh* (London, 1995), on Waugh's self-reviewing of *Labels* in the *Graphic* ('The book that interests me most this week is a new travel book issued by Duckworth's'). Waugh also wrote to his publisher, 'When are review copies going out? I should like to inscribe personal copies to Harold Nicolson and the other more influential critics.' Nicolson duly reviewed it enthusiastically in the *Daily Express*. See also Valentine Cunningham in *British Writers of the Thirties* (Oxford, 1988), 145–7, on Auden, Isherwood & Co. 'booming' and 'puffing' each other, persuading friends to accept other friends' work, and on John Lehmann speaking of his 'key position' of influence at the Hogarth Press. Geoffrey Grigson, Wyndham Lewis and Q. D. Leavis all notoriously attacked England's 'closed literary society run on Civil Service lines' for the benefit of boys from the public schools and the ancient universities.

[18] Cf. John Middleton Murry, who promoted and employed his wife Katherine Mansfield in the pages of the *Athenaeum*. Claire Tomalin, *Katherine Mansfield* (Harmondsworth, 1988), 241.

quite shamelessly.[19] Virginia Woolf was not guiltless in this respect, but she was queasy about it.

Today I got Desmond's book, sent, I'm sorry to say, by request of the author. Richmond, when I asked for D's and L's books said 'Certainly—if you can keep it secret.' I couldnt promise to do this, & therefore wrote to tell him not to send them. And now I must inform Desmond & Lytton. They won't suffer really I believe, but they will be anxious instead of safe, & I'm in two minds as to whether I'm glad or sorry. I think I could have said some very clever things, & a few true things, but undoubtedly one cant avoid a certain uneasiness in writing formally of people one knows so well.[20]

And she wrote to Lytton Strachey in 1918:

I wrote to ask Richmond [the editor of *The Times Literary Supplement*] to let me do your book [*Eminent Victorians*]. He answers that though willing and anxious that I should, he has to make it a rule that reviewers dont review their friends—not that he's afraid I should be partial, but that people would guess, and *say* I was partial, which he admits to be base on his part, but he's afraid he must stick to it. I'm very sorry.... If I review yours, then why not Clive's, Desmond's, Molly's and Fredegond's, which would be more than I could stand.[21]

Similarly, Leonard Woolf would, as a literary editor, be mostly—but not entirely—careful not to seem to promote Hogarth Press books.[22] The Woolfs did not repeat one unfortunate early piece of self-promotion, when in 1919 they reviewed, anonymously and jointly, two of their own Hogarth Press publications, Eliot's *Poems* and John Middleton Murry's critical essay. Murry was the editor of the magazine they were writing for, the *Athenaeum*, and had commissioned the piece. As might

---

[19] e.g. Vita Sackville-West reviewing her girlfriend Dorothy Wellesley's poems, *Lost Lane*, in the *Nation* for 9 May 1925, with gushing praise for 'a talent full of vigour'; or Raymond Mortimer, Desmond MacCarthy, and E. M. Forster praising their friend VW in reviews. See Raymond Mortimer in *Vogue* on *Mrs Dalloway*: 'Mrs Woolf is in love with life: that is her genius.'

[20] *Diary*, 18 Apr. 1918, i. 142.

[21] VW to Lytton Strachey, 15 [in fact 18] Mar. 1918, *The Letters of Virginia Woolf*, 6 vols., ed. Nigel Nicolson and Joanne Trautmann (London, 1975–80), ii. 914, 224. At various times she reviewed or wrote on the work of Forster, Eliot, Fry, Vanessa Bell, Molly McCarthy and Violet Dickinson.

[22] See James Strachey to Alix Strachey, 16 Jan. 1925: 'Leonard ... is afraid of being suspected of favouring Hogarth Press publications.' *Bloomsbury/Freud: The Letters of James and Alix Strachey 1924–1925*, ed. P. Meisel and W. Kendrick (New York, 1985), 186.

be expected, the review read somewhat stiffly, and when Virginia Woolf twice referred in it to the 'uncompromising' nature of the Hogarth Press's 'little books' she may have been prompted by feeling that this was, indeed, a compromised review.[23]

But the Woolfs did use the pages of the *Nation* in the 1920s to promote the Press, and her books in particular. When the literary pages of the *Nation* would have a review by Virginia side-by-side with a round-up of the month's books by Leonard, or when its front page would advertise *To the Lighthouse* and Leonard's *Essays* prominently on its 'Just Published' list, it was difficult not to perceive the *Nation* and the Hogarth Press as part of a cabal.[24] Virginia Woolf's reputation in her lifetime, and after it, was affected by this.

There were other kinds of complicity and compromise in the world of literary journalism which affected Virginia Woolf, and which she disliked and resented. Issues of censorship—internal and external—preoccupied her. In the diary for 7 August 1939 she wrote:

I have been thinking about Censors. How visionary figures admonish us. Thats clear in an MS I'm reading [the memoirs of the American actress Elizabeth Robins]. If I say this So & So will think me sentimental. If that . . . will think me Bourgeois. All books now seem to me surrounded by a circle of invisible censors. Hence their selfconsciousness, their restlessness.

(She identifies this as a contemporary phenomenon, comparing it with the unselfconsciousness of Wordsworth.) The invisible censors may be the modern descendants of the Victorian Angel

---

[23] *Essays*, iii. 54.

[24] *Nation*, 16 May 1925, for example, printed a quarter-page advertisement for *The Hogarth Press*, including *The Common Reader*, 12s. 6d., with quotes from good reviews, including from the *TLS*: 'A lively zest for human beings runs through this volume. The wit and charm are very seductive. It has the breadth which only a real possession of the past can give and the vitality of a fresh imagination.' The *Nation*, 13 June 1925, had as its front-page piece Virginia Woolf on Harriette Wilson, and contained the notices for *The Common Reader* and *Mrs Dalloway*: 'secures a double triumph'; 'Mrs Woolf is perhaps our most brilliant *interpretative* critic'; 'Mrs Woolf is one of the finest critics of our time'. Leonard Woolf's 'World of Books' editorial in the *Nation* for 12 Mar. 1927 noted *To the Lighthouse* as one of the five outstanding novels of that month. The Hogarth Press advertisement on 14 May 1927 on the front cover of the *Nation* noted *To the Lighthouse*, under 'Just Published', with LW's *Essays* underneath.

in the House, that earlier invisible—but highly audible—censor who stood over her when she started to write reviews, telling her to be nice to the menfolk. Like the Angel in the House, the invisible censors seem to be both external and internalized. And the debate between authorial desire and the pressures which make the modern author self-conscious is one of the main stories of Virginia Woolf's writing life.

Her criticism, particularly in her early years, was to an extent complicit with the current conventions in essay-writing. She often found herself inhibited, forced to write 'stiffly, without spontaneity', too aware of her audience or her editor. Sometimes she was censored, or censored herself: Bruce Richmond wouldn't let her use the word 'lewd' in a review of Henry James's ghost stories in 1921; she had to be 'discreet' about lesbianism in an eloquent piece on Geraldine Jewsbury and Jane Carlyle in 1929.[25] 'A crooning domestic sound like the purring of a kitten or the humming of a tea kettle seems to rise, as we turn the pages of Mrs Carlyle's letters, from the intercourse of the two incompatible but deeply attached women.'[26] Though in 1931 she said she had learnt to throw the inkpot at the Angel in the House, she sometimes chose not to throw hard. For these sorts of reasons (reasons which motivated her feminist essays), she resented the pressures and constrictions of reviewing for money (particularly in the early 1920s when she was thinking so much about fiction and the market-place[27]), and used *The Common Reader* as a place where she could write about literature to please herself.

For the woman reader-critic—as for the woman writer—there was conflict and peril in the literary market-place. Virginia Woolf was right to think of the British literary world of the 1910s and 1920s as a male-dominated culture. Almost all the literary editors, magazine owners, publishers and reviewers were men.[28] So was a woman reader and reviewer to disguise herself, to suppress her sexual character and inclination in

[25] *Diary*, 19 Dec. 1921, ii. 152; *Essays*, iii. 324–5; VW to John Hayward, 4 Mar. 1929, *Letters*, iv. 30 (2007).
[26] CE iv. 35–8.
[27] e.g. *Diary*, 8, 15 Sept. 1920, ii. 63 and 65.
[28] With a few notable exceptions, such as Harriet Weaver, Sylvia Beach, and Dorothy Todd.

reading, or to read and write *as a woman*?[29] Virginia Woolf
partly wanted reading to have nothing to do with sex, to be
ungendered and impersonal. But when she writes about reading,
her metaphors for reading are all of slipping, skipping, loitering,
weaving. They are all feminized. There *is* a kind of reading as a
woman which is different from 'the man's way', she seems to
suggest, even while she says that reading should be as androgy-
nous as writing. As a biographer, as a critic and essayist, and as
a novelist, she shows us that there is a distinct way for a woman
to read, and write about, other women's lives.[30] *A Room of
One's Own* is a history of a woman's reading, and is written in
tandem with her history of literature, 'Phases of Fiction'. *Three
Guineas* makes a woman's reading of biographies the basis of its
attack on patriarchal culture. The question of whether women's
reading is a form of difference, and can or should be so expressed, is continually being formulated, as much in her non-
fictional writing as in her fiction.

In 1920, she wrote a feminist story called 'A Society', in a
'violent temper', stirred up by Arnold Bennett's book *Our
Women*.[31] She imagines a women's society set up in order to
infiltrate male domains and to ask questions of their male
'superiors'. Among the women is one who has been left her
father's money on condition that she reads all the books in the
London Library, and another who dresses as a man in order to
be taken as a reviewer. But their enquiries into male superiority
prove disappointing. Like Caliban cursing Prospero for teaching
him to speak, the daughter who has read her way through the
London Library (where women, to Virginia Woolf's fury, were
not allowed on the committee) asks: 'Why, why did my father
teach me to read?' And her friend Castalia, who is pregnant,

---

[29] See Kate Flint, *The Woman Reader 1837–1914* (Oxford, 1994), especially pp.
35, 43, 273 and 327, on the construction of the woman reader in the 19th and early
20th cent.; and see Lyndall Gordon, *Virginia Woolf: A Writer's Life* (Oxford, 1984),
181–2, on VW's reading as a woman.

[30] A marvellous example of a woman's reading of a woman's life is 'Miss
Ormerod', 1924, *Essays*, iv. 131–40.

[31] 'A Society', *The Complete Shorter Fiction of Virginia Woolf*, ed. Susan Dick
(London, 1985 (hereafter *CSF*)), 124–36. See also VW to KM, 13 Feb. 1921,
Congenial Spirits: The Selected Letters of Virginia Woolf, ed. J. Trautmann Banks
(London, 1989), 1167a, 128: 'Like an idiot I lost my temper with Arnold Bennett for
abusing women, and wasted my time writing a foolish violent, I suppose unnecessary
satire.'

decides it would be better for *her* daughter not to read at all. ' "Once she knows how to read there's only one thing you can teach her to believe in—and that is herself." "Well, that would be a change," said Castalia.'

The rage at Bennett's dismissal of women's intellects in *Our Women*, which fuelled 'A Society', flared up again a few years later after his review of *Jacob's Room*. The literary manifestos Virginia Woolf wrote in the mid-1920s are usually read as aesthetic descriptions and defences of the modernist methods she was currently evolving in her fiction. But they are as closely embedded in the literary journalism of their time as Lockhart's reading of Johnny Keats. 'Modern Fiction' and 'Character in Fiction' came out of Woolf's arguments with Bennett, MacCarthy and Murry.[32] In his essay 'Is the Novel Decaying?' in *Cassell's Weekly* for March 1923, Bennett complained that she 'couldn't create characters that survive' in *Jacob's Room*, and that this is typical of the modern novel. This, coming on top of *Our Women* (and Desmond MacCarthy's support for him in the *New Statesman*), and combined with Middleton Murry saying that *Jacob's Room* had 'brought the novel to an impasse',[33] fuelled her literary essays on character in fiction. These famous formulations about modern fiction have now dropped completely out of their journalistic context: we read them as self-ignited, free-standing meditations on what she felt the novel should do and be. But they were, in their inception, angry reactions to reviews of her own work.[34]

The contemporary quarrels with 'crimes of criticism' found their way into the fictions, too. Orlando's poem opens the way for a thinly concealed satire on contemporary, male-dominated journalism. This is more direct in the manuscript of *Orlando*, which has a great deal to say about literary politics: censorship, men's opinions of women, the corruption of the literary market-place, the idiocy of the Burdett-Coutts literary prize, and the embargoes on women writers. There is a bold angry moment in *Orlando* where Orlando joins a 'society' of eighteenth-century

---

[32] See Mepham, *Virginia Woolf*, 84–90, who is especially good on the literary context of VW's work.

[33] For Bennett's attack in *Cassell's Weekly*, 28 Mar. 1923, see *Diary*, 19 June 1923, ii. 248; *Essays*, iii. 437, 388; for Murry's in the *Nation & Athenaeum*, 10 Mar. 1923, see *Diary*, 2 Aug, 17 Oct. 1924.

[34] e.g. on Bennett's critique of *Jacob's Room*, 18 May 1924, *Essays*, iii. 503.

women of the town and they tell each other their adventures.
(Men ask, what can women do without men? Only 'scratch'.) In
the manuscript, she is even more scathing. (Square brackets
show what she was cutting as she wrote.) '[Let] the gentlemen
have the field all to themselves; let them write book after book
in dispraise of the other sex; [let them adduce every reason they
can for thinking vilely of them.]'[35] She names one of these gentlemen as—sure enough—Arnold Bennett. He is, she says, one
of the tribe of 'our modern masculinists': 'tho' they flatter us,
they despise us'.[36] Virginia Woolf is named too, as a minor
writer, a 'poor scribbler', immortalized only by Arnold
Bennett's brilliant articles. A pity: 'She would have been forgotten anyhow, & the half hour spent on her might have given us
another of his masterpieces.'[37] All this revealingly personal
material was excised, but the feeling that went into it lies under
the final version of *Orlando*. And it remains in *To the Lighthouse*, when Lily Briscoe's broodings on 'masculinist' critics of
women return us again to the offence Virginia Woolf has taken
at her male colleagues in her literary world.

'Why did one mind what he said', Lily Briscoe thinks to
herself of the male chauvinist who has said that women can't
paint or write, in the manuscript of *To the Lighthouse*.[38] 'I doubt
that I mind very much', Virginia Woolf said to herself, painfully
anticipating the publication of *A Room of One's Own* and the
possible attacks on her as a 'feminist' and a 'sapphist'. 'Minding'
is the subject of *A Room of One's Own*, in both senses: women
writers minding about being kept out and kept down; women
writers finding a mind of their own. Lily Briscoe, like Virginia
Woolf, 'minds' being patronized. And 'minding' is one of the
most painful aspects of her involvement in the market-place. If
as a reviewer she felt herself suppressed or circumscribed, as a
writer she also had from the first to negotiate with the pressure
of being reviewed. She was exceptionally thin-skinned. But she
knew this was a weakness, and struggled to understand it and to
make some good use out of 'minding'.[39]

[35] *Orlando: The Holograph Draft*, ed. S. N. Clarke (London, 1993), 177.
[36] Ibid. 169.
[37] Ibid. 252.
[38] *To the Lighthouse: The Original Holograph Draft*, ed. Susan Dick (London,
1983), 136.
[39] She was always very interested in which other authors 'minded' about reviews:

In the early 1920s, this struggle was particularly acute. The reviews of *Night and Day*, especially that of Katherine Mansfield, which was cold; her move from being published by Duckworth's to being published by their own press; the publication of *Monday or Tuesday* in April 1921; her own reviewing, and her work on *Jacob's Room*, all intensified a preoccupation with reputation. Her feeling that she was now, at the age of 40, on the right path and in the right context for her work was accompanied by a desire to pull back from the market-place, to be more 'free'. A meeting with Lucy Clifford, the widow of an old friend of Leslie Stephen's, a woman in her sixties who earned her living as a writer, filled her with (probably unjustified) revulsion: 'What an atmosphere of rancid cabbage & old clothes stewing in their old water!'[40] This was not what she wanted to be like in twenty years' time. 'Never write for publishers again anyhow.' She cut down on journalism between 1920 and 1924. But she was also extremely concerned with 'the psychology of fame'.[41] Like her father she disliked conversations about how none of them (except possibly Shaw) would be read in a hundred years' time.[42] But she found it hard to free herself from a desire for popularity, to say genuinely to herself: 'I'm to write what I like; & they're to say what they like.'[43] All this came to a head when *Monday or Tuesday* came out in 1921 to scrappy reviews. (It was badly printed by McDermott, and turned down by the American publisher who had accepted her first two novels.[44]) Meanwhile Lytton Strachey got three columns of praise in the *TLS* for the very popular *Queen Victoria*. A Leslie Stephen-like outburst followed: 'I'm a failure as a writer.'[45] She then tried to be honest about 'this question of praise & fame': whether popularity made a difference, how to control the 'despicable' promptings of vanity, and how to hang on to the real feeling that there was 'something which I want to write; my own point of view.' If that point of view meant low

---

e.g. in 'Reviewing', *CE* ii. 206, she notes that Dickens always 'minded' his bad reviews.

[40] *Diary*, 24 Jan. 1920, ii. 13.
[41] *Diary*, 10 June 1919, i. 280.
[42] *Diary*, 25 Nov. 1921, ii. 145.
[43] *Diary*, 18 Feb. 1922, ii. 168.
[44] George Doran. Harcourt Brace took *Monday or Tuesday*.
[45] *Diary*, 8 Apr. 1921, ii. 107.

sales of difficult and unpopular books, and a small, élitist reputation, so be it. But her jumpiness about reputation was exhibited in her decision to print, at the back of the first edition of *Jacob's Room*, a collection of hostile (as well as good) reviews of *Monday or Tuesday*. It was a way of 'drawing the sting' of adverse criticism; but it looked defensive.[46]

She was determined not to be drowned by the 'splash' of the reception of *Jacob's Room*. She minded that she had become known for minding what was said about her—when Lytton Strachey, for instance, talked to her about Max Beerbohm's literary tastes, 'he thought it necessary to explain that Max had not read me—which was uncomfortable'.[47] These 'uncomfortably' obsessional responses to criticism were linked to her horror of being laughed at or looked at, her resistance to being put right or put down, especially by men, and her desire to be loved and admired, especially by women; above all perhaps to her fear of being thought mad.

As, with the publication of *Jacob's Room*, she began to be better known, she set out to 'make out some rule about praise & blame'.[48] She urged herself not to be for ever 'totting up compliments, & comparing reviews'.[49] If her friends praised the novel (and they did) that had to make up for the mixed critical reception. She resigned herself to the fact that it was 'too experimental' to be generally acclaimed or to sell widely. But the criticisms she took deeply to heart could also be profited from. She would try to incorporate them usefully into her work, just as she incorporated the reviews of her earlier work into the back of

[46] *Diary*, 15 May 1921, ii. 118. 'Books by the same author: Some Press Opinions', *Jacob's Room*, 1st edn., 1922. These were two of the critical reviews (of *Monday or Tuesday*): 'Mrs Woolf, in these sketches, seems to have mistaken literature for mathematics. . . . She tumbles out words and ideas in the hope that they will convey some impression other than that Mrs Woolf has a disorderly mind and does not know how to write. She gushes drivel . . . Mrs Woolf, like the mathematician, does not know whether what she is saying is true; neither do we, nor do we care. In her own style, we retort: Lobatchevsky! Guru!! Miaow!!!' (*New Age*). 'The leading papers speak of the genius of the writer, but I must confess that the product of that genius is unintelligible to me. It marks an altogether new method of indicating thought and emotion . . . I fear that I cannot wax very enthusiastic about this work. It is not of specific Jewish interest.' (*Zionist Record*).
[47] *Diary*, 10 Sept. 1921, ii. 135.
[48] *Diary*, 15 Apr. 1920, ii. 30.
[49] *Diary*, 29 Oct. 1922, 7 Nov. 1922, ii. 209, 210.

Jacob's Room. That determination made *Mrs Dalloway* a deeper book, closer to the feelings and lives of its characters, than *Jacob's Room*. At the same time its strong design and startling adventurousness showed that she had convinced herself she did not need to 'mind' what was said. 'Certainly I'm less coerced than I've yet been', she noted after a year of writing *Mrs Dalloway*[50]—using the same word for literary pressures as she often did for the treatment of madness. Six months later, at the top of her second manuscript book for *Mrs Dalloway*, she wrote, in brackets: 'A delicious idea comes to me that I will write anything I want to write.'[51]

She would never not 'mind'. But when she reviewed her contemporaries, she was not always so attentive as to whether *they* might 'mind' or not. An equivocating piece on Hemingway, for instance, pretended to objectivity, but was scathing and dismissive.[52] She began her review by airing, again, the difficulties for the modern critic in judging contemporary writing, but made her judgement plain: from reading *The Sun Also Rises* she could see that 'if Hemingway is "advanced" it is not in the way that is to us most interesting'. There was something fake about the writing, she thought, and something wrong with the people. Of *Men without Women*, she said:

As the publisher put it . . . 'the softening feminine influence is absent— either through training, discipline, death, or situation.' Whether we are to understand by this that women are incapable of training, discipline, death or situation, we do not know. But . . . Tell a man that this is a woman's book, or a woman that this is a man's, and you have brought into play sympathies and antipathies which have nothing to do with art.

She described him as courageous, candid, highly skilled, modern in manner but not in vision: 'So we sum him up. So we reveal some of the prejudices, the instincts and fallacies out of which what it pleases us to call criticism is made.' Hemingway, reading this review in Sylvia Beach's bookshop, Shakespeare &

[50] *Diary*, 15 Oct. 1923, ii. 272.
[51] 'Mrs Dalloway', MS, written under this heading: 'The Hours or Mrs Dalloway, Good Friday, April 18 1924', British Library.
[52] 'An Essay in Criticism', *New York Herald Tribune*, 9 Oct. 1927, *Essays*, iv. 449–56.

Company, was so furious that he punched a lamp and broke it. Sylvia Beach made him pay for the lamp.[53]

Virginia Woolf didn't break up bookshops, but she might have liked to. Both as a novelist and a critic, she found the public relationship between writers and readers as uneasy and frustrating as any private relationship could be. In 'Byron & Mr Briggs', her 1922 draft of what was to turn into the start of *The Common Reader*, she said that 'the writers of England & the readers of England are necessary to one another. They cannot live apart. They must be forever engaged in intercourse.'[54] But that love-affair was set about with voyeurs and go-betweens. Virginia Woolf is equally hostile to academic appropriations of literature and to 'middlebrow' literary journalism. Her books— especially *A Room of One's Own* and *Orlando*—are full of savage play at the expense of (male) cultural coteries: professors, editors, literary hacks. She becomes increasingly scornful of what one of her biographers has called 'the massive confidence-trick perpetrated by the middlemen of the book trade'.[55]

In spite of these frustrations, the 'intercourse' of author and reader preoccupied her as much as any of her personal relationships. She wanted to write—essays as well as fiction—*for* someone. She thought of conversation between like-minded lovers of literature as an ideal model for literary criticism,[56] but she did not want her criticism to be merely 'random chatter',[57] or— worse still—just talking to herself. She was keenly concerned, both as a novelist and a critic, with the question 'For whom should I write?' 'To know whom to write for is to know how to write', she said in 1924.[58] If, as a novelist, you were too cut off from your public, too indifferent to it, your art became like some weird, tortured, malformed growth (like Meredith, or late James). If you were too much at one with the public, you

---

[53] McNeillie notes, *Essays*, iv. 456: For Hemingway's reaction to Woolf's review see his letter to Max Perkins, *c*.1 Nov. 1927, in Carlos Baker, ed., *Ernest Hemingway: Selected Letters* (New York, 1981).

[54] *Essays*, iii. 499.

[55] Lyndall Gordon, *Virginia Woolf: A Writer's Life* (Oxford, 1984), 262, who writes powerfully about VW and the market-place. See also Rachel Bowlby, ed., *Virginia Woolf: A Woman's Essays* (Harmondsworth, 1992), pp. ix–xxxiii.

[56] e.g. in 'Byron & Mr Briggs', *Essays*, iii. 494; 'Mr Conrad: A Conversation', 1923, *Essays*, iii. 376–80.

[57] 'How Should One Read a Book?', 1923, *Essays*, iii. 354.

[58] 'The Patron and the Crocus', 1924, *Essays*, iv. 214.

became faded and dusty, like a wayside flower. 'Undoubtedly all writers are immensely influenced by the people who read them.'[59] But those readers also had to be resisted, and not always given what they expected. If the 'great British public' was sitting out there saying in its 'vast and unanimous way' that this was what they thought novels should be like,[60] then one of the writer's jobs was to change its expectations. So the mutual intercourse of writer and reader which she so much desires is also a highly problematic union, set about with conventions and hypocrisies. And the question of who to write for was no longer a simple one:

For whom should we write? . . . The present supply of Patrons is of unexampled and bewildering variety. There is the daily Press, the weekly Press, the monthly Press; the English public and the American public; the best-seller public and the worst-seller public; the high-brow public and the red-blood public; all now organised self-conscious entities capable through their various mouthpieces of making their needs known and their approval or displeasure felt.[61]

In her forties and fifties she became increasingly impatient with the job of reviewing; and in the 1930s she identified its compromises more and more with her satirical analysis of patriarchy. So there's a very close link, in the late 1930s, between *Three Guineas*, and an essay called 'Reviewing' which was published as a Hogarth Press pamphlet in 1939. Her settled dislikes of literary journalism—the compromises of a small circle, the mutual puffing, the censorship, the suppressions of a female point of view, the stranglehold of the establishment, the ineffectiveness and contradictoriness of criticism of contemporaries, and the dire effects that a review could have on an author—became bound up with her analysis in *Three Guineas* of a society which she did not feel she could belong to or identify with.

In *Three Guineas* she referred to reviewing (and lecturing, and literary prizes) as a form of 'brain prostitution', 'intellectual harlotry', since it took place within a culture which was not disinterested. In a long footnote, she expounded her theory that current literary journalism could not be changed without

---

[59] 'Reading', 1919, *Essays*, iii. 157.
[60] 'Byron & Mr Briggs', *Essays*, iii. 514; 'Character in Fiction', *Essays*, iii. 433.
[61] 'The Patron and the Crocus', *Nation & Athenaeum*, 12 Apr. 1924, CE ii. 149.

changing 'the economic structure of society and the psychological structure of the artist'. You could not abolish public criticism:
'Vanity and the desire for 'recognition' are still so strong among
artists that to starve them of advertisement and to deny them
frequent if contrasted shocks of praise and blame would be as
rash as the introduction of rabbits into Australia; the balance of
nature would be upset and the consequences might well be
disastrous.'[62]

The solution was to supplement public criticism by 'a new
service based on the example of the medical profession': a panel
of critics would practise like doctors and in strictest privacy.
(The advantages of this for writers were clearer than for readers.) 'Reviewing' pursued this theme, but with so much intoler-
ance and bravado that Leonard Woolf thought it necessary to
print a note at the end, moderating and 'modifying the conclu-
sions' of her essay. Even so, she had already 'modified' it from
its original version, a savage twenty-seven-page manuscript containing a caricature of a Hitlerian literary editor demanding his
article from the servile reviewer, who is like an animal in a cage,
dogged by the fear of poverty: 'But then unpaid the bill; unpaid
the bill; It is the bill—the bill—.' This is all cut out in favour of
a cooler discussion of the uselessness and lack of authority in
contemporary criticism. Better for it to be replaced by a 'Gutter'
(to précis the work) and a 'Stamp' (to award an asterisk or a
cross). So the 'poisoned fang' of the 'louse' reviewer might
disappear in favour of the thoughtful essayist, and the writer
could pay—three guineas, of course—for a private 'reader-
service', and sink back from fame and ignominy into the 'obscurity' of the workshop. Thus 'his self-consciousness would
diminish'.[63]

She was taken aback (even if Leonard Woolf was not) by the
outraged scorn which greeted this satire on the literary market-
place's investment in prejudices and personalities. The *TLS* reviewer ('tart & peevish'), Robert Lynd in the *New Statesman*,
Malcolm Elwin writing a letter to the *TLS*, the *Spectator* and the
Sunday Times, all leaped in to say what a 'contemptuous' and
ridiculous idea this was, and how essential reviewers were for

[62] *A Room of One's Own and Three Guineas*, ed. Hermione Lee (London, 1984),
298.
[63] *Reviewing* (London, 1939), 23, 25.

the health of the culture. She felt 'stung', 'rasped & injured', 'snubbed & put in my place', and had to keep telling herself this was what she wanted: it was part of her campaign to be an 'Outsider'.[64]

'Reviewing' and the reactions to it confirmed her in the attitude of her last years towards the literary market-place. The chapters she began to write for her last book, *Reading at Random* ('Anon' and 'The Reader'), showed her increasing preoccupation with anonymity, folklore, oral history, and drama, her move away from written forms of literature. They set the desire of the writer, and the instinctive desires of the 'common reader', against the interference of the middlemen. Woolf's notes for *Reading at Random*, made in September 1940 (at a time when she was feeling very acutely the loss of her own audience) say that it is 'about the germ of creation; its thwartings; our society; interruption; conditions'. In 'Anon' she describes these pressures as 'those innumerable influences that are to tug, to distort, to thwart'.[65] The history of printing, she says, has been a history of hostility to the unselfconsciousness of Anon: Anon was not 'self conscious', but now that he is named, and his audience has become his reader, that unselfconsciousness is lost.

In her essays, Virginia Woolf likes to describe the ideal intimacy of reader and writer, and to ask what reading can be at its best. She wants, for one thing, to break down any imposed hierarchies of reading. When she is putting her reading in order, Virginia Woolf asks a great many questions about canon-formation, and insists that great books must be set in the context of inferior, ordinary, forgotten books: trashy novels, obscure memoirs, especially of womens' lives, dust-gathering volumes of letters, mediocre biographies, minor plays. 'A literature composed entirely of good books' would soon be unread, extinct: 'the isolation is too great'. We need 'trivial ephemeral books'. 'They are the dressing-rooms, the workshops, the wings, the sculleries, the bubbling cauldrons, where life seethes and steams and is for ever on the boil'. They fertilize our minds and

---

[64] 'Reviewer or Gutter?', *TLS*, 4 Nov. 1939; Robert Lynd, in *New Statesman*, 4 Nov. 1939; VW to Lynd in *New Statesman & Nation*, 11 Nov. 1939, *Letters*, vi. (3566); Malcolm Elwin in *TLS*, 11 Nov. 1939; *Sunday Times* review, 19 Nov. 1939.

[65] 'Anon and The Reader: Virginia Woolf's Last Essays', ed. Brenda Silver, *Twentieth Century Literature* (Fall 1979), 356–429.

get them ready for the big masterpieces.[66] We can't always be reading Keats or Aeschylus or *King Lear*.[67] So—even though she has spent her life reading great books and major authors as well as lesser works—she defends the pleasures of bad books, the historical importance of the rubbish heap.[68] She argues for serendipitous, random reading from the shelves of second-hand bookshops and public libraries: 'I ransack public libraries & find them full of sunk treasure.'[69] All her life she celebrated the function of the public library as a necessary resource for a democratic culture. The public library is the university of the non-specialist, uninstructed reader; it is the reading room for the common reader.

When she describes an ideal reading, she recommends that one should read as if one were the writer: 'I believe one should try to read books as if one were writing them . . . Do not begin by being a critic; begin by being a writer. Try to understand what a writer is doing. Think of a book as a very dangerous and exciting game, which it takes two to play at.'[70] Her own project in reading is to undo the finished printed work, to get back underneath it and find out what historical factors or personal conditions might have brought it into being, or to read so as 'to try to track your author down—To see what he goes in for. . . . To catch him out.'[71] She herself—knowing exactly what it is like to be a writer who feels constrained and self-conscious—is interested in the unwritten novels beneath the published texts.

In her own readings, she tries to connect reading and writing. She gets inside the writer, feels her way to the essence, saturates herself, and then tries to communicate that saturation. The signs of this saturation are everywhere in her books. From small magpie-stealings to larger schemes (like the literary pageant of *Between the Acts*), her work is permeated with her reading, both what she had read for pleasure and for literary editors.

---

[66] 'Lives of the Obscure', 1925, 1st version, *Essays*, iv. 140.
[67] 'On Being Ill', 1926, *Essays*, iv. 325.
[68] 'Bad Writers', 1918, *Essays*, ii. 328; 'How it Strikes a Contemporary', 1923, *Essays*, iii. 325.
[69] *Diary*, 9 Aug. 1921, ii. 126.
[70] MS, 'How Should One Read a Book?', 1926, The Virginia Woolf Manuscripts in the Henry W. and Albert A. Berg Collection at the New York Public Library (henceforth, Berg).
[71] Notebook, 1925, Berg.

Her retentive, absorbing mind keeps hold of and transforms (misquotations are as valuable to her as quotations) what it needs. In her essays, the distinction is eroded between reference, imitation, tribute, and stealing; she works up her subjects out of a tissue of quotation and paraphrase. Her mind is full of echoes.[72]

When the book is closed and the saturation process is over, the 'after reading' begins. 'Making up' turns into 'making whole'. This is not just an interesting part of the process, it is an urgent personal necessity: 'one must, for one's own comfort, have a whole in one's mind; fragments are unendurable'.[73] Over and over again she insists on the need to 'make it whole'. 'A book is all on top of us. Before we can grasp a single detail, we have to possess ourselves [of] the whole.'[74]

'Making whole' is, again, partly a passive process: 'the whole book floats to the top of the mind complete'.[75] But it also involves the effort to communicate, to say what she thinks about the book. And this is when reading turns from a private 'intoxi-cation'[76] to a process of public explanation. The heat of the notebooks cools into the essays, and the intimate 'union' be-tween one reader and one book opens out into comparisons and contexts. Now she needs to consider the different demands made by different kinds of books—how the reader is forced to respond in one way to the ruthlessness and generality of Greek tragedy, in quite another to the sense of familiarity and ordinari-ness in Chaucer.[77]

So critical writing, like reading, must be a form of intercourse. And the critics she most admires are those who do what she wants to do—'to spear that little eel in the middle—that mar-

---

[72] e.g. reading the weekly essayists like J. C. Squire or E. V. Lucas, she says, 'one feels that a common greyness silvers everything'. The quotation of Browning's line invokes his whole discussion in 'Andrea del Sarto' of the relationship between patronage and the market-place and artistic mediocrity. 'The Modern Essay', 1925, *Essays*, iv. 223.

[73] 'Byron & Mr Briggs', *Essays*, iii. 483.

[74] Notes on *Robinson Crusoe*, 1926, Berg. The idea occurs again in 'Notes on an Elizabethan Play', *Essays*, iv. 166; 'On Re-Reading Novels', *Essays*, iii. 341; the preface to 'The Common Reader', *Essays*, iv. 19.

[75] 'How Should One Read a Book?', *Essays*, iv. 397.

[76] Ibid, 396.

[77] 'On Not Knowing Greek', 1925, *Essays*, iv. 42; 'The Pastons and Chaucer', 1925, *Essays*, iv. 33.

row—which is one's object in criticism'[78]—to get at the essence of the writer through intimacy and saturation:

> That is memorable and stimulating criticism [by George Moore] because, even if one had not read the praises of Turgenev which precede and partly inspire it, one would know that it is the fruit not of coldness, but of love.[79]

> Even in his [Hazlitt's] most perfunctory criticism of books we feel that faculty for seizing on the important and indicating the main outline which learned critics often lose and timid critics never acquire... He singles out the peculiar qualities of his author and stamps it vigorously... And if such criticism is the reverse of final, if it is initiatory and inspiring rather than conclusive and complete, there is something to be said for the critic who starts the reader on a journey and fires him with a phrase to shoot off on adventures of his own... That is not criticism... It is loving and taking the liberties of a lover. It is being Hazlitt.[80]

This process of 'seizing', of 'making whole', closely resembles the process she describes in her life of responding to 'shocks' by making sense of them in description and explanation. It resembles, too, the way in which she shapes her novels by retrospective summings-up: 'I have had my vision', says Lily, concluding *To the Lighthouse*; 'Now to sum up', says Bernard in *The Waves*, 'Now to explain to you the meaning of my life.'

---

[78] *Diary*, 8 Sept. 1930, iii. 317.
[79] Review of George Moore's *Avowals*, *TLS*, 30 Oct. 1919, *Essays*, iii. 119.
[80] 'William Hazlitt', *New York Herald Tribune*, 7 Sept. 1930, *CE* i. 155 ff.

8

The Times Literary Supplement in the Second World War and How to Fill Some Gaps in Modern British Cultural History

JEREMY TREGLOWN

The Times Literary Supplement is among the most important literary journals in the world: catholic in subject-matter and in its responses to the rival claims of innovation and traditionalism, specialism and mass appeal; cosmopolitan; exceptionally durable. For almost a century, despite some critical mistakes and outright omissions, it has reviewed more books more thoroughly than any other paper. Yet to literary historians of the twentieth century the *Lit. Supp.*—as it was once universally called—might as well have been invisible.

One reason is anonymity. Until 1974, *TLS* reviews and articles were unsigned, though there were a few exceptions, notably in the Second World War. Much literary history is inevitably a form of collective biography and its practitioners can seem as uneasy faced with a review lacking a by-line as with poems of doubtful attribution. There is also the practical difficulty of summarizing and assessing the role of any complex, long-lived institution, where the primary material is dauntingly large and judging success is among other things a matter of percentages. This in turn helps to account for another obstacle in the way of a fair assessment of the paper: the interest critics in our century have taken—often for strong critical reasons as well as ones of practicality, but with increasing automatism—in the wayward, the anti-authoritarian and the obscure. 'Little', in 'little magazine', began by being one of those terms of mild, unconvinced self-deprecation which have marked English literary life ever since Chaucer's envoy to his 'litel bok'. But it has ended up ranking with hallmarks like 'radical' and 'subversive'. To be any good, it seems, a magazine, like a Romantic poet, has to be of erratic appearance, insult the respected and die young. *The Modern Review* suffered one of the more recent of such fatalities. But the *TLS* itself gave currency to a premature fear that they might be catching. 'The birth of the Little Magazine', it worried in 1952, 'may . . . be seen in retrospect as heralding the decline of the greater.'[1]

F. R. Leavis was one of the critics who, through his own little magazine *Scrutiny* and his derisive attacks on the London literary establishment, had helped to sustain the cliché of oppositionalism with which Ezra Pound had earlier contributed to the *Lit. Supp.*'s inferiority complex. (Both Pound and Leavis none the less took its shilling.[2]) Yet writers with more inclusive approaches than Leavis's have done little to repair the damage. Robert Hewison, for example, in his generally valuable surveys of the cultural history of Britain since 1939, makes no more than glancing references to the *TLS*.[3] And Paul Fussell, in *Wartime: Understanding and Behavior in the Second World War* (1989)—an attempt to provide a comprehensive, revisionist account of the literary production of that crucial period—devotes a chapter to *Horizon* but doesn't once mention the *TLS*.

The Second World War provides a useful vantage-point both on the *Supplement*'s history and on the broader questions raised by its neglect. Wars bring into focus negotiations between artistic individualism and social responsibility which are less obvious at other times; and for the Western European Allies, the issue of

---

[1] 29 Aug. 1952, xlvii. The author was Ian Scott-Kilvert.

[2] For Pound's dealings with the *TLS* see Jeremy Treglown, 'Literary History and the *Lit. Supp.*', *Yearbook of English Studies*, 16 (1986), 132–49. Leavis's complex relationship with literary journalism is discussed by Stefan Collini in Chapter 9 below.

[3] *Under Siege: Literary Life in London 1939–45* (London, 1977); *In Anger: Culture in the Cold War 1945–60* (London, 1981); *Too Much: Art and Society in the Sixties, 1960–75* (London, 1986); *Culture and Consensus* (London, 1986). In the third of these volumes, Hewison gives an account of Ian Hamilton's little magazine *The Review* which includes the parenthesis: '(Hamilton also held the influential position of poetry and fiction editor at the *Times Literary Supplement* from 1965–72.)' He says nothing more about the nature of that influence or how it compares with that of *The Review*: a particularly marked instance of the *TLS*'s invisibility even to its own contributors, since at the time when Hewison was writing the book he had a regular column in the *Supplement*.

responsibility was more straightforward than it had been, for example, in 1914–18. Questions can be asked about the kinds of statement and discussion which might have been hoped for from the high-cultural journalism of the time, whether in relation to anti-Semitism, the future of Europe and its old empires, or the fate and the responsibility of high culture itself. The few comments which have hitherto been made about the wartime *TLS* have mostly originated with admirers of Stanley Morison, editor from 1945 to 1948, who claimed that his predecessor had fatally 'lightened' the paper and who liked to boast that when he took over, he made it 'difficult to read again'.[4] How does the paper of those years stand up to less partial scrutiny? And how did it respond to the social changes which the war brought?

As it happens, Nazi Germany was the source of one of the few purportedly systematic studies which have been made of any aspect of the *TLS*. *Deutsches Schrifttum der Gegenwart in der Englischen Kritik der Nachkriegszeit* ('Modern German Literature in Post-[First World] War English Criticism'), by Hans Galinsky, published in Munich early in 1939, set out to analyse the reception of German writing in Britain between 1918 and 1935, as represented by four leading journals: the *TLS*, the *Criterion*, the *London Mercury* and the *Bookman*. Galinsky's thesis was that between the First World War and the rise of Nazism, German literary production had been conveyed to English readers principally through the work of Jews, rather than by what he described antithetically as *völkisch* literature. He argued that the British reception of *völkisch* German writing suffered a further set-back in 1933 (the year when Hitler became Chancellor) which, with some boldness, Galinsky regretfully ascribed to a new, nationalistic tendency in English criticism. His 600-page book summarized a large number of reviews in search of proof of these supposed—and supposedly damaging—facts, which he blamed on the Jewishness, or Jewish sympathies, of reviewers. In the case of the *TLS*, though, he conceded that 'How far a jewification—in terms of blood or attitude—of the body of critics has played a part in this

---

[4] See Nicolas Barker, *Stanley Morison* (London, 1972), 404, and Adolf Wood, 'The Lure of the *TLS*', in William Roger Louis, ed., *Adventures with Britannia: Personalities, Politics and Culture in Britain* (Oxford, 1995), 141.

cannot be ascertained . . . because of its policy of anonymous criticism.'[5]

The book had begun as a doctoral thesis and appeared as the second publication of the Länderausschüsse, or Foreign Committee, of the Deutsche Akademie. John Middleton Murry (writing anonymously, of course) commented drily in his *TLS* review, 'We should like to know more about these committees and their functions. . . . [The work] indicates that in National-Socialist Germany Academy and University regard themselves as entirely at the service of the new State.' This was on 4 March 1939, six months after the Munich Agreement and only a few days before Germany invaded what was left of Czechoslovakia.

Reviews like this one made a cumulative contribution to raising awareness of the realities of Nazism. The war, meanwhile, played a major role in the survival of the *TLS*. During the 1930s, sales had dropped from around 30,000 to below 20,000.[6] At the end of 1937, the paper's long-serving editor and in effect its founder,[7] Bruce Richmond, then in his mid-sixties, retired. His successor was someone who was intended to popularize the paper: D. L. Murray, a successful novelist and a racing man who, like Stanley Morison, had been on the staff of *The Times* since the 1920s. Morison had a hand in the appointment and—improbable though this seems in the light of his later reputation for mandarinism—it was partly on his advice that Murray introduced large numbers of illustrations and gave prominent space to likely bestsellers.[8] Sales promptly plunged still further and closure, which had been threatened at least once before, in 1922, seemed inevitable.[9]

That disaster was averted was partly a result of Murray's instinctive if not unerring editorial responsiveness to new circumstances, but more of three external consequences of the outbreak of war. Paper shortages necessitated restrictions in the

    [5] 'Wieweit eine blutmässige und gesinnungsmässige Verjudung der Kritikerschaft hineinspielte, ist mindestens im *T.L.S.* wegen seiner anonymen Kritik nicht festsellbar.'
    [6] Interview with Arthur Crook—see below.
    [7] The first issues were in fact edited by J. R. Thursfield.
    [8] Interview with Arthur Crook.
    [9] Treglown, 'Literary History'. Morison adopted a very different approach when he himself became editor after the war, perhaps having learned from the near-catastrophe which he had helped bring about.

size of daily newspapers, which found themselves having to reduce space for book reviews and to turn away a proportion of their advertising. Publishers consequently bought more space in the *TLS*. Meanwhile, the journal found a growing readership among a population forced to sit around in barracks and air-raid shelters, often bored and with little to do but read books and magazines. And some smaller literary journals which had previously represented competition, if only at the margins, closed down under the various pressures of the time: among them the *Bookman*, the *London Mercury*,[10] T. S. Eliot's *Criterion* and Geoffrey Grigson's *New Verse*.

Had the apolitical Richmond stayed on, he would have found it difficult to adapt to the new circumstances of the war. Following the line of Geoffrey Dawson, who remained as editor of *The Times* until 1941, he had found himself among Fascism's passive fellow-travellers. It was under Richmond that a front-page article appeared in a 1934 issue of the *TLS*, hymning the new Italy and comparing Mussolini's speeches with the poetry of Hardy.[11] But if the robustness of wartime cultural discourse, as well as the accommodations the period brought with socialism, would have taxed Richmond, his successor was not only a populist, at least by the *TLS*'s standards, but a pragmatist.[12]

At the outbreak of war, D. L. Murray's *TLS* declared a new agenda: 'to man the strongholds of the mind. Against the poisoning of human relationships, we oppose [*i.e. set up as a form*

---

[10] The *London Mercury* had been founded in 1919 by J. C. Squire, who died in 1934. Both it and *Bookman* were merged with *Life and Letters* in 1939.

[11] 'Fascism and Italian Thought', 21 June 1934. The works under review included Mussolini's article on Fascism in the new *Enciclopedia italiana* and Giovanni Gentile's *Origini e dottrina del fascismo*. The reviewer, Harold Stannard, wrote: 'The lover of Italy . . . is aware of a coherent vitality in the country as a whole, whereas fifteen years back he was all too conscious of the abundant but conflicting energies of groups. Whatever else it may be, Fascism is an extraordinarily potent synthetizing force.' The passage on Mussolini's style explores the literary dimensions of this force, which Stannard calls 'the will to literary power': '[Mussolini's] thought demands an austerity of expression; and remembering Caesar, he achieves it in curt sentences very different from his journalistic days. . . . The sentences may not be particularly well shaped, but beyond doubt they have backbone. Words, as it were, hurled into the place where they will tell; and the effect, for English readers, is not dissimilar from that which so often comes in Hardy's poetry.'

[12] D. L. Murray wrote a book on the subject, *Pragmatism*, published in 1912, and his ideas may have found scope for development in the First World War, which he had spent in the War Office Intelligence Department.

of opposition] the spirit of Europe.'[13] One form taken by this opposition was increased coverage of such foreign books as could be obtained—especially, until they stopped appearing, books from European countries threatened by Nazism. There was also a strong emphasis on debates concerning the post-war future of Europe, including the possibilities of unification. In May 1940, a *Times* leader-writer, Dermot Morrah, wrote a sympathetic piece for the *TLS* on William Beveridge's pamphlet *Peace by Federation*[14] and this apparently quixotic kind of optimism was particularly evident in a special issue celebrating the paper's 2000th issue, which appeared on 1 June 1940, within days of the retreat from Dunkirk. Under the subheading, 'Germany's place in the new Europe', E. H. Carr reviewed a book on *French War Aims* by Denis Saurat, director of the French Institute in London. 'M. Saurat assumes as his starting-point that Western and Central Europe must somehow be welded into a single Europe,' Carr wrote. 'The Germans are trying to do this in their way. We must do it in a way which we believe to be better than theirs.'

Long, argumentative reviews were preceded by informative snippets in a weekly front-page 'News and Notes' section compiled by Arthur Crook—a printer's son who had joined *The Times* as a clerk in the 1920s and was eventually to become editor of the *Lit. Supp.* From this section, readers learned, for example, that royalties in the English translation of *Mein Kampf* were being diverted to the Red Cross;[15] that the Germans had destroyed Tolstoy's house but that, alas, the flattening of the house in Lübeck which Thomas Mann used in *Buddenbrooks* was caused by the RAF. The section also carried information about the literary work of exiled Europeans in England: new foreign-language publications such as *Poètes casques*, an anthology of poems by French soldiers; or a scholarship scheme offered by PEN to potential translators of Polish literary works into English.[16] There were regular reports of the effects of anti-Semitism, not least in literature and scholarship—for example,

---

[13] Editorial, 2 Sept. 1939. The author was Philip Tomlinson, a staff writer on *The Times* since 1928 who became an assistant editor of the *TLS* soon after outbreak of the Second World War. He retired in June 1947. See *Times* obituary, 3 Mar. 1955. Tomlinson was a close associate of John Middleton Murry, with whom he had worked on the *Athenaeum* and the *Adelphi*.

[14] 25 May 1940, 254.   [15] 30 Sept. 1939.   [16] 21 Feb. 1942.

the fact that the Nazi Party Commission of Examination for the Defence of National-Socialist Writing required authors to separate work by Jewish and Aryan authors in their bibliographies.[17] Another piece pointed out that 'the Germans are not a race at all but a nation ... and a nation to which Germany's Jews belonged'.[18] Meanwhile, it was reported that in Croatia, the Czech propaganda board had conferred what the *TLS* wryly called 'the honour of the index' on writers including Karel Čapek, Sigmund Freud, Maxim Gorki, Sinclair Lewis, Upton Sinclair, André Maurois and Emile Zola.[19]

Censorship wasn't, of course, confined to the Axis Powers and the *TLS* took a stern line with publications thought likely to harm the war effort. It was not unusually subservient. The paper published signed articles by J. B. Priestley after his enthusiastic promulgation of socialism had brought questions in Parliament which led to his being dropped by the BBC.[20] And it was notably uncensorious about W. H. Auden's departure for the USA. In 1932, the *Supplement* had described *The Orators* as 'insolently but exhilaratingly new'[21] and although in its reviews of Auden's wartime publications, increasing admiration for his poetry was tempered by some qualms about its obscurity, his escape from England—much criticized in the *New Statesman* and elsewhere[22]—was not held against him. A heavy hand was, though, applied to some dissident authors—including Middleton Murry, who was eventually dropped as a reviewer because of his pacifism.[23]

The kinds of political correctness elicited by all-out war against Fascism weren't always misdirected. It's hard to feel sorry for Stephen Spender in November 1940—shortly after the Coventry firestorm—when he was attacked by the *TLS* for his

---

[17] The author of this piece was Donald McLachlan, formerly in the Foreign Department of *The Times* and from 1939 editor of *The Times Educational Supplement*. (McLachlan later became editor of the *Sunday Telegraph*, appointing as his literary editor a former *TLS*-staffer, Anthony Curtis.)

[18] 13 Jan. 1940, 14. The author was Harold M. Stannard, a regular contributor since 1922.

[19] 30 May 1942.

[20] Robert Hewison, *Under Siege*, 43. Churchill is said to have been behind the decision.

[21] 9 June 1932. The reviewer was Alan Clutton Brock.

[22] See Richard Davenport-Hines, *Auden* (London, 1995), 180, 207.

[23] Interview with Arthur Crook.

suggestion that 'Compared with bourgeois leaders, the gang-
sters, hard-headed business crooks, Mussolini and Hitler are
highly poetical figures.'[24] But similarly rough treatment was
dealt out to a more defensible argument by David Cecil, published in the *TLS* itself.[25] Cecil's article criticized the domination
of the wartime book trade by political subjects and complained
of a decline in what he called 'real' literature—a debate which
touched many of the arts at the time. Cecil made a claim for art-
for-art's-sake, even when

those who . . . still defend the artist's right to live in his ivory
tower . . . [know] he may at any moment be bombed out of it. . . . A
man is admired who escapes from a German prison camp. Why should
he be blamed for escaping out of the dingy, bloodstained prison of
contemporary events into the fertile garden of his creative fancy?

An editorial in the same issue thundered back that artists must
buckle to: 'Is not the Nazi threat to men's liberty . . . sufficient to
move them? . . . Here are themes enough, full, rich and complex.
We can dispense with the perfumery.' This was the voice of one
of the *TLS*'s assistant editors and most prolific contributors,
Philip Tomlinson.[26] A similar line, comical to readers living in
less urgent circumstances, was taken by another frequent contributor, the elderly E. E. Mavrogordato, in a review of Evelyn
Waugh's satire *Put Out More Flags*:

The period of which he is writing is that of the present war; the people
are rogues or inept—people such as in the years after the last war were
drawn by authors dubbed young intellectuals, to the weakening, as
some think, of the nation's faith in itself and with general disruptive
effects from which its enemies are now profiting. In fact, in its render-
ing of those to whom the nation has to look for orders and guidance
this book would be mischievous, but that it is unlikely to impress
readers whose value to the community would be reduced by accepting
its implications.[27]

Orotundities like these, with their echoes of the First World
War, were consistent with a more subtly conformist and optimistic approach in reviews of political books, especially those
on foreign policy. There was a noticeable shift, for example, in
the paper's attitude to the Soviet Union after June 1941. Many

[24] 23 Nov. 1941.   [25] 11 Jan. 1941.
[26] See n. 13.   [27] 21 Mar. 1942.

criticisms of Soviet totalitarianism were voiced in the *TLS* during the time of the Nazi-Soviet Pact and earlier—not least in a review of Arthur Koestler's *Darkness at Noon*[28]—but after mid-1941, when Germany turned against the Soviet Union, the note became one of respectful enthusiasm for Soviet military strength and the greatness of Russian literature. The novelist William Gerhardi, who had been born and educated in Russia, contributed a signed piece which, though not wholly uncritical of the Soviet system, emphasized its coherence, resilience and admirable rejection of class distinctions. This new and unexpectedly durable line has sometimes been put down to the sole influence of E. H. Carr, who joined the staff of *The Times* in January 1941. But his views were widely shared at the time by other members of the British intelligentsia and the *TLS*'s weekly stockbooks show that most of the pro-Soviet pieces published by the paper during the war were written not by Carr but by another regular contributor, R. D. Charques.[29]

Given what has happened to the communitarian hopes raised in Britain at that time, there's an extra resonance in the way that wartime *TLS* contributors advocated social-democratic programmes.[30] On 6 September 1941—three months before Pearl Harbor finally brought the United States into the war—a special issue appeared, entitled 'England Looks to the Future'. A woodcut on the front page depicts a big-eyed woman holding the hands of a departing man, against the background of a storm-

[28] 21 Dec. 1940. The reviewer was R. D. Charques.

[29] At this time the stockbooks were handwritten quarto notebooks in which each double-page spread listed all the unused material which had been set in type and was therefore available to the editor for the issue whose date appeared at the top. Items were divided into broad categories—general pieces, fiction reviews, poems, leaders, letters, special sections, and so on. Each entry consisted of the surname of the contributor (but see below, p. 146), the title of the book under review or another short heading and the length of the piece in inches. When a piece went into the paper, it was crossed out in pencil. The remaining entries were copied out again for the next issue. The other main source of information about contributors is the 'marked copy' of each issue, in which every piece has the contributor's name written on it for the information of the accounts department.

[30] Wartime propagandism played a part even here, of course. Beveridge himself admitted that his revolutionary report, *Social Insurance and Allied Services*, was prompted, among other considerations, by the question of 'what is needed to make a democracy whole-hearted in war. Democracies make war for peace, not war for its own sake. They fight better if they know what they are fighting for after the war.' (*The Pillars of Security and Other Wartime Essays and Addresses*, quoted in the *TLS*, 19 June 1943, 294.)

lashed coast. Inside, Edith Sitwell's poem 'Still Falls the Rain' was published for the first time, along with resolute analyses of books on the links between England and Russia and the future of Anglo-American relations, as well as other more or less undisguisedly propagandist works by established literary figures—*War in the Air*, by David Garnett, for example, and Margery Allingham's *The Oaken Heart*, an account of English village life aimed at stirring nostalgia in American readers. The main piece, though, was by J. B. Priestley, prophesying a post-war future in which 'England will . . . be the eastern outpost of a new oceanic English-speaking power . . . [in] a democratic pioneering kind of world . . . creative rather than subtly appreciative. It will be rough-and-ready rather than smooth and finished. Its culture will rest on a broader base.' Much of what is anticipated here sounds like an idealized version of Priestley himself but it proved none the less accurate for that. He hastened to reassure *TLS* readers that he wasn't looking forward to 'an orgy of "proletarian" literature with hymns to concrete mixers'. On the contrary, he hoped that 'it may well be a far more deeply philosophical culture'. Whatever form this vaguely imagined philosophicality might have taken, he was confident that it would belong to 'a better world than the one that is currently being blown to pieces'.

While Priestley and others were looking to the future, the *TLS* also gave space to authors who found sources of strength and hope in the past. There's something touching about the blithely unruffled air of business as usual which comes across in the more scholarly literary articles, though Arthur Crook takes a sceptical view of it: 'I'd love to think it was based on anything other than "Nothing can possibly happen it'll all be all right in the end" kind of thing.' On 2 September 1939, for example, just after Germany invaded Poland, the journal published a letter from Maynard Mack elucidating a couplet in Pope's *Epistle to Dr Arbuthnot*. Britain declared war the following day. At the beginning of 1940, Georgina Battiscombe asked for information relevant to her biography of Charlotte M. Yonge. The early years of the war also saw correspondence about a forged letter from Peele to Marlowe, and about 'A line in Baudelaire'. On 2 May 1942, immediately after the 'Baedeker raids' on the cathedral cities of Exeter, Bath, Norwich and York, in which 1,000 civilians were killed, *TLS* readers were treated to the text of a lecture given by Dorothy Margaret Stuart on 'Minor Verse of the Regency Period'. Week by week they learned, too, about new books on Etruscan sculpture, medieval music, ancient Greek drama, ornithology and bibliography. Meanwhile, some of the material culture being discussed was sold off. The *TLS*'s literary versions of war-casualty lists reported sales of rare books and manuscripts. January 1942, for example, saw a first edition of *Lamia* inscribed to Hazlitt, offered at auction in London, along with a first edition of *Leaves of Grass* (Brooklyn, 1855). *Tom Jones*, six volumes in a contemporary calf binding, went for £30; more than 1,300 original woodblocks made by Thomas Bewick, in four wooden chests, for £300.[31] 'They have presumably gone . . . to some American museum or library', the paper noted.

Clearly, the value of these and other aspects of the *TLS*'s wartime coverage lay at the time in their *not* being opposed to the national culture. This point was spelt out movingly in the 'News and Notes' section in the last issue of 1941:

The Nazis not only have destroyed their native literary output, but already they have deeply affected the significance of the literature of the lands still free. By which is meant not the current of to-day's writings, which inevitably is directed along the channels of war, but the point of so much that was written in the past.

The work of all the greater writers of the nineteenth century and later expressed protest in varying degrees and for various reasons against conformity to conditions which, in their view, fall short of civilization. When we turn to them to-day they seem to dwell in some capricious atmosphere, remote from the dread realities of life. They were in revolt against conditions which seem some centuries in advance of our own. . . . Thoreau proves an American case. He was allowed to speculate freely by his pond, and his broodings seemed positively anarchical till yesterday. Now they lead us nowhere, except to some kind of fairyland.[32]

Such were the conditions against which the *TLS* stood, week by week, year by year, in more than 300 wartime issues, containing between them about ten million words. Who wrote them?

It's hard for modern readers to imagine how intensely

---

[31] 2 May 1942.
[32] 20 Dec. 1941. The author, once again, was Philip Tomlinson.

clubmanlike the *Times* offices at Printing House Square were before 1939. This atmosphere was slow to change. Unlike in recent years, when the *Supplement* and *The Times* have become editorially more separate, *TLS* pieces were often written by salaried *Times* critics and leader-writers. D. L. Murray had worked for Bruce Richmond. Most of the able-bodied young were directly involved in warwork so Murray was to some extent obliged to use the personnel Richmond had built up. Edmund Blunden, for example, not only wrote for the paper often during the Second World War but was brought on to its staff. Other well-established literary and academic figures who appeared included Laurence Binyon, R. M. Dawkins, Ifor Evans, Roger Fry, Roger Fulford, Philip Guedalla, John Hayward, Christopher Hollis, Lewis Namier, Mario Praz,[33] Peter Quennell, Herbert Read, Michael Sadleir and R. A. Scott-James. The youngest of these—Fulford, Hayward, Hollis, Quennell—had been boys during the First World War and were now in their mid- to late thirties. Most of the others could remember the reign of Queen Victoria.

In the rapidly changing social circumstances of the time, though, an increasing number of those enlisted to help 'man the strongholds of the mind' were women. In the paper's records for the early months of the war, they are easily identifiable. Men appear by their surnames only (except in the cases of duplicate names and contributors of signed pieces). Women are generally 'Miss' or 'Mrs'. You can see social change even in details like these: by 1944, regular female contributors such as Georgina Battiscombe, Naomi Royde-Smith and Marjorie Hessell Tiltman were recorded by their surnames, like the men. Some thirty women wrote for the paper in the first fifteen months of the war alone. About a third of these still appear in the contributors' lists in 1944, by which time others had been introduced. A few—among them Royde-Smith and Tiltman, as well as Elizabeth Sturch and Leonora Murray (who was married to the editor)[34]—wrote pieces almost every week.

[33] Praz was at this time married to Vivyan Eyles, a stepdaughter of D. L. Murray. In this inner network of kindred and affinity Murray's wife, Leonora Eyles (see n. 34), wrote regularly for the paper, and her daughter, Merle—later Merle Knox—was a frequent contributor.

[34] Under her previous married name, Leonora Eyles, she was the regular author of a widely syndicated agony-aunt column.

It's important not to exaggerate their impact. Only a sixth of the contributors were female,[35] although by this time women were far from being newcomers to British literary and academic life. As one of the older of them, Gertrude Woodthorpe, pointed out in a *TLS* review, it was not the Second World War but the First which had secured most of these emancipations, and indeed for many women 1939 brought an interruption to established careers.[36] Again, there's plenty of gender-stereotyping in how reviewer is matched to subject: children's books and books about clothes, for example, were invariably reviewed by women.[37] On the other hand, almost every work on the pressing topic of the British colonies and their future was reviewed by Margery Perham, one of the leading conservative authorities (at this time, she was Reader in Colonial Administration at Oxford[38]). The *TLS*'s main wartime reviewer of books on the sea and sailing was a woman. A high proportion of the poems published in the wartime *TLS* were by women, especially Vita Sackville-West and Edith Sitwell. Other well-known female contributors included Clemence Dane and Elizabeth Middleton Murry. Most tellingly, the paper's first major statement on the role of writers in the Second World War was not only written by a woman but appeared under her name: Storm Jameson.

The piece was published on 7 October 1939, with the heading 'Fighting the Foes of Civilization. The Writer's Place in the Defence Line.' Jameson wrote fervently about how the 'forces of regress'—anti-Semitism among them—had persisted throughout the supposedly civilized world since the First World War, and warned of how easily a new conflict might produce other regressions, particularly in the form of censorship. For her as for many writers of the time, one prediction about the war was that in combating Fascism, the Allies would find themselves taking on some of its colouring. Authors could be useful, here: 'The writer, because he is used to breaking through his own solitude in order

[35] Again, this figure is based on Sept. 1939–Dec. 1940, only.

[36] Review of Peggy Scott's *British Women in War*, 16 Nov. 1940.

[37] Children's books principally by Naomi Royde-Smith and Elizabeth Sturch. The expert on clothes and the history of costume was the social historian Muriel St. Clare Byrne. There was also a corner in books about dogs, all of which were reviewed by Catherine Garvin, daughter of the editor of the *Observer*.

[38] After the war she became Director of the Oxford University Institute of Colonial (later Commonwealth) Studies.

to speak, is more able than other men to reach the individual in time to save him from choking in the officially induced fog.' It was essential, Jameson insisted, to avoid the crudifications of jingoism. 'A correspondent in *The Times* wrote lately, "We have no other aim than to destroy Hitlerism, and no elaboration of that simple purpose should be permitted." The writer cannot allow himself to share this comforting simplicity.' Literature's task, she continued, was nothing less than that of 'imagining for Europe a future from which the poison of nationalism has been drawn. . . . The rest is to experience despair as a stage in courage . . . the thought of defeat as a reminder that no Dark Age has outlasted, or can outlast, the unquenchable energy of the mind.'

Jameson, then in her late forties, was among the most promi-nent British novelists and cultural activists of her day. A lifelong socialist, she had begun her career as a writer in 1913 with a piece about Shaw for A. R. Orage's journal *New Age*, where she became a regular contributor.[39] By the 1920s she was in effect the editor of a shorter lived little magazine, *New Common-wealth*. An early, consistent and vocal opponent of Fascism (she and her husband, the publisher Guy Chapman, were among those who went to see at first hand what was happening in Germany in the early 1930s), she helped organize practical support for refugees and in 1938 was elected as the first woman president of PEN, a position which she held until the end of the war.

Jameson was a close friend of D. L. Murray, whom she later described as 'like a good-humoured priest, large, soft, delicate in mind and manner, with no vanity and not a great deal of male energy'.[40] It's not precisely clear what kind of male energy she wanted from him but intellectually, at any rate, she seems to have supplied some of what was missing herself. Certainly the ideas expressed in her article at this early stage of the war, though (as she admitted) not entirely original,[41] were to become theme-tunes of the *TLS* in the coming months and years. Arthur

[39] Storm Jameson, *Journey from the North: Autobiography* (2 vols.; London, 1969 and 1970), i. 329 and *passim*.

[40] Ibid. i. 138.

[41] Ibid. ii. 95. One of the issues here is how PEN went about formulating its policies, how far they coincided with those of the *TLS* and what part was played by Jameson in these processes.

Crook recalls that 'Murray admired [Jameson's] novels enor-
mously and also her general attitude and thoughts about the
war. She was quite an important part of the *Supplement*. They
dined together frequently and he took a lot of guidance from
her'—so much so that in 1944, as she later described, Murray
'set me down to write his editorial' on the liberation of Paris,
which took place while she was staying with him, his wife and
father at their home in Brighton, convalescing from an illness.[42]

According to Jameson, Murray was 'deeply proud' of his
editorship of the *TLS* and mortified by what she describes as his
'abrupt dismissal' in 1945. She seems to have thought that both
of these feelings were justified.[43] One result of attending to the
paper's wartime history is to rescue its reputation, to a degree,
from the self-serving criticisms of Murray's successor. Such
issues are only a small part of what a full study of the *TLS*'s
history will help to illuminate,[44] but whilst any diligent
researcher has usually been able to find out from the *Times*
archives who wrote a specific piece, it has been far harder to
search the records in other ways—for example, to see what a
particular author contributed over a whole lifetime, who the
dominant reviewers were in a given genre or on a particular
topic, or what the links were between the paper and other
institutions of the time, such as the British Council, the BBC
and PEN, as well as with the anonymous readers and editors of
publishing houses. It is time to complete the work begun by
John Gross in 1974.[45] Since the *TLS* is part of the material of
several histories—social and economic as well as literary and
intellectual—the process will contribute to our understanding of
many aspects of the culture of which it has been a part.

Not even the memorious Arthur Crook, of course, can identify everyone, and names alone cannot, and perhaps shouldn't,
rescue everyone from oblivion. As a retired Foreign Editor of

---

[42] *Journey from the North*, ii. 139. 'David loved Italy and had little feeling for
France; since he knew I had a great deal, he set me down to write his editorial about
it.'

[43] Ibid. ii. 137.

[44] As this book goes to press, a centenary history has just been commissioned
from Derwent May.

[45] A project has recently been begun at the University of Warwick, with the help
of the Leverhulme Trust, under the joint editorship of the author and Deborah
McVea, which will make the entire index of the *TLS* from 1902, including the
identities of contributors, electronically available.

The Times said, after the *TLS* had abandoned anonymous reviewing, 'They tell you their names, now. None the wiser. What I want to know is how old they are and where they went to school.' Cultural historians, too, may want information of these kinds—as well as much more besides. But names will be a start.

9

The Critic as Journalist:
Leavis after *Scrutiny*

STEFAN COLLINI

How to have a human civilization in a world of academic specialism? The dominant answer of our century has been: *journalism*, which creates a human world and comments upon it, but only as it uses a language far less capable of showing thought than of providing amusement and stimulation.

> (Editorial, 'One Language', *The Human World*, 1
> (1970), 5)

... journalism (in one form or another) is now the menacing disease of university 'English'.

> (F. R. Leavis, *Nor Shall My Sword: Discourses on
> Pluralism, Compassion, and Social Hope*
> (London, 1972), 64)

Leavis was in many ways more like a journalist of genius ... than like an academic.

> (Michael Black, *Cambridge Review*, 110 (Oct. 1989),
> 132)

We must have mercy on critics who are obliged to make a figure in printed pages. They must by all means say striking things.

> (George Eliot)

I

By pairing the terms 'literary journalism' and 'literary scholarship', one risks exaggerating a conventional distinction into an exhaustive opposition. It may, therefore, be worth beginning by remarking certain asymmetries nestling within this apparently neat antithesis, starting with a telling disjunction between the respective referents. 'Literary scholarship' refers to the disciplined study of a particular subject-matter: the exact definition and limits of that subject-matter may be constantly, and properly, contested, but in principle it has for the greater part of the twentieth century been recognized as the study of 'literature' and not of something else, such as economics or philosophy. But 'literary journalism' is not used to refer to journalism about this same specific subject-matter. 'Literary' here is used in its broader sense of 'to do with books', including, of course, books about economics or philosophy or other comparable 'subjects'. 'Literature' in the narrower sense has for long been at the heart of the concerns of the 'literary editor' of a newspaper or periodical, which no doubt encourages the appearance of symmetry, but none the less literary journalism has not yet become simply the outdoor version of one branch of scholarship.

In similar vein, one must not too readily or neatly map the distinction between scholarship and journalism on to that between academic and non-academic. It is true, of course, that scholarship has become largely the preserve of those employed in institutions of higher learning, though it is even now not quite completely so and was far from being the case during much of the period covered in this book. Conversely, substantial contributions to literary journalism have frequently been made by academics, and a glance at the review pages of the contemporary broadsheet press would suggest that this practice has far from disappeared.

A third complication to the apparent simplicity of the contrast concerns the place of 'criticism'. One implication that can be read into the contrast is that criticism lines up on the journalistic side of the divide against largely historical scholarship on the other. But after the 'Modernist revolution' in the 1920s and 1930s, and especially after the rise of New Criticism to pedagogical centrality in the 1940s and 1950s, criticism was seen as being very much at the heart of the academic study of literature. Where that assumption is endorsed (it has, of course, come in for considerable attack in recent years), 'criticism' seems to change sides in any contrast between the academic and the journalistic, and 'literary criticism' then becomes counterposed to 'book-reviewing'. The distinction between these two activities can be stated most starkly by saying that in the former the assumption is that readers have already read the books being discussed and that in the latter they haven't. But clearly neither presumption is always or strictly true, and, moreover, there continue to be various non-specialist forms of criticism which involve a constant and profitable commerce between the familiar and the novel, and a corresponding exercise of informed judgement, that doesn't line up tidily with either 'literary journalism' or 'literary scholarship'.

So, without losing sight of the possibly fruitful tensions suggested by the pairing of those terms, one might recast the direction of discussion by beginning with the question: where does cultural criticism happen? Where do those debates take place in which a society's conception of itself is fought out and fought over, in which standards of argument, of intellectual and aesthetic excellence, even of general human flourishing, are articulated and brought to bear on the transient issues of the day? Cast in such general terms, the question is in danger of collapsing under the weight of its own abstraction, and even if rephrased in more modest and concrete form, there must be a strong presumption that different answers would obtain for different times and places. At present, for example, much of this criticism may be carried on in media other than that of print journalism, and there is also some reason to think that literature may be less looked to as a source of value or legitimation than when 'literary scholarship' first established itself. None the less, the starting-point for this essay is the suggestion that for the middle decades of the twentieth century in Britain one particularly plausible short answer to this general question would be 'literary journalism'.

Clearly, if that term is taken in its narrowest sense, then this will seem an implausible and bathetic answer: could a society's sense of its identity really be so dependent upon, say, the reviewing of new novels? But, as I've suggested, the term does also connote a larger terrain, embracing a wide range of contributions to those cultural and intellectual discussions that are carried on in the 'literary' pages of newspapers and periodicals. There, alongside much else, one finds the aspiration to bring a 'non-specialist' perspective to bear, the aspiration that is the hallmark of the cultural critic or intellectual. Of course, the phrase 'non-specialist' begs too many of the relevant questions, and one of the recurrent themes of debate in Britain in the mid- and late twentieth century has precisely been the peculiarity of the claim of literary criticism to escape or transcend the defor- mation that is alleged to be the fruit of specialization in other disciplines. But such discussion has only served to increase rather than diminish the centrality of 'literary journalism' in the broad sense. And it is in this setting that the role of the literary critic as social critic invites consideration.

In speaking of this role, I intend to draw attention to ques- tions of performance. We recognize that the power of the best literary criticism is inseparable from the effect on us of a sense of the critic's distinctive voice, a voice that is both impressively 'achieved' yet irresistibly 'natural'—one thinks of, say, the unfussed worldliness that accompanies Empson's most delicate discriminations, or the combination of self-conscious *gravitas* and engaged modernity in Trilling. Less obvious, perhaps, is the part played by some such effect in making the critic a persuasive contributor to public discussion of non-literary issues. Yet effec- tive cultural criticism does aim, in a similar way, to make a distinctive voice (an expression of a particular view of the world) tell in public discussion, as much by the indirect effect of its attractiveness as by the irrefragability of consecutive argu- ment. This may be particularly important where (speaking for the moment in terms that are bound to seem clumsily general) the beliefs and values which the critic is trying to uphold are neither readily acknowledged and shared nor susceptible of brisk propositional statement. In such circumstances, the ques- tion of the tactics by which the reader is cajoled or manœuvred into starting to look at the world in unaccustomed ways be- comes central.

In this essay, I address these issues by focusing on the later polemical writings of F. R. Leavis (from the period, that is to say, after the closure of *Scrutiny* in 1953 until his death in 1978). But I should make clear from the outset that I am far from regarding Leavis as a model or exemplar in the role of literary critic as social critic. Indeed, part of my concern here will be to try to discriminate some of the more general and enduring features of that role from what I find to be the mis-judged and ultimately self-defeating aspects of Leavis's actual performance in it. Although Leavis was too powerful a presence and too idiosyncratic a voice to be comfortably handled as a 'case study', his later polemical writings do raise in a particu-larly intriguing and forceful way the questions of tone and authority in cultural criticism as practised by the literary critic. In particular, his example crystallized what is at the least a tension and even for some a dilemma: if one believes that the public conversation matters but that most of the media in which it is carried on are constraining or distorting—that they are, one might say, part of the problem rather than of the means to the solution—then how is one to participate? In addition, Leavis had, for better or worse, a major influence upon the ways in which the relations between metropolitan literary journalism and academic literary criticism were conceived in, roughly, the three decades after 1945. For these reasons he cannot but be one of the major points of reference in a book such as this.

2

One of the difficult choices the cultural critic always has to make is whether to try primarily to use the existing cultural media, with all the attendant drawbacks of potential collusion and vulgarization (or even, at the limit, of censorship or exclusion), or whether to seek to establish a vehicle over which one has some control, but where the corresponding disadvantage is that of potentially failing to reach an audience beyond the already converted. It could be said that, up until the closure of *Scrutiny* in 1953, Leavis had largely followed the second of these strat-egies: *Scrutiny* was never a narrowly professional journal, but it made much (at times too much) of its oppositional or even sectarian character. Its circulation never exceeded 3,000 and was usually considerably smaller. After its closure, however, Leavis was increasingly driven to writing in the kind of main-stream periodicals whose laxity he relentlessly denounced. At the same time, his sympathies continued to be engaged by the ambition to found a journal which would stand out against both the superficiality of contemporary literary journalism and the narrowness of contemporary literary scholarship. Initially, it seemed as though *The Cambridge Quarterly* (founded by a group of younger Cambridge admirers in 1965) might go some way to reviving this ambition, though it was perhaps the short-lived *The Human World* (founded by his former pupil, Ian Robinson, in 1970) that came closest to satisfying it. Notoriously, Leavis fell out with the founders of the first of these and refused to contribute after the opening number, but the second provided a home for several of his most embattled later pieces. Still, it remains largely true that after 1953 Leavis was increasingly driven to participate in that larger world of literary journalism that was so much the target of his criticism, and so although there are, needless to say, many deep continuities between the work of his earlier and later periods, a special interest attaches to the latter within the frame of the present volume.

One striking index of the change of condition that accompanied, even if it did not wholly determine, the shift in direction of Leavis's later polemics is given by the following figures (these are my calculations, based on the very full annotated bibliography edited by Maurice Kinch *et al.*): before 1953, Leavis published seventy-eight reviews and nine letters to the press, while after 1953 he published nine reviews but sixty-six letters.[1] These figures signal several changes: the reviews in the earlier period were nearly all in *Scrutiny*, of course, while it was Leavis's increasing fame, or notoriety, that provided the occasion for many of the letters to the press in later years. But the change could also be seen as a decision to adopt guerrilla tactics rather than conventional warfare, or, changing the metaphor slightly, the tactic of choosing one's own ground on which to fight rather than letting it be determined (once he no longer commanded his own journal) by the opportunistic decisions of review editors.

The direction of his polemical energies in the second half of his career can be illustrated in a further way. In the twenty-five

---

[1] This may understate the number of letters, especially in the later period, since I have excluded the apparently minor ones mentioned in Kinch but not included in Tasker; see M. B. Kinch, William Baker, and John Kimber, *F. R. Leavis and Q. D. Leavis: An Annotated Bibliography* (New York, 1989); and *Letters in Criticism by F. R. Leavis*, ed. John Tasker (London, 1974).

years between the closing of *Scrutiny* and Leavis's death, he published twenty-two essays or articles of some substance. (Inevitably, the classification must be somewhat approximate here: a case could be made for treating one or two reviews as essays, and I have omitted a couple of short notes. But the general picture these figures presents seems to me beyond dispute.) The largest single category (six items) is made up of pieces that appeared in American literary and cultural reviews such as *The Sewanee Review* or *Commentary*. Five appeared in Robinson's self-consciously *Scrutiny*-emulating *The Human World*. Three were published in *The Times Literary Supplement*, and two in *The Spectator* (including his 'Two Cultures?' lecture). Two more appeared in *The Universities Quarterly* and its successor, and the remaining four appeared in miscellaneous periodicals, two of them published in India.

One immediately noticeable feature of this list is the absence of scholarly articles in the professional 'Eng Lit' journals: the nearest (which is not, after all, very near) was the appearance of his Anna Karenina essay in the first number of *The Cambridge Quarterly*. The list also suggests that Leavis did not find it all that difficult to get his pieces published in some of the leading 'general' periodicals. His relations with the various journals were not constant, and the appearance of a piece by him sometimes reflected the editorial initiative of an old pupil or some other personal connection. Two other facts are less clear from the list itself. The first is that Leavis republished practically all the significant essays of his later years in book form. And the second (which can be documented from MacKillop's biography and other sources as well as from the Kinch bibliography) is that the majority of these pieces first began life as some kind of public lecture. Finally, it is worth remarking that, though the ostensible topics covered are very various, in practice a small group of topics is reworked over and over again—the familiar Leavisian themes about cultural decline, the need for an educated public, the role of universities, the place of the teaching of English.

The overall picture—and, without going into them in similar detail, I suggest that this is borne out by the pattern of his other kinds of writing during this period—serves as a reminder of the distance separating Leavis from the conventional academic literary scholar (even though he has been taken by some subsequent literary theorists to represent the 'approach' of the allegedly dominant scholarly practice). The pattern of his later writing was not at all that of the professional academic contributing to learned publications in his or her 'field'; it suggests, rather, the cultural critic or intellectual who seizes on the occasions which his reputation brings his way to reiterate a small number of cherished truths to a non-specialist audience.

Leavis exemplifies, in a characteristically insistent way, what I have suggested is bound to be one of the central dilemmas of serious cultural criticism: by which means and with which tactics can one make a persuasive critical case about the low standards of contemporary cultural debate if one is obliged to use the very media whose standards one is criticizing? If one's charges about the shallowness and corruption of contemporary literary journalism are well-grounded, will that journalism provide a receptive vehicle for one's attacks, and if it does so on any kind of regular basis, should that be seen as calling the accuracy of the hostile picture into doubt? Moreover, if, like Leavis, the critic believes that the state of literary journalism is merely an expression of a more general absence of attention to serious cultural standards, then the dominant concerns and idioms of public debate will seem to set limits to what is likely to be found acceptable or persuasive as a contribution to that debate: how then is one to be persuasive in attempting to mount a critique of the very standards that determine what is to count as persuasive? The more fundamental one's objections, the less likely it is that they could effectively be expressed within the confines of the public debate one is objecting to.

This general dilemma was particularly acute in Leavis's case, since he could not take advantage of two responses that, in different ways, might seem to offer some relief. The first, a position taken not just by academics but by several varieties of mandarin social criticism in the twentieth century, is to be dismissive of the importance of public debate, disdainful of 'mere journalism', and to consider oneself to be addressing a handful of other superior minds or perhaps, more loftily still, posterity. The other possible response is to consider oneself to be writing in the role of 'expert' or upon subjects on which one's acknowledged professional qualifications authorize one's criticism of more popular treatments. Both these identities, or strategies, afford the critic a comforting sense of vindication independent of general contemporary response. But 'comfort' was never Leavis's way, and some of his most deeply held convictions denied him either of these forms of solace.

To begin with, he never lost his passionate belief in the importance of 'an educated public', and he repeatedly insisted that cultural standards and values were only 'there', only realized, in so far as the conversation between writer and readers was genuinely reciprocal, with the response of an educated public being expressed in serious critical judgements.

It is only in a coherent, educated and influential reading-public, one capable of responding intelligently and making its response felt, that standards are 'there' for the critic to appeal to: only where there is such a public can he invoke them with any effect. A great fact of the literary history of our time is that such a public no longer exists. The fact is manifested in the difficulty of establishing and keeping alive any serious critical organ.[2]

As this last sentence indicates, Leavis could never be indifferent to or dismissive of the importance of would-be 'serious' literary journalism.

Leavis's concern with journalism was, of course, of long standing, predating even the foundation of *Scrutiny*, never mind its closure. It is worth remembering that the topic of his Ph.D. thesis was 'The Relationship of Journalism to Literature Studied in the Rise and Earlier Development of the Press in England'; as completed, the thesis concentrates on the seventeenth and early eighteenth centuries, but Leavis's original proposal had been to devote at least as much attention to the relations between literature and journalism in the nineteenth and twentieth centuries.[3] Throughout the *Scrutiny* years, the Leavises (this is one of the areas where it is appropriate to speak of them together) constantly sniped at the so-called 'quality' daily and Sunday newspapers and the literary and political weeklies, deploring their betrayal of the critical function but never regarding them as insignificant or beneath notice. In his celebrated 1953 exchange

---

[2] Letter to *The London Magazine* (Mar. 1955), in *Letters in Criticism*, ed. Tasker, 44.
[3] See Ian MacKillop, *F. R. Leavis: A Life in Criticism* (London, 1995), 71.

with F. W. Bateson on the function of criticism, Leavis asked rhetorically whether Bateson thought that as long as journals like *Scrutiny* and *Essays in Criticism* existed it did not matter how bad the reviewing in the weeklies and Sundays was, and then answered: 'If so, I cannot take seriously his idea of the function of criticism, or his interest in literature . . .' and so on.[4] These newspapers and periodicals (even more than the BBC, another of the Leavises' constant targets) constituted the chief terrain on which the battle for an educated public could be fought, and in his later years Leavis returned with a wearying frequency to his sense that this was where the corruption of contemporary culture was most shamefully exhibited. As he put it in the prefatory note added to the American edition of his 'Two Cultures?' lecture, speaking here specifically of the Sunday papers:

They maintain in their review pages—an aspect of this cultural phenomenon that, with my eye on my theme, I have to emphasize—the air and the reputation of performing the critical function at the highest level, their reviewers being (it is to be understood) of the intellectual elite. And indeed they are, if anything properly to be called an intellectual elite anywhere presents itself in British journalism. The critical function is performed at no higher level in the intellectual weeklies, where in fact we find not only the same kind of writer, but very largely the same names.[5]

But Leavis could be as savage about the misplaced positivism and moral evasiveness of academic literary scholarship as he was about the vulgarities and corruptions of literary journalism. 'The academic is the enemy', as he pithily put it in his Richmond Lecture of 1962 (referring to a quality or style, not a person); 'a solidarity of professional philistines' was one typical characterization of orthodox literary scholars.[6] Though he supported closer relations between the study of literature and the study of history than his later reputation as a one-eyed exponent of 'practical criticism' might suggest, in public debate he never

[4] 'The Responsible Critic: or the Function of Criticism at Any Time', *Scrutiny*, 19 (1953), 180.
[5] F. R. Leavis, *Nor Shall My Sword: Discourses on Pluralism, Compassion, and Social Hope* (London, 1972), 69.
[6] Ibid. 63; 'Introduction to the 1976 edition', in F. R. Leavis (ed.), *Towards Standards of Criticism: Selections from 'The Calendar of Modern Letters'* (London, 1976 [1st edn., 1933]), p. xvii.

claimed to speak on the basis of the authority conferred by the accumulated learning of literary *scholarship*: Leavisian criticism explicitly rested on the kinds of judgement and recognition open to any educated reader willing to engage in collaborative critical discussion, and he always firmly repudiated the idea of a separate realm of 'literary values', insisting, rather, that what literature expressed and the standards by which it should be judged were those of 'life'. There was a claim to authority here, though not to expertise, but it was a claim that could only be vindicated by his success in persuading the non-professional reader. It did not license either assertions of incontestable competence or of self-protective withdrawal.

Of course, it is notorious that Leavis invested unrealistically high hopes in the university as society's 'centre of consciousness', but this was not as much at odds with the characterization I have just given as it may at first seem. Leavis idealized the university, a Cambridge of the mind that never in fact assumed any terrestrial form, while detesting the academic ethos; you could say that he looked to an idealized notion of the university to counter the ills of which the current state of academic specialization was a major symptom. In a similar way, it is also true that he promoted the claims of literary criticism as a discipline, deserving of its place in the university, and that he was to that extent identified with one specialism among others. But here, too, his stand was consciously anti-academic: his constantly reiterated justification for an education in literary criticism was precisely that it was, as he put it in one of his earliest essays, 'the best possible training for intelligence—for free, unspecialised, general intelligence'.[7] English, as he declared in one of his last major lectures, is 'a discipline *sui generis* that is special though not specialist'.[8]

Given that Leavis was thus committed to the intellectual equivalent of bare-knuckle street-fighting, it was a handicap, to which he often drew attention, to be trying to maintain a general position that was not readily susceptible of succinct propositional statement. Philosophers and literary theorists have given a certain amount of attention to the logic of 'tacit knowledge' and to the role of 'recognition', and, more

---

[7] F. R. Leavis, *For Continuity* (Cambridge, 1933), 54.
[8] *Nor Shall My Sword*, 203.

practically, there is a long tradition which maintains that the best literary criticism is in the end little more than a matter of pointing and saying 'notice *this* in its relation to *that*' and so on. But how a position based on these related styles of thinking might be made effective in general cultural criticism is a teasing question. If the persuasiveness of a view is only to be conveyed indirectly by tone, detail, and juxtaposition, mere programmatic assertion will not do. But mere programmatic assertion may be all that the limited space and the polemical requirements of journalism allow.

As Michael Bell says in his excellent study of Leavis's literary criticism, his emphasis on 'recognition' meant that he was always steering a course between the ineffable and the banal.[9] In engaging in the activity of criticism, Leavis could 'enact' (to use one of his favoured terms) the values he wished to uphold, but they inevitably seemed schematic or obvious if reduced to bald statement. Moreover, on his own showing, they could only be enacted in so far as there took place something like the genuinely collaborative exchange signalled by his catch-phrase 'This is so, isn't it?' followed by the response 'Yes but . . .'. As Bell again suggestively remarks, for Leavis 'reading depends on the reader and is more comparable to musical performance than it is to musical connoisseurship'.[10] In these terms, Leavis had to make cultural criticism 'happen'; it was not reducible to a few simply stated propositions.

Leavis deliberately drew attention to this predicament. 'If, of course, one is challenged to stand and deliver and say' what one means by various references to human values, 'it is hardly possible to answer convincingly at the level of the challenge'. This is from his 1966 'Luddites' lecture, and a few pages later he repeats: 'This is not a simple answer; no serious answer *could* be.'[11] Or again in his 1971 lecture 'Elites, Oligarchies, and an Educated Public', having quoted a passage from one of his own earlier books on the way 'modern civilisation' was shaped almost entirely by technocratic considerations, he observes: 'For a disease of that kind there is no remedy that can be made to sound simple, immediately convincing, and easy to apply.'[12]

---

[9] Michael Bell, *F. R. Leavis* (London, 1988), 137.
[10] Ibid. 130.
[11] *Nor Shall My Sword*, 92.   [12] Ibid. 202.

Or yet again, in grimly reflecting on the conditions imposed when 'a circulation of a million isn't large enough to sustain a newspaper', he acknowledges that 'it is hard to explain to anyone who needs to have it explained' what a real educated public would be like. The necessary circularity of 'recognition' operates as a constraint here.

Leavis also displayed a constant sense of the limitations of the available polemical genres. Speaking of a point in an article in the *TLS* which his critics misunderstood or found too condensed, he observed: 'But I was troubled enough by my sense of the complexity of the essential argument that had to be presented, and in so brief a space.'[13] He was alert to the constant possibility of journalistic distortion, and sought ways to preempt it. Replying to the allegation that he had 'excluded' journalists from his Richmond Lecture 'in order to be protected against critical reactions', he claimed that the press would have given it an 'ugly kind of publicity', and went on: 'And I was intent on ensuring that my actual theme and argument should be really attended to. I should have indeed been a fool if I had thought that giving the journalists an opportunity was likely to further that aim. My purpose was to see to the publication of the full text myself.'[14]

But 'attended to' by whom? His later lectures, essays, and letters constitute a relentless onslaught on the dominant 'literary intellectuals', that 'metropolitan literary world' which, following the paranoid logic of self-conscious 'outsiderdom', he claimed exercised so much power that it was almost impossible to get dissident views attended to. And at the same time, these writings were a sustained denunciation of the 'statistico-egalitarian reductivism' (a variant, though perhaps scarcely an improvement, on his more familiar phrase, 'the technologico-Benthamite ethos') which he regarded as so completely possessing contemporary opinion that it was difficult to find a foothold for a critique or an alternative. This bleak diagnosis makes the question a pressing one: to whom is the Leavisian cultural critic speaking? Leavis himself described the violence of his attack on Snow as an attempt 'to get some recognition for the inadequacy' of the views he took Snow to represent. But from whom is he

[13] Letter to the *TLS*, 9 Aug. 1963; in *Letters in Criticism*, ed. Tasker, 104.
[14] *Nor Shall My Sword*, 74.

trying to get this recognition? Hardly from Snow himself and his attendant lords (Annan, Plumb, Robbins *et al.*), nor from the opinion-formers among the metropolitan literary élite. It can only be an appeal to the already half-converted: only they could recognize the argument.

Thus, when referring to a letter he had sent to *The Times* about the shallowness of contemporary thinking about 'student unrest', Leavis assumed that the audience of teachers and students of English to whom he was lecturing would share his sense of 'what is perhaps the most formidable problem we confront— the impossibility (even if given much more space than a print-able letter) of stating it in a newspaper or to a politician . . . or to a committee presided over by Lord Annan or Lord Robbins, so as to get it intelligently attended to'.[15] His use of the collusive first-person plural here presumes an audience that *could* 'intelli-gently attend to' his unfashionable position. Similarly, his pre-ferred form of reply to the bullying use of the cliché about politics being 'the art of the possible' was to insist that '*we* create possibility', where, he acknowledged, the 'we' was made up precisely of those able to recognize the values he was asking them to recognize. Once again, the logic of Leavis's polemics implies an ungathered church of potential true believers, those who are not yet so utterly corrupted by the prevailing sophistries as to be incapable of recognizing the force of an appeal to other values.

This limited optimism continually surfaces in the otherwise all-damning pessimism of his later polemics. In trying to draw attention to the kind of creativity he believed was at the heart of cultural continuity, as opposed to the humanly uncreative mat-erialism of orthodox 'enlightened' opinion, he restated his long-held view: 'Only in terms of literature can this truth be asserted with effect in our world, and the asserting must be, not a matter of dialectic, but itself, in a patently illustrative way, an assertion of life'.[16] The ambition signalled by the quiet phrase 'with effect' should not be overlooked here. Another indication of the kind of 'success' Leavis was hoping for may be suggested by his own description of his Richmond Lecture as a 'failure' because, des-pite his criticisms, 'the debate about the two cultures' was still

---

[15] *Nor Shall My Sword*, 105.   [16] Ibid. 120.

a standardly prescribed sixth-form topic.[17] (To lose the battle in the sixth-forms was, for Leavis, a particularly telling defeat, so much did he still look to them as his recruiting-ground.)

In considering what, for Leavis, counted as 'success' in these polemics, the metaphor of 'guerrilla warfare' that I used earlier naturally suggests itself, a strategy of small, nagging engagements that slowly undermine the position of an enemy much stronger in conventional terms.[18] It was rather in these terms that he described, in his 1969 lecture ' "English", Unrest, and Continuity', what could be hoped for in the fight against 'the world of enlightenment': 'There is no Stalingrad to be achieved over that enemy, but we can discredit its clichés, disturb its blank incuria, and undermine its assurance.'[19] Once again, one has to consider whether the implicit logic of such tactics is, in fact, to undermine the '*enemy*'s' assurance, or whether it is not, rather, to sway others who already had some doubts about the legitimacy of that assurance.

Indeed, in Leavis's ontology at this point, it almost seems as though it is the power of 'the metropolitan literary world' which prevents a real 'educated public' even from existing.

The 'literary world', in fact, with its command of all the means of publicity, virtually shuts off the educated public from effective existence. The public, in any serious sense of the noun, is only a potential public. It has no part in the formation of contemporary taste, no power to influence or to check—I am thinking of what passes for educated taste.[20]

At other times, however, he allowed the implicit optimism to show. Noting, in one of his last public lectures, that he had 'slipped into the present tense' in speaking of the 'educated public', he allowed, in a phrase revealing of a significant identification, that 'the educated public that Matthew Arnold's ironies, castigations and admonitions assumed hasn't yet wholly disappeared'.[21] Only that belief, acknowledged or not,

---

[17] *Nor Shall My Sword*, 141.
[18] Referring to the lecture ' "English", Unrest and Continuity' which he had hurried to Wales to deliver, fresh from giving a lecture in Newcastle, Leavis said: 'It was an opportunity—a hazard—taken in the field: *c'est la guerre*' (letter to John Tasker 19 June 1969, quoted in MacKillop, *F. R. Leavis*, 376). Similarly, he spoke of his later lectures and polemics as 'field-performances'.
[19] *Nor Shall My Sword*, 107.
[20] Ibid. 72.   [21] Ibid. 213.

prevented Leavis's later cultural criticism from being nothing more than a message put in a bottle and flung overboard.

3

In many of his later writings, Leavis begins by directly address-ing questions of tone and of authority, and here, too, his ex-ample illuminates a general feature of the role of the literary critic as cultural critic. A critic in his position needs to deploy a variety of tactics to deprive the prevailing orthodoxies, however identified, of their appearance of naturalness (what another idiom would call the 'unmasking of ideology'). One way in which he did this was to confront what he termed the enlight-ened élite's possession of 'unquestioned moral authority'.[22] In a letter to *The Listener* taking issue with a leading article in a previous number, Leavis focuses on just this question by saying 'you implicitly offer yourself as speaking for an authoritative central body of the right-thinking and sane', and he goes on: 'What distinguishes your own position, it seems to me, is a readiness to rely upon empty phrases and inert preconcep-tions—which look like something else to you because of your consciousness of enjoying massive support.'[23]

Leavis did not write as somebody who could take such 'support' for granted, nor, as I have already suggested, did he attempt to lay claim to public attention primarily on account of his credentials or expertise: his writing had to establish its own human authority. Of course, by the period I am discussing here, Leavis's name *was* his claim on readers' attention. But this could also have the self-defeating effect that people thought they knew what his 'line' was, and were able to discount it in advance. Trading on the recognized distinctiveness of his own voice was, therefore, a high-risk strategy, but it could, at its most success-ful, be a way of shifting the idiom and focus of debate to favour positions for which it was difficult to argue in the established terms of public discourse.

Consider the opening words of the introduction to *Nor Shall My Sword*: 'No-one will suppose me to have forgotten how

[22] *Nor Shall My Sword*, 166.
[23] Letter to *The Listener*, 3 Nov. 1960; in *Letters in Criticism*, ed. Tasker, 75.

Blake's stanza continues . . .'. The reader is immediately treated as being a member of a community which not only recognizes that Leavis's title comes from Blake and how the stanza continues, but which is also already familiar with Leavis's general position. The form of his opening sentence raises, only to dismiss, a question that may have crossed the minds of such readers: it constitutes an immediate rebuke to anyone tempted to a superior or amused thought at an implication Leavis himself may have missed. From the start, an almost conversational intimacy is established, but at the same time Leavis's own rhetorical presence is kept at the centre of attention. As the introduction unfolds, a familiar Leavisian case is presented about how the kind of creativity represented by Blake serves as a benchmark against which the inadequacies of the 'technologico-Benthamite' assumptions dominating contemporary society may be measured. But the tone and, so to say, angle of attack of Leavis's writing are part of an effort to prevent that familiar case being dismissed as naïve or indeed as merely familiar. The reader is addressed in a direct, personal way, is put on the spot.[24]

Take another small example, this time from that genre that Leavis almost made his own, the letter to the press vindicating himself against criticism or misrepresentation. In 1963 he wrote to *The Spectator* to correct an account given in the previous week's issue of his estimate of James's *The Princess Casamassima*. He quoted the relevant passage from his *The Great Tradition*, and then immediately followed this with: 'I know, of course, of the wide agreement that I write badly, but I don't think I'm commonly charged with lack of care to be precise.'[25] Again, one is immediately treated as being *au fait* with a continuing conversation, and again one is not being allowed the luxury of any knowingness at Leavis's expense. In effect, the reader is personally challenged, forced to reflect whether, in the light of such a sentence, they haven't perhaps been merely

---

[24] One is reminded of the many anecdotes about Leavis pressing in this direct, personal way in public discussion. Chairing a committee meeting, Raymond Williams hedged about his own position. Leavis was relentless: 'No, I am putting it to you directly'; Williams gave an impersonal, official reply: ' "To *you*", Leavis repeated.' Raymond Williams, 'Seeing a Man Running', in Denys Thompson, ed., *The Leavises: Recollections and Impressions* (Cambridge, 1984), 117–18.

[25] *Letters in Criticism*, ed. Tasker, 106.

conventional in sharing the 'wide agreement' that Leavis writes badly. At the very least, the possibility is raised that in the relevant passage he had been more exact than his critic assumed. It becomes, if only for a moment, harder for the reader to allow any sense of superiority about Leavis's prose to prejudge the issue, and this then makes it that bit more difficult *not* to accept the authority of his own account of what he previously wrote about the James novel.

In illustrating the general point here, I have deliberately concentrated on relatively minor details, since it is through the accumulation of such small touches that much of the distinctiveness of Leavis's cultural criticism is built up. For an example of a frontal attack on the question of cultural authority, one could not do better than turn to the opening paragraphs of his 'Two Cultures?' lecture, a bravura performance which raises in an acute way the question of the persuasiveness of such tactics, since the attack was so widely condemned as unpardonably *ad hominem*. That performance, and the responses it evoked, would need to be discussed at greater length than is possible here,[26] but I do want to draw attention to the ways in which, in that lecture and its sequels, Leavis constantly chips away at the issue of authority.

Thus, when the historian J. H. Plumb, a friend and colleague of Snow's, supported Snow's breezily positive assertions about the effects of the Industrial Revolution in England, Leavis deliberately cited the title of Plumb's chair in a show of mock-amazement that such manifestly ill-grounded historical views could be held by a 'Professor of Modern British History in the University of Cambridge'. The mere juxtaposition of Plumb's view with a passage from Thomas Hardy is treated as sufficient to dispose of his 'authority' on the matter.[27] But in fact, Leavis shows himself not content with this tactic, since he, exceptionally, added three appendices to the published form of his lecture, containing passages from other historians which supported his own view of the humanly damaging consequences of the Industrial Revolution. Similarly, when he speaks of Lord Todd (who

---

[26] I hope to treat this episode in more detail on another occasion; for a preliminary discussion, see my 'Introduction' to C. P. Snow, *The Two Cultures* (Cambridge, 1993), esp. pp. xxx–xli.

[27] *Nor Shall My Sword*, 188.

had made some widely cited remarks about science as one cultural pursuit alongside others) he asks 'the rude-seeming question' of whether Todd's distinction as a chemist does signify any deeper understanding on his part or whether he is just pronouncing 'with the confident modesty of one who, bringing to bear the intellectual grasp of the trained mind, says what can't be disputed'.[28] As with Snow, the route to disputing 'what can't be disputed' is to begin by undermining the implicit claim to authority.

The responses to his Richmond Lecture also emphasize how Leavis was representative of the dilemmas of this tradition of cultural criticism in having to face the charge of attempting imperialistically to extend the sway of literary criticism over all other disciplines. He frequently referred to the charge against him of 'literary bias'.[29] This allegation was a way of making his views on matters like 'the two cultures' seem one-sided or un-realistic, but it also raised the question of what, in contemporary society, constituted an appropriate form of cultural authority. His frequent citation of the work of Michael Polanyi on 'tacit knowledge' was one expression of Leavis's concern with this issue. It was clearly important to him that Polanyi was, as he pointedly repeated, a Professor of Physical Chemistry, and so his views could not so easily be dismissed as those of a literary Luddite. At the same time, one is bound to wonder whether Leavis was wise to make so much of the authority of Polanyi, since there was a danger that the latter's unorthodox career and idiosyncratic views could make him seem merely a crank in the eyes of professional philosophers. It was a nice calculation: Leavis wanted to challenge the standing of 'professional phi-losophers', among others, yet to do so he needed to deploy some countervailing cultural authority.

Here, we return by another route to one of the central dilem-mas of the cultural critic in an age of academic specialization. The premiss of the cultural critic's activity is the possibility of a certain 'general' or non-specialist perspective, yet at the same time the authority to pronounce on any given topic will in the first instance be given to the specialists in whose domain it falls. Despite his frequent disclaimers, Leavis was, and still is, widely

---

[28] *Nor Shall My Sword*, 173-4.   [29] e.g. ibid. 21.

taken to exemplify the imperial ambitions of literary criticism to set itself up as a general cultural arbiter, but he can perhaps more justly be seen as struggling with the conundrum of trying to escape the deformation of specialization while retaining the kind of authority accorded to the specialist. One revealing and representative sign of this dilemma was his continual hankering after some kind of general or non-specialist journal. *Scrutiny* had carried several admiring pieces about the great Victorian reviews, which Leavis continued to idealize into the 1970s.[30] Although he maintained that the conditions which had made it possible to start *Scrutiny* had now disappeared, the notion of 'launching a review' makes an almost shy entrance in his last lecture, and he begins to warm to the theme—speaking of the talent that lies unexpressed 'because there is no organ in which to publish', how if it began properly, 'the word would go round', 'the new influence would tell far beyond the limits of certifiable "circulation"', and so on.[31] Here again, we glimpse the instability in Leavis's representation of himself in this period: on the one hand there is the critic as hedge-priest, eluding persecution to bring the true gospel to a few scattered believers, and on the other there is the critic as tribune, reaching beyond the corrupting sophistries of the ruling oligarchy to the true convictions of the people as a whole.

4

Leavis was, of course, far from ignored. If simple volume of attention were the ultimate measure of a critic's effectiveness, his later polemical career would have to be judged a success. In the three decades after 1945, what he was supposed to stand for became one of the chief nodes of antagonism in relations between literary journalism and literary scholarship.[32] Or rather, it became one of the chief foci of hostility from the literary journalists, and it was they who identified the discipline of academic literary criticism as a whole with his and his followers' work; most academic literary scholars always recognized what a mi-

---

[30] *Nor Shall My Sword*, 218.   [31] Ibid. 218–19.
[32] For extensive illustration (combined with some highly partisan analysis) see Garry Watson, *The Leavises, The 'Social', and The Left* (Swansea, 1977).

nority pursuit Leavisism remained. But a glance at the literary-journalistic controversies of the late 1960s and early 1970s, in particular, reveals how Leavis's name could be used to exacerbate the conflict between Grub Street and Academe (in an article of that title in *The New Review* in July 1974 Peter Porter called it 'the topic of the hour').[33] There were, of course, more than purely personal or contingent reasons for this focus. Precisely because he did concentrate on the question of the cultural authority of the literary critic, as well as because he upheld an ambitious ideal of the university's social function, Leavis appeared to be threatening to take over the domain of the literary journalist in a way that few other academic literary scholars did. After all, the metropolitan critic, to use Clive James's proud self-description, had little to fear from the textual editors of *Piers Plowman*. This may also have been a particularly sensitive question at a time when university expansion provided a new focus for the familiar lament that it was becoming impossible to sustain life as a freelance man of letters.

In assessing Leavis's performance as a cultural critic, we should not restrict ourselves to the most obviously functional measure of 'success'. Needless to say, the governing rationale of the controversialist's activity is persuasion, and there is little evidence that Leavis did, through this medium (as opposed to through his teaching), persuade many of the not already converted, while there is plenty to suggest that the effect he chiefly wrought was antagonism and irritation. But there can be other measures, such as forcing certain issues on the attention of a public, and, beyond that, still less tangible goals some of which are perhaps best indicated by slightly old-fashioned phrases about 'keeping the faith' and 'bearing witness'. In maintaining an unpopular position, there can be a fine line between bloody-minded obstructiveness and heroic defiance. Indeed, it may be that the later Leavis, though he would no doubt have angrily repudiated the suggestion, should be thought of as having more in common with that subset of social critics known as prophets

[33] Peter Porter, 'Grub Street versus Academe', *The New Review*, 1 (July 1974), 47. Another important locus of this conflict had been the penultimate chapter of John Gross's nostalgic-celebratory study of literary journalism, *The Rise and Fall of the Man of Letters* (London, 1969), which, alongside some more positive judgements, included a sustained assault on Leavis's narrow and (allegedly) characteristically academic dogmatism.

or doomsayers, railing at the heedlessness of a pleasure-
bent world, drawing strength from an uncompromising
Manicheanism, and aiming at something more like conversion
than persuasion.

None the less, it seems to me that Leavis exhibits in a particularly striking form several of the weaknesses of the tradition of
cultural criticism to which he belongs. (It is an open question, of
course, whether these defects, let alone additional ones, might
not be equally evident in cultural criticism as carried on by those
who were primarily, say, historians or political theorists.) To
begin with, there is the absence of any adequately sociological
understanding of his own society, and a consequent inability
to estimate social and political forces at their true strength.
This also, I think, blunted his cultural perceptions: when he
inveighs against the 1960s, for example, he becomes too
undiscriminating (and 'discrimination' was meant to be his
ace of trumps), sounding all too like a *Daily Telegraph* leader-
writer: 'violence, destructiveness, condoned irresponsibility in
regard to sex, drug-addiction, "student unrest"' and so on.[34]
Arnold famously criticized the Romantic poets on the ground
that 'they did not know enough', but perhaps a similar charge
can be laid at the door of the main exemplars of the tradition
of literary critics as social critics that descended from Arnold.
Related to this in Leavis's case was the tendency to posit the
existence, homogenize the nature, and exaggerate the power,
of an 'Establishment' hostile to him and his ideas. Self-
dramatization is the inevitable consequence here.

Another of the common sins of cultural criticism carried out
in this mode is that of setting the stakes too high. There is an
inherent unpersuasiveness, which is only compounded by repeti-
tion, in being told that the fate of civilization, or the possibility
of living a truly human existence, depends on the quality of
reviewing in the literary weeklies. Getting the level right is, as
always, partly a matter of tone. This danger is all the greater
when, as in Leavis's case, the cultural critic contends that the
existing public discourse only recognizes the values of utilitar-
ianism and commercial calculation, since attempts, within the
constraints of the genres of public polemic, to characterize alter-

[34] *Nor Shall My Sword*, 181.

native conceptions of human flourishing have a constant tendency to degenerate into coercively prescriptive generalities. Here one might echo John Gross's judgement at the conclusion of his largely unsympathetic account of Leavis: 'What is galling about the Leavises and their followers is not that they are altogether wrong, but that they give a cause which deserves a wider hearing a bad name through distortion, omission, and strident over-statement.'[35] In seeing the 'metropolitan literary world' as a 'system', capable of imposing a uniform set of values on a range of associated institutions from the Sunday papers to the BBC, Leavis surely did exaggerate its power, homogeneity, and intent. (Apart from anything else one might say here, it is worth remarking the number of Leavis's ex-pupils who were increasingly influential in that world: to take only the most notable example, Karl Miller, who had chosen Downing College in order to be taught by Leavis, was successively literary editor of *The Spectator* and of *The New Statesman* and editor of *The Listener*.)

But perhaps Leavis was not *wholly* wrong to think that the values and practices encouraged by the conditions of life determining commercial literary journalism were inhospitable to the taking seriously of what he so passionately believed needed to be taken seriously. Equally, could any university teacher in a humanities subject genuinely believe that Leavis was *wholly* wrong in identifying something fundamentally misguided about the industrialization of literary 'research'? In a similar spirit, one might also ask whether some of the tensions I have identified in Leavis's practice are not inherent in the role itself. For instance, to reach even that wide minority one might call 'the educated public', there is no practicable alternative to using the major existing outlets of broadcasting, the literary periodicals, and the so-called 'quality' daily and Sunday papers. But the constraints both of commercialism and of the properties of the media themselves make it extremely difficult to present a case that is complex, extended and nuanced. It would be to fall into a modern form of that over-dramatization I have alleged against Leavis to say simply 'sound-bites rule', but the requirements of brevity, 'liveliness', and 'punchiness' are certainly much insisted

[35] Gross, *Man of Letters*, 271.

upon.[36] So again, the dilemma is similar: how to make the case against these constraints while working within them? Persuasively to expose the fatuity of the requirement of 'punchiness', must one be punchy?

Moreover, one does not have to subscribe to Leavis's end-is-nigh-ism to remark some discouraging changes in the available media. When Radio Three replaces talks with talking, when a serious journal introduces irrelevant photographs in the middle of reviews, when a literary editor commits his or her pages to trying to *create* controversy—these and the several other instances one might cite are all symptoms of something similar: a loss of confidence in the ability of a well-presented case to hold the interest of the relevant audience. And then there is, of course, that seemingly perennial source of gloom, the claim that the number of would-be serious critical periodicals is diminishing. Britain is in fact fortunate still to possess a reasonably varied and intelligent broadsheet press, but as 'features people' increasingly replace 'literary people' as editors of the books pages, so the proportion of space devoted to self-advertising 'personalities' and show-biz ephemera rises. The proud tradition of seriously reviewing serious books maintained by the *Guardian* as recently as the 1970s and early 1980s is now beginning to look bafflingly archaic. And even in the case of such a generally admirable upholder of the critical function as the *TLS*, one might reasonably have reservations about certain features of its recent incarnation, such as the heavy reliance on a small group of elderly, culturally conservative and politically right-wing reviewers for writing about American topics, the sneering knowingness of the weekly column by 'D.S.' which tended to caricature rather than engage with what it identified as the 'political correctness' of 'literary theory', the already-mentioned placing of unnecessary and distracting illustrations in the middle of reviews, and so on.

To set alongside the continuing high quality of much of the writing in the *TLS*, the most heartening new development in this domain over the past fifteen years has surely been the founding

---

[36] One notably depressing example was the manifesto by the then new literary editor of the *Guardian* outlining various changes he proposed and concluding 'we shall seek to deliver all this with a polemical punch'; Richard Gott, 'Standfirst', *Guardian*, 6 Feb. 1992.

of the *London Review of Books*, whose editorial policies and
very layout presuppose the possibility of engaging non-specialist
readers in the relatively extended and informed critical discussion of a wide range of intellectual and political issues. That
such a periodical should not only be started but should have
achieved and sustained a substantial circulation is a standing
refutation of the gloomiest jeremiads of the cultural pessimists,
though even this generally excellent review has in recent years
occasionally been marred by its evident presupposition that
disagreement and antagonism are always intrinsically more interesting than agreement and appreciation, and by its consequent tendency to substitute artificially provoked controversy
for the considered assessment of achievement. The *reductio* of
this implicit policy seemed to have been reached when the paper
printed a letter by veteran *agent provocateur* Tom Paulin com-
plaining that there hadn't been any outraged letters in response
to his earlier review, itself containing a good deal of rather
laboured and exaggerated provocation, of Anthony Julius's
book on Eliot and anti-Semitism.[37] Reservations of a similar sort
might be expressed about various other less significant or less
generally laudable publications, and clearly the increasing concentration of ownership of newspapers and periodicals by multinational financial conglomerates intensifies certain kinds of
commercial pressures.

None the less, it seems to me that the contemporary cultural
critic is better advised to extrapolate from the optimistic logic of
Leavis's principles rather than from the pessimistic model of
his practice. This would, in turn, involve developing a more
discriminating view of modern societies than he did, as well as
adopting a more inviting critical voice, a voice that does not
immediately repel all but the most devoted sectaries. I do not
subscribe to 'the general opinion' that Leavis 'wrote badly', and
his armoury included command over an arresting and telling
polemical register. But the way in which he exaggerated his well-
aimed barbs into a lament about total and irreversible cultural
decline was self-defeating. Although he constantly championed
the need for a responsive educated public, he too often wrote as
though 'the system' was now powerful enough to make such a

---

[37] *LRB*, 18/11 (6 June 1996), 4.

public an impossibility. But the premiss of any cultural criticism that is genuinely engaged with its own society has to be that there are some ears that are not deaf, some mouths that are not stopped; even my own detailing of discontents with certain aspects of the present state of literary journalism presumes the possibility of assent and, at the margin, of improvement. In letting Leavis have the last word, I am not presuming to quote him against himself, but rather offering a reminder of the logic of his own best practice. 'Criticism, with all it stands for, is collaborative and creative. Mere lonely intransigence is barren.'[38]

[38] Letter to the *Guardian*, 12 Apr. 1960; *Letters in Criticism*, 74.

10

Saving Lives: Kenneth Tynan and the Duties of Dramatic Criticism

JOHN STOKES

Speaking behind their backs Laurence Olivier would call theatre critics 'bastards', though he cared enough about their presence to aim a blow at James Agate when, in 1945, he returned late to his seat at a Vivien Leigh first night.[1] Olivier knew as well as anyone else that without a critical notice a production soon dies. According to Richard Eyre, a successor of Olivier's as Director of the Royal National Theatre, critics are 'the only people in our world who pay no penalty for failure',[2] his resentment at their relative security reinforcing his belief that the pleasures and displeasures of critics are fundamentally dissimilar from those of anyone else in an audience.

There seems to be a constant refusal among theatre people to admit that critics have several duties: to the artists certainly, but equally to themselves and to their readers. At the Olivier Awards ceremony in 1995, the actor Tony Slattery (not presumably intending to honour the man after whom they are named), said that theatre critics were 'barking bloody mad';[3] in the same year, another young performer, Julian Clary, about to open in a 'lost' play by Jean Genet, announced that he didn't like reviewers, 'so if they ... have a horrible evening, then that's a jolly good thing'.[4] The survival of a traditional loathing is proof in itself that the practice of writing about live performance has to be distinguished from the day-to-day business of book or even

---

[1] See James Harding, *Agate* (London, 1986), foreword and 179; and Anthony Holden, *Olivier* (London, 1988), 239.
[2] *Utopia and Other Places* (London, 1994), 209.
[3] See Milton Shulman, 'Hurrah for Theatrical Thuggery', *Evening Standard*, 30 June 1995.
[4] *Evening Standard*, 8 June 1995.

film reviewing. A sense of dependence has much to do with it. Unlike the other arts, theatre requires an immediate critical report if it is to find, and maintain, an audience. Nor, without its critics, would theatre ever survive in the long term, enter the historical record.

Even that responsibility can be diminished. Conceding that some critics have a gift for evoking performances, Eyre still believes that 'however vivid their powers of description they are doomed to the status of obituarists'.[5] A heady rhetoric of life and death seems inescapable.

Kenneth Tynan, who once described reviewing as 'writing letters to posterity',[6] thought he knew better. A critic, he insisted, was 'neither a ticket salesman nor a weather vane'; his job was 'to record a unique experience as it impinged on his mind and sensibility'. From the longer perspective of the theatre scholar, who must rely upon critics for documentary evidence of a production, Tynan's choice of preposition—'to posterity' rather than 'for posterity'—may suggest an eye on the future that betrays an over-developed sense of his own importance as intermediary. While it's true that the uniqueness he speaks of belongs to the spectator every bit as much as it does to the theatrical moment, there will usually be more than one critic present, and historians are able to record a more complicated response, build up a more composite picture. Even so, this rarely means consensus, and historians will still tend to rely for authenticity upon the imaginative responses of those exceptional individuals who seem to be the symptomatic or prophetic voices of their time. It is precisely because he understood the workings of this principle, and exploited it to the full throughout his career, that Tynan has left us with the most vivid picture of British theatre in mid-century.

Tynan undoubtedly saved lives in a far more vital way than Eyre's notion of the 'obituarist' allows, generously fulfilling his own criterion that good criticism tells you 'what it was like to be in a particular theatre on a particular night'.[7] The reviews first

---

[5] *Utopia and Other Places*, 138.

[6] *Tynan on Theatre* (Harmondsworth, 1964); hereafter, *TOT*. A very full account of Tynan's career is available in Kathleen Tynan, *The Life of Kenneth Tynan* (London, 1987) and from *Kenneth Tynan: Letters*, ed. Kathleen Tynan (London, 1994).

[7] *TOT* 12.

collected in *Curtains*,[8] subtitled *A Critic's View of Plays, Players and Theatrical Events 1950–1960* (1961), amount to an animated picture gallery in which the reader is encouraged to see performers as Tynan saw them, vibrant and three-dimensional, fulfilling, exceeding or failing his special expectations. One reads and rereads that book because his sensibility seems right for his times; his criticism is historical in that double sense.

Yet *Curtains* belongs to a dying genre since the habit of collecting reviews is no longer automatic—though both Michael Billington of the *Guardian*[9] and James Fenton, who had a brief but turbulent period as theatre critic of the *Sunday Times* in the 1980s,[10] have received the accolade. The economics of publishing are presumably to blame, and a changed media culture, rather than critical humility. Perhaps there is simply too much competition. Memoirs, biographies and autobiographies, interview books, and 'production journals' crowd the foyer bookstalls. But critics are not considered to be practitioners, and a collection of reviews, if it is to be of any value, should serve a function quite other than the provision of insider information. Reviews are the record of outsider opinion—or so we like to believe.

The custom of gathering them up in books developed in the late nineteenth century when, along with a general expansion of the newspaper and publishing industries, critics grew in power and importance. William Archer and A. B. Walkley were prominent (Archer published annual volumes), though the two critics from that period who are now best remembered are Shaw and Beerbohm, both of whom had their pieces collected by other people some time after they were originally written. The great

---

[8] Hereafter, *Curtains*. Despite the new prefaces, *Tynan on Theatre* is a reduced version of this book. Tynan also published later collections including *Tynan Right and Left* (London, 1967) and *The Sound of Two Hands Clapping* (London, 1975).

[9] *One Night Stands* (London, 1993); hereafter, *ONS*.

[10] *You were Marvellous* (London, 1983); hereafter, *YWM*. Fenton's collection fell foul of theatre people. The playwright, Simon Gray, who felt that he had been roughly treated by Fenton, reviewed the author's photograph. He looked, wrote Gray, like 'yet another Faustus eternally ex-communicated from what he yearns for, while seeming to be always attendant upon it'. (*TLS*, 2 Sept. 1983, 927.) Subsequent controversy included Bernard Levin in *The Times*, 30 Aug. 1983; Arnold Wesker in the *Listener*, 25 Aug. 1983; a reply by Fenton in the *Sunday Times*, 4 Sept. 1983; a follow-up letter from Wesker in the *Sunday Times*, 18 Sept. 1983; and a summarizing article by Richard Boston in the *Guardian*, 24 Sept. 1983.

Edwardians were followed, for good or ill, by James Agate, Tynan's chosen mentor, whose autobiographical journal, *Ego*, ran to nine volumes between 1935 and 1948.

Hard covers confirm authority. The other effect of collection is to construct a sequential narrative out of what, at the time, must have been more like a bundle of surprises. Archer's volumes, and to some extent Shaw's, have that aura and any theatre historian who relies upon them must be alert to the stories they purport to tell, the historical hindsight that may be imposed by the compiler. In this respect Tynan's *Curtains* is relatively unprogrammatic, though for the revised paperback edition in 1964 he did add short prefaces in which he indicated overall trends in world theatre. Reducing the number of items from his early, pre-1956 phase, he also disarmingly acknowledged his own inconsistencies. Even within the now quite sharply defined phases of his career Tynan's tastes still varied considerably. Then again, as he put it himself, many years later: 'The only constant critic is a dead critic.'[11]

Along with the wit and erudition of his predecessors, Tynan brought to the job of reviewing a contemporary political awareness and he claimed, immodestly, to represent his generation. In the exhausted post-war years he would demand from established actors barely feasible displays of emotional heroism and physical daring (the same qualities as would draw him to bullfighting); in the 1960s, after the discovery of Brecht, at the time of the Vietnam War and student upheaval, he espoused revolutionary Marxism; finally, in the 1970s, he turned to a kind of Reichian faith in the universal possibilities of sexual liberation. He was consistent, though, in the kind of theatre he admired. It had to be courageous, outrageous, above all alive—the qualities he had famously seen in Jimmy Porter in 1956 with his 'evident and blazing vitality'.[12]

It was Agate who, at Tynan's own invitation, first spotted him as 'a great dramatic critic in the making'.[13] This was in response to an astonishing book, *He that Plays the King*,[14] published in 1950 when Tynan was 23, before he had become a professional

---

[11] From an interview included in 'Reputations: Kenneth Tynan' (hereafter, 'Reputations'), written and presented by Anthony Howard, produced by Philip Speight, first broadcast in 1982 on BBC2.

[12] *Curtains*, 131.   [13] Harding, *Agate*, 211.   [14] Hereafter, *HTPK*.

journalist. The tribute was undoubtedly intended to suggest a paternal succession flattering to both men, but Tynan was already outstripping his inheritance. One way of measuring those changes is to put *He that Plays the King* alongside some gentlemanly mutterings from an older generation compiled by the writer of poetic dramas, Christopher Fry, in a volume called *An Experience of Critics*, published in 1952.

Tynan's first book is a proclamation made up of fervent impressions and wild polemic, obviously designed to draw attention to his own unique gifts, in which he takes—preening delight. There are passages of adolescent purple—the best moments in English tragedy are 'like our glimpses, on February evenings, of the monstrous, pacific sun, prying for a moment under the grey circus tent of twilight'[15]—coupled with an oddly old-fashioned pomposity. Not once is he whimsical, and he never apologizes. In absolute contrast, it's their very self-restraint that gives the older men away. The ideal critic, says Ivor Brown, is 'an enthusiastic introducer',[16] the flatness of the language denying the definition. 'His damns must follow deliberation and his curses be tempered by courtesy',[17] which seems well put until one tries to imagine how a courteous curse might sound. 'The general level [of criticism] is not despicable—it is just fairly low or fairish',[18] says Alan Dent—in which case, from the artists' perspective, it is surely despicable. But Dent opens by saying that the great line of critics 'began with Leigh Hunt and concluded with the age of Agate', and so, in comparison with someone of Tynan's ambitions, condemns himself before he even begins.[19]

Theatre criticism in the immediate post-war years was at one not only with the state of the theatre itself (thrown into a panic when John Whiting's *Saint's Day*, against considerable opposition, won a critic's prize in 1951), but with a self-mocking tendency within the country as a whole: the backward-looking aspect of the Festival of Britain, epitomized by Roland Emmet's quaint jumble-sale sculptures which mocked modernity. With his precise observation, Tynan challenged that indulgently haphazard mood.

---

[15] *HTPK* 220.
[16] Christopher Fry, *An Experience of Critics* (London, 1952), 35.
[17] Ibid. 36.   [18] Ibid. 41.   [19] Ibid.

He that Plays the King was intended to preface a great theatrical career, not necessarily as a writer, but after some attempts
at direction (not unsuccessful) and at acting (calamitous), journalism took over. Tynan worked for a while on the *Spectator*,
then for the London *Evening Standard*, initially in 1951 on an
ad hoc basis, replacing the resident theatre critic Beverley Baxter
in 1952. After that there was a brief stint on the *Daily Sketch*.
By no means all his reviews from this period were to be considered worthy of inclusion in *Curtains*. He was never entirely
happy on the tabloids, although the time he spent working on
them did teach crucial lessons: how to create for his readers a
sense of occasion, how to make theatre seem like news. The
popular journalism, written before Tynan became professionally secure, reveals the origins of much that came later, and gives
a broader, less settled, view of the post-war scene than the more
confident progression implied by the collections.

Tynan always argued that critics should be sensitive to the
uniqueness of each performer, each performance:

What our critics need is a steady cultivation of response to uniqueness
on the stage; to the strange inflexion, the unexpected stance, the new,
accusing fire in the eyes, the mordant strangeness of diction, or any of
the marks by which we recognise a new experience in theatre. It calls
for great flexibility of reaction, and above all, great flair and cocksure-
ness; and on the intellectual level, it means the abandoning forthwith of
an assumption fatal to a proper appreciation of players: the assumption that every performance of a given role is an approximation
towards an ideal, pre-existent interpretation of it. By this premise, all
acting is a shot at the same target and you judge it by its nearness to the
ideal, which is, of course, in your mind.[20]

Accordingly, even in his earliest pieces of journalism, his
openness to each theatrical event, his eye for an individual actor
matched by his ear for a phrase, is everywhere, sometimes
lavishly, sometimes cruelly, apparent: 'When Olivier enters a
stage, lions pounce into the ring and the theatre becomes an
arena. Gielgud, on the other hand, appears; he does not "make
an entrance," but looks like one who has an appointment with
a portrait painter.'[21] Should they fall short of the heroic potential Tynan had accorded them, actors, however distinguished,

[20] *HTPK* 30–1.   [21] *Evening Standard*, 29 June 1953.

were granted no mercy whatsoever: Orson Welles's Othello terminally damned as 'Citizen Coon',[22] Donald Wolfit in a long-forgotten play called *Lords of Creation*, all pretension punctured:

In the midst of this disaster stands Mr Wolfit, playing a retired admiral in the same spirit as other men play rugby football in the pouring rain.

In a part which must have been intended as a lovable old rogue, he was at once bellicose, noisy and cheerless, and there were times when I thought he was about to spit directly into the orchestra.

The old-fashioned technique of squinting, wrinkling up your nose and raising your voice to the grating pitch of a knife-grinder when delivering a comic line has won Mr Wolfit considerable applause for his Falstaff and his Malvolio; and it occurred to me frequently last night that Shakespeare, as well as being the hardest trial of good acting, can often be the easiest refuge of bad.[23]

Though Tynan could be considerably more admiring of Wolfit's barnstorming style than this passage would suggest (Wolfit had actually been a boyhood hero), the actor was sufficiently goaded to sue for libel.[24] In Tynan's scheme of values, to betray one's recognized talent was bad enough; to present oneself to the public lacking all the basic resources was unforgivable—and if the public still accepted you, no matter. Anna Neagle in *The Glorious Days*, for instance:

Here she is, anthologised at last, available once nightly in the large economy size; dipping into the fabled store of her talents, and bringing up a horn of plenty. From this she pours, with cautious rapture, three dwarf acorns.

First, she acts, in a fashion so devoid of personality as to be practically incognito; second, she sings, shaking her voice at the audience like a tiny fist; and third, she dances, in that non-committal, twirling style once known as 'skirt-dancing,' which was originally invented to explain the presence on the stage of genteel young women who could neither sing nor act.[25]

Neagle was a national treasure, in Tynan's eyes a china figurine waiting to be smashed, and the ensuing fuss made his name—

[22] *Evening Standard*, 19 Oct. 1951; *Curtains*, 14.
[23] *Evening Standard*, 25 Apr. 1952.
[24] Kathleen Tynan, *Life*, 104. The case was never heard; the *Standard* backed off and paid Wolfit's costs.
[25] *Evening Standard*, 6 Mar. 1953; *Curtains*, 40.

initially in publicity stunts dreamed up by the editor of the *Evening Standard*, who gave over whole pages to readers' letters for or against Tynan's 'impertinences'. Tynan ingenuously complained about exploitation, and was promptly sacked. He moved briefly to the *Daily Sketch* from where he launched some of the most devastating assaults of his whole career, including a renewed attack on Neagle to mark her forty-ninth birthday in which he suggested that *The Glorious Days* might become 'an annual event, like the Braemar Gathering'.[26] His very first piece in the *Sketch*, headed 'Down with scarecrows, snobs and sniggers!' lists the sixteen things he would most like to see in the theatre. These range from Laurence Olivier as Macbeth to 'a scriptwriter equal to the obstreperous demands of Frankie Howerd's talent', from '*Pal Joey*, the most adult of the American musicals' to 'A marital farce in which an outraged husband does not round on his wife and bellow: "Don't change the subject!"', finally to 'a new play by Angus Wilson, Ivy Compton Burnett, Nancy Mitford or Henry Green. In fact, a new play by a novelist. In fact, a new play.'[27] The agenda was in place: the following year, 1954, he became theatre critic of the *Observer*.

Tynan's experience on popular papers that were accustomed to rapid switches from adulation to attack had also taught him basic lessons in the delineation of personality for public consumption. The *Evening Standard* sometimes ran features on prominent performers which combined biographical information with critical comment on their professional achievements. Tynan took to the idea at once. In 1953 he wrote a series of five articles called 'The Queen's Players' on 'top personalities of today's theatre', mixing research, commentary and interview in a way that he would rely on all his professional life. His last book, *Show People*, published in America in 1980, made up of *New Yorker* 'profiles', derives directly from these early pieces. By that stage, the choice of subject was all his own: those who remembered his loathing of bland entertainment were likely to be taken aback by the reverence he now professed for the repartee of Johnny Carson, the American TV host; if they then

[26] *Daily Sketch*, 16 Oct. 1953.   [27] *Daily Sketch*, 2 Oct. 1953.

recalled his long-standing admiration for the sang-froid of the true professional—bullfighters, jazz musicians, certain boulevard actors—their surprise might have dissolved in recognition.

Even in the early period Tynan had been susceptible to assured signs of success in others. Any display of personal style, especially when accompanied by luxury, especially when it came gilded with pre-war glamour (Beaton, Coward, the Lunts), could dazzle, sometimes making an objective judgement hard to form. Writing about Terence Rattigan he introduces his subject as 'handsome, tactfully urbane, and transparently Harrovian; you might imagine him to be an immensely fashionable psychiatrist'.[28] Rattigan belongs to the Bachelor's Club and to the Garrick; 'what is more (much more) he lives in Eaton Square and has his wallpaper specially designed for him'. Nevertheless, this entranced portrayal—so knowing that it's hard to tell when a salute turns into a sneer—culminates, at it might not have done, with a wrenched return to judgement:

Last year Rattigan hit his stride with *The Deep Blue Sea* which for two acts (the third lacks resolution) is a masterpiece of pure theatre.

Impatient of false humility he believes that on his day he is the equal of any playwright alive except Anouilh; and here he thought, he had made his point. Yet still, from some quarters, the old cry went up: 'Good theatre, *but . . .*'

One hopes it may be Rattigan's mission to take the curse off that snide, dismissive phrase. It smacks of condescension, of giving a hack his due; and it implies that for a play to fit its chosen medium is somehow not quite respectable.

Nobody denies that the best plays, the palaces of drama are more than just 'good theatre.' But (as Coleridge said) however decorative a palace may be, it must first of all be a house. And Rattigan is a master builder.

The matching elegance of approach to his subject, the tributes to craftsmanship and the literary invocations are already typical, enhancing the 'profile' of the sitter while masking that of the observer. Only a year later, in the cooler, franker air of a book review, Tynan was to complain, in the context of Rattigan's 'Aunt Edna' campaign, of the 'negative virtues' of his plays on

[28] *Evening Standard*, 1 July 1953.

the page: 'tact, understatement, avoidance of cliché—the hall-marks in fact of the gentleman code which holds so much of West End playwriting in curious thrall'.[29]

An alternative way of responding to established talent was to pay matinée favourites the kind of over-heated tributes, close to camp, that engulfed their gentility with his extravagance. Edith Evans, for instance:

The noise she makes is a kind of heavenly burbling, as if the leading soloist in a celestial choir has taken a nip too much nectar.

I can still hear her best modulations in *Waters of the Moon*; and I can restage in my mind all her entrances in the same sad little play. Each of them was like the arrival of Dalila in Milton's *Samson Agonistes*: 'But who is this, what thing of sea and land?' you murmured—and suddenly, shuddering with coloratura ecstasy Dame Edith would be upon you, and the scene would start to glow.[30]

One senses here the widening distance between the young critic and Evans's theatrical world: N. C. Hunter's *Waters of the Moon*, Tynan's 'sad little play', was generally much admired for its English-Chekhovian style; so too was Hunter's *A Day by the Sea*, a piece of 'pseudo-Chekhov' which Tynan dismissed in the *Sketch* as 'as about as close to the real thing as an aspidistra to a woodland fern'.[31] The time was up for English Chekhov, which had long been a favourite mode on Shaftesbury Avenue, and Tynan, based in the rougher end of Fleet Street, was in the right place to sound the death-knell. The lasting effect of these probationary jobs on the tabloids was to propel him towards a more rumbustious approach, almost if never entirely free of pre-war mandarin, that would prove broadly hospitable to the 'impertinent' kinds of drama he would encounter when writing for the *Observer*.

'My ideal critic is something between a latter-day substitute for Lorenzo de' Medici, and a terrible Judex of an aesthetic Dies Irae', he had already pronounced. 'He must be patron and judge, capable of dealing out rewards and blisses with one hand, and infernal aches and penuries with the other.'[32] In the middle and late 1950s Tynan turned the *Observer* into the highest theatrical court in the land. Now he entered his own heroic

---

[29] *Curtains*, 74.   [30] *Evening Standard*, 4 July 1953.
[31] *Daily Sketch*, 27 Nov. 1953.   [32] *HTPK* 22.

phase, championing Brecht with a most un-Brechtian passion, elevating apprentice writers like Osborne, Wesker and Delaney into national spokesmen, declaring unfashionable (but hilarious) ambivalence in the face of Beckett and outright, entirely straight-faced, hostility to Ionesco. He judged all who came before him, whether revered artists or well-loved entertainers, with carnivalesque conviction. Like those who controlled the world he wrote about—the impresarios, the publicity men—Tynan relished his chance to make extravagant, even irresponsible, claims.

At the same time, following on from Beerbohm—who saw in Dan Leno someone 'perplexed but undaunted in the struggle for life'[33]—and from Agate—who wrote of the *farceur*, Robertson Hare, that 'his prototype was known to Bunyan'[34]—Tynan continued to value popular performers for the ways in which they can embody moral insights that are not always easy to assimilate. He put the straight actor who 'appeals to the sophisticated mind, which compares and contrasts him with the thing he is personating' alongside the music-hall star who 'goes to something more primitive, the simple joy of discovery':

I shall be happier about our theatre when there is a place in straight plays for the personality which nowadays is being drawn more and more towards revue; and that can happen only when we go to the play and find, with the wondering shock that a child feels at its first visit to a circus, that all the people on the stage are unrecognisable: that we have never seen them before, that they are not just extensions of tricks and traits we are familiar with, but that they are strangers, un-looked-for foreigners whom we cannot relate in any way to ourselves.[35]

If the week's round of duties meant a mixture of high culture and popular tat, then so much the more inviting, since the contrasts would oblige the critic to reveal his own capacity for enthusiasm. Back in 1952, on the *Evening Standard*, he had found himself confronting, in the same week, the Crazy Gang, a great British institution already beginning to creak, and Jean Genet, tyro of the Parisian avant-garde. His aesthetic was wide enough to encompass both: the Crazy Gang, he said, belonged

---

[33] *More Theatres* (London, 1969), 528.
[34] *The Contemporary Theatre: 1944–45* (London, 1946), 164.
[35] *HTPK* 158.

to the archaeology of farce, but had gone a little soft: 'I hope they will recover their old grip on that fundamental secret of comedy: man's inhumanity to man, and his positive inhumanity to woman'; Genet's *The Maids* is 'that rarity on English stages, a play which consciously sets out to leave an unpleasant taste behind. To see it is like watching an adhesive bandage being repeatedly torn off an unhealed wound.'[36] A taste for the nastily subversive runs through the comments on both performances; indeed, rather shockingly, one could almost swap them around. 'It is nice', he said of Genet, 'to make the acquaintance of a highly articulate dramatist in whose vocabulary the word "nice" does not exist.' At the *Observer*, from 1954 to 1963, Tynan set about his self-appointed task of ridding the English theatre of 'niceness', of gentility and restraint, with a display of critical outrageousness that not only reflected the sexual demands of post-war youth but, coincidentally, served a theatre industry that had identified a new market.

Inevitably, Tynan's posthumous reputation is coloured by the libertarian, even lurid attitudes to sexual freedom that ruled his later career: the sex revues *Oh! Calcutta!* (1969) and *Carte Blanche* (1976), and his curious mission to be the first man to say 'fuck' on television. Quite soon after his death from emphysema in 1980, Jonathan Miller, as alert as Tynan himself to the po-faced pieties of other people, was ready to compare his evangelical fervour to that of Marie Stopes, Havelock Ellis or some other high-minded Edwardian sexologist.[37] Since then the priorities have shifted even more. If much of what he advocated—total nudity, erotic demonstration, physical frankness—has become breezily commonplace in mainstream dance and performance art, his subversive Reichian theories have lost whatever force they once possessed.

Tynan never himself expressed any embarrassment, let alone repentance, about his commitment to theatre as an erotic art. It was there from the start. One of the funniest pieces he wrote for the *Sketch*, 'Bald Men and Bikinis', a review of a show at the Windmill Theatre, makes unfavourable comparisons between what London has to offer in the field and 'such American burlesque shows as "Julius Teaser" and "Panties Inferno." '[38] (He

---

[36] *Evening Standard*, 14 Nov. 1952.   [37] 'Reputations'.
[38] *Daily Sketch*, 5 Feb. 1954.

did concede that the Windmill bill had 'a good roller-skating act'.) Already a connoisseur of what he liked to call 'genial carnality',[39] he had written in the previous year, 1953, that Peggy Ashcroft's 'ability to convey, on the stage, an intelligent interest in sex' was 'rare among English actresses, most of whom, when called on to express passion, behave with a sort of nervous perplexity, rather as a debutante might behave if she turned up in error at a vampire hunt in Transylvania'.[40] This dewy-eyed appreciation of those who revealed themselves on stage could be as fervent as the itemized, some might say obsessive dismissal of high-strung Englishness (not just Anna Neagle, but above all Vivien Leigh). As the heroine of Rattigan's *The Deep Blue Sea*, Ashcroft made Tynan think of 'a melted candle, burned down but still beautiful; and nobody could have given it but Miss Ashcroft, a player of whom it might be said that her soul is showing'.

For Tynan, good theatre was always the place where gender construction is unravelled. 'No good actor is ever wholly masculine', he wrote.

Something, some vocal or physical trick, betrays his debt to woman-kind, the debt which every man owes, but which most of us, out of some primitive animosity, do our best to hide. The actor is different because he bestrides both worlds, and is able out of his sophistication to call a truce in the normally interminable battle of the sexes.[41]

He composed a sensitive obituary of Vesta Tilley in 1952—'to a Bacchanalian business she brought finesse'[42]—and his dedicated critique of Olivier was often focused within a masculine/feminine dialectic. Olivier's Justice Shallow made him wonder 'whether one root of comedy is not the exposure of all that is womanish in man, the unveiling of feminine traits beneath the masculine exterior',[43] whereas his interpretation of Hamlet suffered from 'a perverse desire to amputate every trace of fatal effeminacy from the part'.[44] Always the ideal, even when he lapsed, Olivier, alone of modern actors, took the physical risks necessary to explore our sexual natures.

It was in order to work with Olivier that in 1963, after some twelve years of constant activity, Tynan brought his full-time

[39] *Daily Sketch*, 5 Feb. 1954.   [40] *Evening Standard*, 30 June 1953.
[41] HTPK 24.   [42] *Evening Standard*, 16 Sept.   [43] HTPK 78.
[44] HTPK 134.

reviewing career to a close and became literary manager of the new National Theatre. As a critic he had willingly inherited demands for a state-subsidized theatre first voiced by Archer and Granville-Barker in 1907. When the Comédie Française visited London in 1953, he had immediately drawn comparisons between its stability and the fate of an outstanding *ad hoc* company led by John Gielgud and Peter Brook, whose *Venice Preserv'd* he had much admired. After a few short weeks the company would be 'broken up and resold': 'Nobody, of course, will complain. The English tradition of improvidence will have been upheld; and I, in the English tradition of understatement, will have to confine myself to a scream of rage.'[45]

As the early years of the National are written up,[46] so Tynan's contribution will be re-evaluated—and the signs are that his historical significance as its first *dramaturg* will be much contested. Similarly, his uniqueness as a critic is most apparent in the rather patchy nature of his influence. Michael Billington frequently cites him, but nowadays in the manner of an old and much annotated textbook. Many have taken up the challenge of his style, reaching for the same combination of wit and wonder, straining for that snappy last line, hoping to spin their whole review on a single startling pun. Yet, for some time, the truly Tynanesque strain has been heard most unmistakably not so much among theatre critics as among writers about television (Clive James's early work for the *Observer* is the most obvious instance) and among a younger generation of cultural observers, who have shown little or no interest in the theatre. The early Billington may have been crammed with Tynanesque puns— 'hold the mirror up to Nietzsche',[47] 'irony and steel'[48]—the mature journalist has found his own more ruminative style.

Some critical habits do remain in place. Like Tynan, Billington respects a select group of popular entertainers— Frankie Howerd among them. Like Tynan, like most male critics, Billington sometimes favours the old stage-door manner, the chivalry of Shaw and Agate, forever promising fidelity to the

[45] *Evening Standard*, 22 May 1953.
[46] See e.g. John Elsom and Nicholas Tomalin, *The History of the National Theatre* (London, 1978) and John Dexter, *The Honourable Beast: A Posthumous Autobiography* (London, 1993).
[47] *ONS* 90.   [48] *ONS* 254.

infinite variety of his heroines, though these days with some qualifications. Judi Dench's Cleopatra may be 'capricious, volatile, the mistress of all moods'; this ensures that her 'sexual magnetism lies not in any Centrefold posturing, but in emotional extremism'.[49] Awestruck attitudes to actresses, a Tynan trait, continue to hold sway in a field of journalism where women have, even now, made relatively little headway.

In the theatre itself much has changed since Tynan's heyday, sometimes vindicating his view of the future, sometimes not. In the 1950s there was still widespread faith in the regenerative possibilities of an English verse drama; Tynan was always sceptical, writing of a revival of *Murder in the Cathedral* in 1953:

Mr. Eliot's admirers have a habit of referring to him as a leader in the movement towards 'the new language' in the theatre by which of course they mean poetry.

At this my historical sense rebels because the new language, the really recent adventure, is prose. The Greeks would have none of it; Shakespeare reserved it for servants' chatter and idle comedy; and it was, in fact, less than eighty years ago that prose was accepted as a respectable instrument for serious dramatic expression.[50]

Despite a retrospective tribute to Christopher Fry by Billington ('he brought a neo-Elizabethan linguistic exuberance to a rather drab, post-war English theatre'[51]) and widespread praise of Tony Harrison, stage 'poetry' is these days mostly a matter of atmospherics, the only modern kind Tynan was prepared to contemplate. James Fenton, a poet himself, even selects Harold Pinter, a writer of prose, as his favourite 'stage-poet', explaining that the 'poetic qualities' he admires in Pinter are fundamental to all serious literature: 'something irreducible, something untranslatable into any other terms'.[52]

In any case, for Tynan, the matter of 'poetry', like that of theatrical impact in general, was always inseparable from an actor's delivery: 'The one unquestionably heroic thing in English drama', he insisted very early on, 'is the sound of Laurence Olivier's voice.'[53] By placing the emphasis on personalities

---

[49] ONS 279. [50] *Evening Standard*, 4 Apr. 1953. [51] ONS 291.
[52] YWM 80. [53] HTPK 250.

rather than plays,[54] he extended the boundaries of critical interest whilst defining the social significance of contemporary methods of acting. In this respect, it is certainly true that younger critics have tended to follow him. Billington comes into his own, and even goes beyond Tynan when, as in his description of John Wood as 'the spirit of the Seventies: ironic, inquisitive, anti-heroic',[55] he relates acting styles to their cultural moment.

Tynan's Brechtianism remains as problematic as ever. What had begun, in his own words, as 'an intense fascination with birds of bright plumage' became, after the discovery of the German playwright in the mid-1950s, a more complicated enterprise: 'I came to a different concept of theatre, the theatre militant, which told me not only about the crisis of the individual but the crisis of a society.'[56] But Tynan was far from the first British writer to recognize the significance of Brecht's methods,[57] and, in comparison with someone like Ewan MacColl, a Brechtian since the 1930s, his Marxism looked jejune. Tynan did, though, instinctively appreciate the Brechtian principle that modes of presentation engender ways of seeing. This enabled him to indulge his precise and skilled aestheticism—'I defy anyone to forget Brecht's stage pictures'[58]—alongside generalized proclamations about the material basis of social organization. In a crafty way he transferred his love of surface glitter, and what that might imply, to Brecht's canvas workclothes; the shift characteristically enabling him to remain faithful to his own nature while keeping up with the new.

In the long term, Tynan's contributions to the British appropriation of Brecht are probably best seen as part of a long-established, still continuing, preference for stylish realism over rigorous and doctrinaire ideology. In 1979 Fenton was to complain that a Caucasian peasant at the end of the Second World War, forced to watch Brecht's chalk-circle parable about the politics of ownership, would surely have been justified in pelting the stage;[59] even in 1956 Tynan had confessed to being unmoved

[54] 'The Critic Comes Full Circle', *Theatre Quarterly*, 1/2 (Apr.–June 1971) 37. Further references are to TQ.
[55] *ONS* 77–81.
[56] *TQ*, 37–48, 37.
[57] See Nicholas Jacobs and Prudence Ohlsen, eds., *Bertolt Brecht in Britain* (London, 1977).   [58] *Curtains*, 452.   [59] *YWM* 28–9.

by what Brecht had to say in that play, though he was 'over-whelmed by the way in which he said it'.[60] When, in 1995, David Hare adapted *Mother Courage* for the National, he said that Brecht had made the abstract nouns, 'Time and War', central characters;[61] more than forty years earlier Tynan had described it as a play in which 'the squalor of all wars is somehow compressed'.[62] The British theatre as a whole has often only been able to express its admiration for Brecht by applying to his plays an ahistorical notion of the universal: the political implications have been felt to be either too extreme or simply inappropriate to the local situation. Tynan's reputation as a dilettante Marxist may posthumously have come to his aid.

A Brechtian style of production has, however, often been applied in genuinely radical ways, as Tynan well realized when he wrote of the influence of the Berliner Ensemble during the 1950s upon young Shakespearean directors such as William Gaskill:

If the tale is a fable (as in the comedies it often is), anchor it to earth with solid objects and unsentimental acting. If it is tragic in content, anchor it in place and time. If it is a chronicle, anchor it in historical perspective. Prefer social fact to poetic fiction, the touch of truth to the hypnotic gesture of illusion; and above all, never fall into the error of supposing that high-born characters merit attention and respect more than the rest simply because they sometimes express themselves more beautifully.[63]

What's powerful about that prescription is its practicality as much as its politics. Nevertheless, from the mid-1960s into the early 1970s, social drama invariably meant left-wing drama, suspected, in some quarters, of being the only kind of drama that would ever win critical approval. Though no longer a full-time critic, Tynan was held personally responsible for this situation. As a reminder of a now distant atmosphere, here is the playwright William Douglas Home, eager to be seen as the unofficial spokesman for middle-class, middle-brow theatre, speculating in 1979 on

---

[60] *Curtains*, 390.
[61] Ironically the production was severely criticized by Billington for falling short of Brecht's intentions. *Guardian*, 17 Nov. 1995.
[62] *Curtains*, 386.   [63] *TOT* 99.

the possibility, remote admittedly, but none the less conceivable, that one day not just some but ALL dramatic critics might be guilty of political or social bias, thus ensuring that no plays by authors on their black list saw the light of day, except perhaps for a short time. Such censorship, in one form or another, has occurred and still occurs in other countries. It could happen here. The price of its avoidance is eternal vigilance. . . .

Imagine, for example, Miss Vanessa Redgrave being signed up by some London paper as their drama critic. Think of Messrs Wedgwood Benn, Clive Jenkins, Tariq Ali—any left-wing characters, in fact, you might care to mention—manning the rest. 'What chance then,' one might ask, 'for any playwright tarred with the establishment brush?'[64]

'Mr Home (pronounced Hume), made me foam (pronounced fume)',[65] Tynan had once remarked about a writer whom he had never ceased to castigate since his 1953 autopsy of *The Bad Samaritan*: 'It is a commonplace that in the theatre holiness is next to priggishness, so one must be charitable to Mr Douglas Home's good characters, a gently boring lot. But charity expires in the face of his sinners. Where a thousand theologians have failed, he has succeeded; he has made wickedness look unspeakably dull.'[66] No wonder Home felt he had no place, though by the late 1970s he had less to fear from left-wing critics than he thought; they were already shifting ground. In the 1980s, Thatcherism's attacks on the expression of liberal opinion in the media would result in a deepening critical commitment to the theatre as the only open forum for debate. From a radical perspective it's at this point that Tynan finally loses touch. In 1971 he was championing theatre against television which 'is either state-controlled and therefore totally propagandist, or, like our own, meant to be impartial and so emasculated eventually—because the other side has to be given equal time to reply', whereas in the theatre, even the large-scale theatre, 'the independent political viewpoint can be expressed with no censorship and a quite untrammelled directness'.[67] In the 1970s, the radical groups belonging to what was by then called 'The Fringe' went one way, towards a latter day agit-prop; national critics went another. Neither direction would have been inviting to Tynan.

---

[64] William Douglas Home, *Mr Home Pronounced Hume* (London, 1979), 174–5.
[65] Ibid. 178.   [66] *Evening Standard*, 26 June 1953.   [67] *TQ* 38.

By 1979 Billington had developed his preference for impartial analysis over Tynan's 'untrammelled directness' to the point where he could hail a Caryl Churchill play (which a colleague had described pejoratively as 'committed') as exemplary because 'its chief commitment was to truth . . . its great virtue is that it sets the evidence before us and makes no attempt to load the dice through presentational effects'.[68] In 1982 Billington summed it all up: 'I want some instructions in how to live rather than a demonstration of spiritual negativism.'[69]

If we look back over the 1980s through the medium of Billington's collected reviews, David Hare's plays on Tory Britain, performed at a National Theatre which has turned into a very different institution from the one Tynan helped found, seem to arrive with Messianic force. Hare's *The Secret Rapture*, wrote Billington in 1988, 'is partly about the corrosive effect of the Thatcherite ethos on human relationships; but at a deeper, quasi-religious level . . . it is about pain, martyrdom and the idea of fulfilment through death'.[70] This emphasis on spirituality, on areas of experience that lie beyond politics, yet whose form and pressure are clearly determined by the ethical life of a nation, are part of an extended response to that earlier moment, at the start of the decade, the moment, coincidentally, of Tynan's departure for America, when previous nostra—including the sexual revolution—had begun to seem pointlessly utopian, miserably out-of-date. Of course, Tynan had no more been the sole public spokesman for a politically engaged theatre than, in the 1950s, he had been the single-handed engineer of Brecht's ascendancy, but his belief that radical feelings could be, should be, explored in subsidized, let alone commercial settings, now seemed badly off-target. This was certainly the case after the débâcle of Howard Brenton's *The Romans in Britain* at the National in 1980, when Mary Whitehouse, a prominent moral activist, served a summons on the director, Michael Bogdanov, accusing him of 'procuring an act of gross indecency' by staging a scene of homosexual rape. Where a subsidized theatre had gone, few commercial managements were now prepared to follow. One suspects, too, that Tynan would have been slow to see the implications within contemporary feminism for his 'art

---

[68] *ONS* 88.   [69] *ONS* 180.   [70] *ONS* 301.

of titillation';[71] then again, AIDS caught almost everyone unawares.

At the moment of his death the tributes came from all quarters of the theatrical world. Not that this almost unique example of a multiple career—only Shaw exceeds it—has done anything to heal the divisions between critic and practitioner. Tynan was undoubtedly unusual in that writers and even actors were sometimes ready to accept his judgements—in Tom Stoppard's words, 'he made it worthwhile trying to be good'[72]—yet the ancient hatred still festers.

The older hands have certainly been consistent in their conviction that critics are the enemies, not the allies, of creativity. In the light of the Slattery affair of 1995, the playwright Arnold Wesker restated his position using exactly the same words he had used in response to James Fenton's collection *You Were Marvellous* in 1983: 'a newspaper review is only one person's opinion magnified out of proportion by print'.[73] Smarting from dismissive reviews of his own recent work, Wesker complained that print 'has magic properties and carries awesome authority'.[74] So that while it was all very well for Fenton, in a postscript essay entitled 'The Right to be Wrong', to confess his own frailty—'We must be true to our anger, true to our enthusiasms, true to our excitement, true to our boredom'—one could never forget that behind him lay the institutionalized might of the Sunday papers.

Despite Wesker's continued reliance upon it, that word 'magnified' seems wilfully inadequate to the art of criticism as practised by someone like Tynan. This was no more an ordinary person whose opinions had been 'magnified' by print than a great actor is simply 'magnified' by his or her appearance on stage. Tynan worked hard polishing his charisma; here was the critic as talented individual, as performer, as personality, as star. He always, as John Osborne later confirmed, 'considered himself part of theatre and show business'.[75] It is in that respect that

[71] *TQ* 38. See e.g. the account given in Kathleen Tynan's biography of his difficult and aborted attempt at collaboration with Trevor Griffiths.

[72] 'Reputations'.

[73] *Guardian*, 4 Apr. 1995. Wesker's first and most extended reply to critics was 'Casual Condemnations: A Brief Study of the Critic as Censor', *TQ* 16–30.

[74] *Listener*, 25 Aug. 1983.   [75] 'Reputations'.

his example is most potent, and, from Wesker's point of view, surely most dangerous: the fan became a rival, probably always had been one.

The lasting lesson of Ken Tynan is that performer and critic have more in common than most critics, let alone performers, are prepared to admit. Both are on the night shift; both have to deliver on time, with no second chance until the next night (or the next column)—when it will be too late. 'I should like to see both of these performances again in a few weeks' time, when I've had a chance to get over my first-night nerves', Fenton once let slip.[76] Irving Wardle has also described the psychology of reviewing as a kind of stage-fright: 'The piece has got to be written. You do not *try* to write it. You write it.'[77] Both must make an impression, here and now.

Even Wesker, for all his belief in the 'ordinariness' of critics, detects a 'tone of competitiveness: the reviewer in competition with his/her subject',[78] but holds that this will generally lead to a scene-stealingly negative notice. This has long been a worry.[79] When, in 1989, Terry Hands and Michael Billington carried out a role-changing experiment whereby Billington directed a play and Hands wrote the review, Hands couldn't help adding: 'It is hard to criticise. I'd rather appreciate. It requires enormous experience to surrender to a performance and yet retain a pencil in hand or head.'[80] Unexpectedly perhaps, many critics agree with him. Wardle believes that hostile notices are much easier to write: 'Hostility allows you to remain in command, and this generates mental energy. Admiration puts you in a subordinate role—the artist has done something that is beyond you—which may reduce you to gushing drivel or tongue-tied paralysis.'[81] It was for precisely this reason that Fenton, who made a point of noticing Tynan's *Show People* when it appeared in England after the author's death, paid tribute to the critic's gift for unequivocal admiration, noting that praise is difficult because 'many of those with necessary articulacy are too proud to praise.

[76] YWM 227.

[77] Irving Wardle, *Theatre Criticism* (London, 1992), 127.

[78] *Guardian*, 4 Apr. 1995.

[79] For Billington's report of a debate in which he, Fenton and Michael Coveney met with David Edgar, Dusty Hughes, Max Stafford-Clark and others, see *ONS* 179.

[80] *ONS* 314.   [81] *Theatre Criticism*, 36.

They think that some virtue is gone out of them when they praise.'[82] Yet as Fenton also allowed, those who take the act of praising to an extreme might conceivably be practising some obscure, but gratifying, form of self-abasement.

By conceding power with praise critics can, it is true, reclaim their authority. This is more than a paradoxical hypothesis; it can be literally, practically, the case. There's a splendidly vituperative outburst in Rodney Ackland's *Absolute Hell*, revived to great acclaim in the 1980s, in which an author turns on his critic-tormentor: 'My only *real* life, I might tell you, was as a writer, a creative artist, but thanks to you . . . all that is finished, I am nothing, nothing, and less than nothing, my books are out of print, forgotten—and my name means nothing any more.'[83] The end of a '*real*' life': Ackland wrote that in response to the critical drubbing given to an earlier version of his play by Harold Hobson of the *Sunday Times* in 1952.[84] Yet it has been another critic who has been instrumental in reviving interest in Ackland's work: Hilary Spurling, herself once cast into darkness when she was banned by the Royal Court in 1969 for walking out half-way through a performance. Tynan, long-established scourge of the Establishment, undoubtedly enjoyed his power, as critic, as literary manager, and latterly as producer—first of Hochhuth's *Soldiers*, then of his own erotic shows. He may even at times have turned his gift for enthusiasm to his own advantage. Because he led, in every way, a professional life, he was continually caught up in cultural battles, as theatre historians who use him for evidence should always bear in mind. He once said that above all he admired those 'whose god-given or life-developed gift is to be able to mould the consciousness of a thousand people in a room at the same time',[85] believing that only in the theatre are such exceptional individuals given the freedom they need. Yet he probably came closer to that ideal of influence, of moulding consciousness, when working as a critic in the medium of print than he ever did in the theatre itself. He achieved it by writing about other people.

[82] YWM 131–2.

[83] *Absolute Hell* (London, 1990), 63.

[84] Tynan, incidentally, called it 'an intensely atmospheric little play'. *Evening Standard*, 20 June 1952.

[85] TQ 37.

It can sometimes be irritating to be dismissed, in Kenneth Williams's phrase, as 'a pack of parasites',[86] but those of us who write reviews, if only in an amateur way, can always soothe ourselves with the thought that, in nature, parasites are essential to the well-being of the host, that they can save the lives they feed upon. Indeed, without their parasites, hosts might not know what they had to offer. And just occasionally that primal, chafing interdependence is acted out, acted upon. 'How shall we slaughter the little bastard?' Olivier asked Joan Plowright when Ken Tynan applied to the National for the job of literary manager in 1962, falling back on his usual epithet for journalists and applying it to a man who had adoringly stalked every stage of his own career. 'You might do worse,' she replied,[87] sharp enough to recognize that, like it or not, the first Lord and Lady of the English stage now ruled a cultural kingdom mapped out for their benefit, and to their considerable advantage, by a life-saving critic.

[86] 'A pack of parasites who specialise in the sort of treachery that is unspeakable', Kenneth Williams, *Letters* (London, 1995), p. xvii.
[87] Holden, *Olivier*, 437.

11

'Between the Saxon Smile and Yankee Yawp': Problems and Contexts of Literary Reviewing in Ireland

EDNA LONGLEY

Impartial criticism is a more than usually delicate task where a small country like Ireland is concerned. When the intellectual centre is confined within a restricted area, personal relations are unavoidable, and the critic finds discretion imperative, if he is to continue to dwell peaceably in the midst of his friends . . . The effect . . . of this absence of critical judgement, publicly expressed, has been that honest criticism prefers to be silent where it cannot praise. Consequently there is a lack of intellectual discipline which allows the good and the mediocre to struggle on equal terms for recognition. In Ireland we have become accustomed to hearing Irish writers either enthusiastically advertised by the English press, or denounced as charlatans, usurping the fame reserved for genuine heirs of England's glory . . . We cannot expect others to show more discrimination than ourselves.

(Ernest Boyd, *Ireland's Literary Renaissance*, 1916)

I

Most problems of literary reviewing in Ireland are identical with problems of literary reviewing in Britain and the US. The preview and interview try to usurp the review. Other media usurp the book. The obsession with 'theory' produces new variants on old tensions (and sometimes old collusions) between the creative writer and the academic reviewer. The non-academic reviewer clings to 'literature' as to a capsized craft. Chums puff one another's work. The majority of poetry reviews are by people who write the stuff themselves—less because professional, or would-be professional, poets conspire against the public, than because it has become harder to find other reviewers who intelligently follow the art.[1] Discussion of books on radio and television is marginalized or trivialized when it is not abolished.[2] But beyond such common ground and common grievances, special factors condition reviewing in Ireland. These can be traced to an intersection between economic forces, Irish history, Irish literary history, the history of literary studies, and the cultural dimension of Irish politics since the 1830s.

A fundamental factor is scale: the smallness of Ireland's literary-critical, scholarly and publishing base in proportion to the market and audience for Irish writing. Five million people, eight universities or university colleges, and a few dozen small presses are drops in the English-speaking, English-reading, British Studies/Irish Studies ocean. Irish books from UK publishers receive the majority of their reviews outside Ireland. British newspapers, with massive cultural sections, now carry their circulation war into the Republic through Irish editions which domesticate some of the political coverage, but not (so far) the book pages. One effect of the British penetration is to drive native newspapers down in market as well as up in price. A promising young poet, critic and magazine-editor said recently: 'I don't know whether I will stay in Ireland. Although this country prides itself on having a very literary culture, there is just no structure or place for a literary journalist to make any real money.'[3] Scale, then, may not be the only problem. None the less, whereas Yeats desired to found a school of Irish criticism, his own fame, together with that of Joyce, has ensured that

---

[1] The statistics of *Poetry Ireland Review* are similar in this respect to those of *Poetry Review* (London).

[2] The Radio Telifis Eireann (RTE) arts discussion programme, *Black Box*, was presented in 1995–6 by the novelist Glenn Patterson but (as with BBC2's *Late Review*), books were only part of the picture. He was subsequently axed and a 'magazine' rather than critical format proposed. Television in Northern Ireland rarely deals with books on its arts programme. Books do rather better on radio in both parts of Ireland, but tend to be handled in a populist way, as exemplified by the title of the Radio Ulster programme, *You're Booked*.

[3] David Wheatley, quoted in the *Irish Times*, 4 Sept. 1996.

the academics and journalists who comment on Irish literature overwhelmingly come from elsewhere.

Here I might include that often colourful figure, the expatriate pundit. For metropolitan readers, the phrase 'Irish literary critic' probably conjures up Tom Paulin. In 1994–5 the *London Review of Books* published two Northern Irish 'Diaries', one at the time of the IRA ceasefire, the other a year later. Both were written by expatriates (Paulin and the novelist Ronan Bennett). Bennett's single theme, at the complex moment of the ceasefire, was the attitude of the British media to Gerry Adams. He also made Adams more user-friendly to *LRB* readers by recalling an encounter that included 'some small talk about books and publishing, about which Adams, an author, is very interested'.[4] The *LRB* currently employs critics based in the Republic (Fintan O'Toole and Colm Toibín), but none based in the North. In 1995, too, Bennett was given several pages of the *Guardian* to generalize about the arts in Northern Ireland. Meanwhile, Richard Gott, then the *Guardian*'s literary editor, would not give space to Irish-published books.[5] That is a preliminary snapshot of how literary journalism contributes to the tangled threads of representation (who gets to speak where? who is a presumed insider and who an outsider?), at a time when readings of Irish culture are highly politicized.

Of course reviewers in Ireland do not confine themselves to Irish publications, or to Irish writers. Their perspectives on British or American writing help to inform Irish readers, but rarely make much difference to its wider critical reception. Presumably that is one reason why the *Irish Times* has established its rich International Prize for fiction (won by such authors as E. Annie Proulx and J. M. Coetzee), and why its literary editor, the novelist John Banville, moonlights as a reviewer for the *Observer* and *New York Review of Books*. A visiting English publisher told me that he liked the *Irish Times* literary pages because they were more detached about books published in Britain, and he compared the situation to Brussels reviewing Paris. For example, Eileen Battersby, the paper's regular fiction reviewer, began a survey of Booker Prize hopefuls: 'In moments of despair it is easy to [conclude] that literature is well-nigh

---

[4] *LRB* 16/18, 22 Sept. 1994.
[5] Reported to me by the publicist for Blackstaff Press.

dead, and that it lives on only through the determination of publishers to continue producing a seemingly inexhaustible tide of heavily hyped books.' Yet detachment possibly slid into national antagonism when Battersby called *Classwork*, an anniversary collection of short stories from Malcom Bradbury's East Anglia Creative Writing course, 'largely pretentious', and continued: 'Particularly irritating, arrogant and inaccurate is the foolhardy decision made by either Bradbury or his publisher to hype these stories as "the best of contemporary short fiction". The best of contemporary fiction from where, exactly? The world? Surely not Britain? Let's hope not.'[6]

Such irritation arises from the reality that London can afford to ignore Dublin, just as Paris ignores Brussels, or Dublin Belfast. In contrast, reviewers and critics outside Ireland *do* make a difference to the reception of Irish books. Nobody should whinge about the widespread audience that the English language has given to Irish writers. In 1945 the poet John Hewitt pinned his hopes for Northern Ireland's literary future on the fact that there was 'no limit to [the Ulster writer's] potential audience'.[7] Seamus Heaney's international success, which owes something to his poetry's regional flavour, subsequently proved the point. Yeats in 1894 told an unbelieving Ireland what its literature would owe to the 'small group of men of imagination and scholarship which is scattered through many lands and many cities'. He instanced the making of Whitman's reputation outside America, and despite America, partly by the Irish critic, Edward Dowden, who was less receptive to the Revival in his own backyard.[8] Nine years later Yeats reminded his publisher 'of our rule to send no copies of my books to Dublin papers . . . Reviews in Dublin papers sell no copies & I don't see why I should give them the oppertunity of attacking me.'[9] The rule was kept for twenty years. Literary protectionism would, of course, be especially misplaced in a country once prone to censorship and—like other countries—resistant to having its horizon of expectations shifted. The tone of Samuel

---

[6] *Irish Times*, 11 May 1996.

[7] 'The Bitter Gourd: Some Problems of the Ulster Writer', in *Ancestral Voices: Selected Prose of John Hewitt*, ed. Tom Clyde (Belfast, 1987), 115.

[8] *Collected Letters of W. B. Yeats*, ed. John Kelly, i (Oxford, 1986), 408–9.

[9] *Collected Letters of W. B. Yeats*, ed. John Kelly and Ronald Schuchard, iii (Oxford, 1994), 341–2.

Beckett's assault on censorship (written in 1935) suggests how Irish literature has been shaped by complexities of reception and rejection, by multiple interpretive communities. He ends: 'My own registered number [on the Censorship Register] is 465, number four hundred and sixty-five, if I may presume to say so. We now feed our pigs on sugarbeet pulp. It is all the same to them.'[10] The rhetoric of Yeats's poetry, a poetry obsessed with audience, was stretched by the exigencies of moving between readers attuned to nationalism and readers attuned to symbolism; between local hostility and 'men of imagination and scholarship'; between 'Paudeen' and Ezra Pound.[11] There may be implications for literary theory in the extent to which Ireland problematizes inside and outside readings—not least, because of its internal divisions.[12]

None the less, to review Irish fiction and poetry, or related works of criticism and biography, in Ireland itself is to subscribe to an unbalanced literary economy. More mechanisms of control lie outside the country—in the hands of multinational criticism—than is usually the case. This might weaken critical debate *inside* the country, as arguments leak into the sea, and thus prolong elements of the provincialism disturbed but hardly routed by Yeats. Ultimately, however, it is not the ratio between indigenous and foreign views that counts, but the reciprocity and its subtlety.

Absence of subtlety shows itself when the newspapers of independent Ireland come up with headlines like 'London Critics Praise Irish Play'. Not all Dublin reviewers go along with this cultural cringe. John Boland, who writes a crisp column of literary news and opinion for the *Irish Times* ('Bookworm'), was recently annoyed by two characteristic English approaches to Irish authors. On successive Saturdays he wrote: 'I see that the English are at their old game of passing off Irish achievement as their own [a *Sunday Times* review of Roddy Doyle]'; and 'What is it with English writers when they're sent on journalistic

[10] Samuel Beckett, 'Censorship in the Saorstat', reprinted in Julia Carlson, ed., *Banned in Ireland: Censorship and the Irish Writer* (London, 1990), 146.

[11] See Warwick Gould and Edna Longley, eds., *Yeats Annual*, 12. 'Yeats and his Irish Readers: "That Accusing Eye"' (London, 1996).

[12] For a discussion of these issues see 'Introduction: Revising "Irish Literature"', in Edna Longley, *The Living Stream: Literature and Revisionism in Ireland* (Newcastle upon Tyne, 1994).

assignments to Ireland? In the *Independent on Sunday* last weekend, Peter Conrad contributes a profile of Roddy Doyle that's full of the most amazing Oirishy nonsense.'[13] It was not for this that Shaw wrote *John Bull's Other Island*. Irish critics recurrently take issue with English 'Celticism'—for which they usually make Matthew Arnold the scapegoat. Yet Irish writers sometimes profit (in terms of reputation, at least) from sentimental misreadings. Louis MacNeice, in *The Poetry of W. B. Yeats*, used the following anecdote to sum up his exasperation with the 'tear in the eye' that prevents 'many English people' from seeing Ireland clearly: 'only this year [1939] at a London performance of *The Playboy of the Western World* I overheard people in the audience saying to each other "Aren't the Irish *sweet*!" '[14] More recently, Blake Morrison was, perhaps, a little soft on an Irish novel in which 'Magic and folklore swirl around . . . [the child's] aunt tells him stories of possessions and metamorphoses and sleeping warriors; he learns how if you meet somebody with one green eye and one brown you should cross yourself, "for that was a human child that had been taken over by the fairies" '.[15] Powerful forces, indeed, must be at work to perpetuate such impressions: the author of the novel is Seamus Deane, the Irish academic who (in *Celtic Revivals*, 1985) has been toughest on Celticism. The challenge for Irish critics who review on both sides of the water is to mediate between perspectives, as did John Naughton's *Irish Times* review of *St Patrick's People* by the English writer Tony Gray (from whom he quotes a passage about 'the fairy folk liv[ing] on in the Irish people'): 'We Irish are unique. Upon this all authors of guide books and other works of cultural exegesis seem to agree. Quite why we should be unique is less clear.'[16]

But even if twilight swirls and lingers abroad, critical isolationism has never been the answer. The poet and critic Anthony Cronin takes rather perverse pride in the idea that, owing to the Free State's wartime purdah, the reputation of the poet Patrick Kavanagh was made exclusively at home.[17] In fact, Kavanagh

---

[13] Weekend, *Irish Times*, 13 and 20 Apr. 1996.

[14] Louis MacNeice, *The Poetry of W. B. Yeats* (London, 1967 edn.), 46.

[15] Review of Seamus Deane, *Reading in the Dark*, *Independent on Sunday*, 1 Sept. 1996.

[16] Weekend, *Irish Times*, 4 May 1996.

[17] Cronin is the author of *Dead as Doornails* (Dublin and London, 1976), a

did not think his poetry well-served by the critical climate, or
lack of it, in 1940s and 1950s Ireland. He attacked 'Irishness'
as 'a form of anti-art'; founded (in 1952) his own angry,
scattergun, short-lived journal *Kavanagh's Weekly*; and complained, in his valedictory editorial, about 'the absence of an
audience'. He continued: 'It is the need of the audience which
produces the voice. . . . Oddly enough, although there is no
ultimate audience there is just enough coquetry to draw out
writers who are then left with a hunger that cannot be satisfied
within that society.' As for audiences elsewhere, although
Kavanagh often portrayed London's literary environment as a
utopian antithesis to Dublin, he also charged: 'There has
always been a big market in England for the synthetic Irish
thing. . . . Another villainous maw opened for things Irish-and-
proud-of-it is the American literary market.' And as for
subtle reciprocities between home and abroad: 'the unfortunate
peoples of my island home lap up all that vulgarity when it is
dished out to them'.[18]

2

Kavanagh's complaints, if extreme, go beyond self-interest.
They dramatize problems of reception and reviewing, bound up
with twentieth-century Irish history, which have become less
acute without being wholly resolved. One consequence of the
political events of the 1920s was a decline in indigenous publishing houses,[19] and British publishers closed down their Irish
offices. There were also changes to the ethos of literary circles
and magazines. Anne Ulry Colman, in her *Dictionary of
Nineteenth-Century Irish Women Poets* (1996), argues that
Irish feminist theory has maligned the Victorians, and that the

memoir of Kavanagh, Brendan Behan and other doyens of literary Dublin from the
late 1940s to the 1960s. He made the claim in a talk at 'Kavanagh's Yearly' in
Carrickmacross, Co. Monaghan (late 1980s).

[18] See Patrick Kavanagh, *Collected Pruse* (London, 1967), 16, 149, 227, 13.

[19] 'The closure of the Maunsel publishing company in 1926, the company that
had published the work of many of the writers associated with the Revival, was a
chilly omen of Ireland's literary future'. Terence Brown, *Ireland: A Social and
Cultural History 1922–1979* (London, 1981), 124.

real female silence fell in the 1930s. More generally, the mingled literary and political debate that preceded Independence died with AE's (George Russell's) liberal journal *The Irish Statesman*. In fact, taking the century as a whole, the actual number of cultural/literary journals steadily increases, with the main troughs occurring from 1912 to 1922 and in the 1940s.[20] However, the graph of intellectual, creative, and critical energy shows a different curve.

In his useful survey of Irish 'Little Magazines' since 1900, Peter Denman writes:

immediately after the establishment of the new state there was relatively little activity in periodical publishing. *The Irish Homestead* and *The Irish Statesman* continued until 1930. In 1924 *Tomorrow*, edited by Francis Stuart and Cecil Salkeld, lasted for two issues . . . but did not survive the rumpus which followed its publication of a story by Lennox Robinson, 'The Madonna of Slieve Dun' . . . in which a simple country girl fancies that she is to give birth to a new messiah.[21]

Conservative Catholic journals such as the *Irish Ecclesiastical Record* (1864–1968), *The Dublin Review* (1836–1969), and the *Irish Monthly Magazine* (1836–1969) persisted, as did the *Dublin Magazine* (1923–5, 1926–58), edited by the poet Seumas O'Sullivan (alias James Sharkey). Opinions differ as to whether the *Dublin Magazine*, with its adulation of AE, constituted the epitaph of the Revival, or whether it kept the literary scene ticking over until better times should come.[22] O'Sullivan printed some limp poetry (although Kavanagh was a contributor), but the reviews of Irish and British authors maintained serious critical standards. Through Beckett, there was occasional contact with the continental avant-garde. Also, writers such as P. S. O'Hegarty, Austin Clarke (who spent fifteen years in England reviewing for *The Times Literary Supplement* and other papers), and Sean O'Faolain sometimes involved the

---

[20] This information stems from research by Tom Clyde at Queen's University, Belfast. The history of Irish periodicals has been insufficiently investigated.

[21] Peter Denman, 'Ireland's Little Magazines', in Barbara Hayley and Enda McKay, eds., *Three Hundred Years of Irish Periodicals* (Mullingar, 1987), 128.

[22] For various views see Brown, *Social and Cultural History*, 167; Denman, 'Ireland's Little Magazines', 130; Gould and Longley, eds., *Yeats Annual* 12, 130–2.

magazine in more vigorous cultural and literary polemic than it is usually given credit for.[23] The contrast with O'Faolain's *Bell* (founded in 1940), the bracing journal that took on all the Irish sacred cows, should not entirely overshadow the achievement of the *Dublin Magazine* during the 1930s.

That it could be difficult to create space for critical discussion, that the protocols of argument could grow rusty, was proved by the career of *Envoy* (1949–51), set up as 'a forum of Irish creative thought'. The Anglo-Irish essayist Hubert Butler wrote a barbed obituary for *Envoy*, in which Kavanagh, Cronin, and other 'rebellious writers' had scourged literary institutions, including Yeats and the Revival:

> *Envoy* was a serious paper engaged on a real campaign against the Philistine and it was bad management that all the violence went on in the guard-room behind the lines, while the Philistines looked on and laughed. Compared to Patrick Kavanagh, a dashing guerrilla captain, Matthew Arnold [*whom Kavanagh had attacked as a 'well-meaning bore'*] was a great general, a tried campaigner against the Philistines, trained in all the academies of war.[24]

It was as if some of the culture of the literary journal had been lost or rejected, and had to be reinvented.

The Censorship of Publications Act (1929) was a factor in all this. The Act provided for the banning of publications that were 'in . . . general tendency indecent or obscene'; that devoted too much space to 'the publication of matter relating to crime'; and that advocated 'the unnatural prevention of conception or the procurement of abortion or miscarriage'. A board of five members assessed publications which customs officials or citizens brought before them. In effect, censorship manifested the repressive instincts of some of the forces that created the Irish Free State. Protests against the Act were led by Yeats, Shaw, AE, and Gogarty. This history explains why, twenty years later, despite his critique of *Envoy*, Hubert Butler regretted its demise. He wrote: 'An Irish journal is like a sortie from a besieged city. Its effects cannot be measured by its duration.'[25] The same might be

---

[23] See, particularly, O'Faolain's attack on Daniel Corkery's cultural exclusivism, *Dublin Magazine*, 11/2 (Apr.–June 1936), 49–61.

[24] Hubert Butler, '*Envoy* and Mr Kavanagh', *Escape from the Anthill* (Mullingar, 1985), 155.

[25] Ibid. 154.

said of the Belfast magazine *Lagan* (1943–6). Associated with John Hewitt and his project for literary regionalism, *Lagan* broke the repressive silences of the North in a way that had long-term repercussions.

Conversely, perhaps, the effects of censorship should be meas-ured by *its* duration: the last bitter *cause célèbre*, the banning of John McGahern's novel *The Dark*, occurred as lately as 1965. A recent collection of conference papers *On Intellectuals and In-tellectual Life in Ireland* distorts the present situation because, with remarkable historical amnesia, it fails to mention this black hole in the century.[26] Censorship amounted to more than the sum of banned books and emigrant writers. In *Banned in Ireland* (1989), edited for Article 19, Julia Carlson shows that it not only put great burdens on a few brave intellectuals, but induced a shrunken sense of possibility:

> Throughout the thirties, forties, and fifties, the moral fervour that fuelled censorship so dominated Irish life that those who objected to censorship risked being victimized if they protested against it. Supplies in libraries and bookshops dwindled until the books available to the Irish reader consisted of religious works and those that celebrated Irish culture and Irish life. Virtually no serious contemporary fiction was on the shelves.[27]

Carlson prints depressing interviews with writers who re-member the period, and reprints expressions of protest, such as O'Faolain's essay 'The Mart of Ideas' (1942) in which he calls the Censorship 'a smooth machinery to prevent [the] inter-change' of ideas, and to promote 'intellectual indifference . . . as a virtue in the masses'. O'Faolain also stresses the contradiction whereby the hegemonic project of Irish (Catholic) nationalism was devouring its own authors: 'Thirty years ago nobody would have denied the importance of a live intelligentsia here. Then those same people who now deride it made use of it day in and day out to disseminate all those doctrines which have resulted in a free Eire.'[28] The homosexual novelist John Broderick, inter-viewed in 1987, even said: 'Ireland was a much freer place when

[26] Liam O'Dowd, ed., *On Intellectuals and Intellectual Life in Ireland* (Belfast, 1996). O'Dowd's 'Sociological Introduction' stresses the role of Nationalist intellec-tuals, without raising the issue of intellectual liberty or exploring discontinuities between the intellectuals of 1900 and the intellectuals of the 1990s.
[27] Carlson, *Banned in Ireland*, 11.   [28] See ibid. 147–9.

the British were here. The society was more open. The zealots, the narrow-minded Opus Dei, Legion of Mary people took over.'[29]

Censorship pre-empted and prevented the functions of criticism. Ten years on, its inhibiting force facilitated the wartime censorship (under the Emergency Powers Act) that carried the burden of the Free State's neutrality policy. In *Censorship in Ireland: 1939–1945* (1996) Donal O'Drisceoil argues that Irish measures went beyond those taken by other neutral countries, partly to conceal actual cooperation with the Allies, partly to repress pro-German, anti-British feeling in a polity not yet recovered from the Civil War. For O'Drisceoil, 'Ireland's censorship culture, the low priority accorded to freedom of information and expression, and the tradition of "closed" government and administration' further explain 'the relative extremism of its wartime system'. Book reviews, though usually not literary reviews, suffered too: 'The chief culprit in the publication of pro-Allied views was the *Irish Times*. It published, without permission, a series of objectionable reviews, including reviews of books which had been withdrawn from sale in Ireland, like *The Persecution of the Catholic Church in the Third Reich*, which provoked a complaint from Hempel [the German ambassador] and a number of warnings from the Censorship.' The famous *coup* of R. M. Smyllie, editor of the *Irish Times*, who spent the 'Emergency' in a battle of wits with the Censor, was to smuggle into the paper a review previously banned. He did so by changing the book's title from *Worrals of the WAAF* to *Lotte of the Luftwaffe*. O'Drisceoil concludes his valuable study by calling for a full 'history of Irish censorship . . . from the foundation of the state to the present day . . . and addressing, particularly, the role of censorship in weakening the development of a democratic and civic culture in Ireland'.[30]

3

Just as two kinds of censorship had intersected, so, in the Republic of the 1960s, publishing and periodicals began to

[29] Carlson, 48.
[30] See Donal O'Drisceoil, *Censorship in Ireland: 1939–1945* (Cork, 1996), 291, 135, 303.

recover along with the instinct for democratic liberties. Many factors conspired to wreck what the historian Gearóid O'Tuathaigh has termed the project of 'Albanian' Ireland: the reversal of policies of economic isolationism; joining the EEC; the gradual (though still incomplete) displacement of Catholic theology as a basis for state law; penetration by British and American media; the advent of Irish television.[31] A similar movement of articulation in Northern Ireland was geared to a different set of literary, cultural and socio-political dynamics. There, evidently, the political deep freeze of the mid-century has not yet thawed to the same extent.

Jeremy Addis, enthusiastic promoter of Irish publishing and editor of *Books Ireland*, claims: 'The publishing renaissance is a natural development for a small "mid-Atlantic" country with high educational standards and a well-read population.'[32] What had retarded Irish publishing was, in part, the closing down of systems after Independence (as noted above); in part, the proximity of a more populous mid-Atlantic English-speaking island. None the less, Irish-language publishing had also suffered a creative drought, despite government support for educational texts. It is interesting that poetry publishing, a relic of the Revival, should have led the way. The Cuala Press, run by Lily and Lolly Yeats, and initially designed to give a national imprint to their elder brother's work, finally ceased to operate in 1946.[33] In 1951 Liam Miller's Dolmen Press took up the torch, with an emphasis on the poetry of Thomas Kinsella. When the renaissance properly began in the 1970s, Gallery, another poetry press, was prominent.

The publication of fiction proved more vulnerable to limitations of scale. Initially, Ireland could not compete at the popular end of the market, although greater numbers of Irish-oriented books are now doing well there. Nor could Irish lists retain 'literary' novelists who made any reputation. Today, young Irish novelists are being offered large advances by London publishers. The only publisher to succeed as a multi-faceted commercial enterprise (Gill and Macmillan) controls school texts. Brandon

[31] See, for instance, Brown, *Social and Cultural History*; J. J. Lee, *Ireland 1912–1985: Politics and Society* (Cambridge, 1989).
[32] See Edna Longley, 'Free from the Metropolitan Blight', *Times Higher Educational Supplement*, 14 June 1991, 17.
[33] See Gifford Lewis, *The Yeats Sisters and the Cuala* (Dublin, 1994).

Press in Kerry hit the jackpot with two best-selling writers: Gerry Adams, author of *Falls Memories* (1993), and Alice Taylor, famous for *To School Through the Fields* and other memoirs that 'deal with a rural Ireland of still unquestioned values, domestic security and close, almost tribal familial ties'.[34] Here the publishing renaissance taps into nostalgia for the political and cultural forces that delayed it. Elsewhere, the industry survives by a combination of subsidy and the niche-marketing of books that feed Ireland's obsession with its own history and culture. Belfast's Blackstaff Press, a regional publishing house in the fullest sense, though with an all-Ireland scope, has been significant in providing a range of articulation from poetry to autobiography to local history to politics that simply did not exist in the North before 1969. Yet Blackstaff, even with subsidy from the Arts Council of Northern Ireland, the Community Relations Council, and other sources has never been free from financial anxiety. To take an example from the Republic: Gallery Press has done well to keep or poach Irish poets from Oxford University Press or Bloodaxe (though never, it seems, from Faber and Faber). Yet its founder, Peter Fallon, in interviews given to mark the Press's quarter-century (1970–95), spoke of problems with promotion, sales, and reviewing coverage. Gallery receives 63 per cent subsidy from An Chomhairle Ealaion, the Republic's Arts Council, and also subsidy from the Arts Council of Northern Ireland. Cultural prestige, however, is an invisible asset. Gallery's anniversary reading was launched by President Robinson at the Abbey Theatre in an atmosphere of national self-congratulation. The spectacle of authors expressing such public gratitude to their publisher was rather unusual.[35]

The picture is not all one of underlying anxiety sublimated by Irish forms of hype. Academic publishing is starting to expand.[36] Co-publication with British or American firms reaches new readers. Publishers gain financially from being talent-spotters

[34] Brian Fallon, 'Paperback Choice', *Irish Times*, 13 Apr. 1996.
[35] There is an interview with, and a set of tributes to, Peter Fallon in *Irish Literary Supplement*, 14/2 (Fall 1995), 4–6. See also *Poetry Ireland Review*, 34 (Spring 1992), 32–7.
[36] In addition to the well-established Gill and Macmillan, Institute of Irish Studies, and Irish Academic Press, Cork University Press has increased its output during the last five years.

for the metropolis. They often cooperate effectively, for instance, in marketing abroad, although still more could be achieved.[37] Their small-scale enterprises persist as take-over gales sweep the metropolitan landscape. And the plus side of the national or regional stake in publishing is that subsidy will probably continue for the sake of status.

Ireland was the featured country at the 1996 Frankfurt Book Fair: an opportunity accorded very high priority by the An Chomhairle Ealaion. Frankfurt was about national self-image as well as about selling international rights. In the Frankfurt edition of *Books Ireland*, Gerhard Heimler, a German publisher, explains the German 'enthusiasm' for Ireland in a manner that suggests once again the potential and danger of the literary export market as it influences critical reception:

It seems to date back to a romanticised and idealist nineteenth-century image of the Emerald Isle as symbolising everything noble and good. Add to this the experience of an oppressed and enslaved [*sic*] people and there is the recipe for sympathy and solidarity. Peace-loving and innocent, the Irish are seen as devoid of any ambition to dominate world politics, and their heroes fight with words rather than swords.[38]

Gerald Dawe, editor of the literary magazine *Krino*, has criticized the co-option of Irish literature as a national asset, its translation from heretic to icon, and the drift towards a simplistic and cosy view of the writer's public role: 'Writers have been urged to become guru-like figures addressing "historical problems" . . . Somehow, though, the sharp edge of criticism, the exploration of the structure and contemporary meaning of a writer's work, has blurred into a "themey" mist.'[39] For John Boland and others, more publishing can mean worse, especially when joined to the current fashion for Ireland: 'there's far too much Irish writing being published over the last few years . . . [especially] fiction . . . aspirant writers and incapable publishers [are] aided and abetted by an international literary vogue which suggests that Irish writers can do no wrong and by an official ethos at home declaring that artistic creativity is

---

[37] 'The American agencies . . . feel that Irish publishers could do more to boost their performance in the US.' *Books Ireland*, 197 (Sept. 1996), 207.
[38] Ibid. 203.
[39] Gerald Dawe, *A Real Life Elsewhere* (Belfast, 1993), 35.

magically in us all'.[40] Here the problem is 'theme' as in themed (Irish) pubs.

It may be relevant that the most conspicuous way in which reviews of Irish books reached Frankfurt in 1996 was through a special edition of the *TLS*. The majority of literary reviews read by Irish people appear in the *Observer*, the *Independent on Sunday*, the *TLS*, the *London Review of Books*, and *The Times Higher Educational Supplement*. The only Irish national newspaper to have real standing or policy in this area is the *Irish Times*. As for Northern Irish newspapers, the record is mostly dreadful. Over all, the Scottish press does better. The main Irish periodicals that review literary works are either academic journals—the *Irish Review*, the *Irish University Review*—or magazines such as *Krino*, *Poetry Ireland Review*, *Graph*, the *Honest Ulsterman*, the *Linen Hall Review*. All of these have relatively small circulations. *Books Ireland* is essentially a trade journal, more notable for listings and interviews than for the interest of its reviews. The only *New Statesman*-like periodical is *Fortnight* magazine, which lives from hand to mouth, appears monthly (yes) in the North, and sells about 3,000 copies on the strength of its political coverage.[41] Ireland has generally lacked the English left-wing tradition of radical intellectual journals, just as it has lacked a tradition of radical intellectuals. Left-wing parties have rarely been strong in Ireland, and when they have been strong (as in Labour Party membership of the former coalition government), they have hardly been left-wing. Public subsidy is, of course, a factor in the multiplication and stamina of magazines: in 1954 Hubert Butler could not find enough money to establish a cross-border journal to be called *The Bridge*.[42] The

---

[40] *Irish Times*, 6 Apr. 1996.

[41] The *Irish Review* is currently published by Cork University Press. The *Irish University Review* is edited by Christopher Murray, Department of Anglo-Irish Literature, University College, Dublin. *Krino* is edited by Gerald Dawe, PO Box 65, Dun Laoghaire, Co. Dublin. *Poetry Ireland Review* is published by Poetry Ireland, Dublin Castle, Dublin 2. *Graph*, recently revived, is published by Cork University Press. The *Honest Ulsterman* is edited by Tom Clyde at 49 Main Street, Greyabbey, County Down BT22 2NF. The *Linen Hall Review* is published by the Linen Hall Library, Donegall Square North, Belfast BT1 5GD. *Books Ireland* is published by Jeremy Addis at 11 Newgrove Avenue, Dublin 4. *Fortnight* magazine is published at 7 Lower Crescent, Belfast BT7 1NR.

[42] See 'Crossing the Border', in Hubert Butler, *Grandmother and Wolfe Tone* (Dublin, 1990), 64–8.

Honest Ulsterman, founded by James Simmons, has lasted since 1968; the bi-annual *Krino* and *Irish Review* since 1986. A special fiftieth issue of *Poetry Ireland Review* (discussed below) came out in summer 1996. Some of these magazines grew up in close association with new generations of writers, North and South; and the *Honest Ulsterman* in particular has usually maintained an independent-minded critical edge.

To what extent do reviews and critical articles in the literary magazines connect with public debate about Irish culture and politics, or manifest intellectually 'an international emphasis and spread of concerns'?[43] Such were the ambitions of *Atlantis* (1970–3) and the longer lasting *Crane Bag* (1977–85) edited by the philosopher Richard Kearney. The *Crane Bag* was not a review of books, and the literary items that appeared there sometimes dissolved into Gerald Dawe's ' "themey" mist'.[44] Conversely, in the mid-1980s the *Honest Ulsterman* sponsored a 'Critical Forum' on cultural politics edited by John Wilson Foster, who claimed that 'traditions of expression, thought, and behaviour—which some regard as Ireland's lifeblood—are currently being placed in the critical centrifuge'. After several lively interventions, however, the Forum lapsed into silence.[45] *Fortnight*, *Irish Review* and *Graph*, addressed to different audiences, keep a foot in both camps, but there are strong pressures in the direction of specialism and there is no equivalent of the *LRB*. Peter Denman, who diagnoses a post-war shift from 'predominantly social and polemical to . . . predominantly literary and critical' magazines, argues that, in a state the size of the Republic, the 'broadcast documentary, interview, and latterly phone-in, have in many respects made the journal redundant as a forum for debate'. Meanwhile the 'little magazine' struggles on as 'the *samizdat* of the imagination, a literary undergrowth that flowers in conditions of neglect'.[46] Nevertheless, as Dawe implies, more precise negotiations between literary criticism and other Irish forums are desirable. Given the historical prominence of the literary intellectual, to which an age of sociologists,

---

[43] Denman, 'Ireland's Little Magazines', 142.

[44] See Richard Kearney, *The Crane Bag Book of Irish Studies* (Dublin, 1982).

[45] *Honest Ulsterman*, 82 (Winter 1986), 29. This issue, which inaugurates the Forum, features a dialogue between Foster and Richard Kearney.

[46] Denman, 'Ireland's Little Magazines', 135, 145.

economists and cultural studies has not quite succeeded, literature will be co-opted in any case.

4

The *Irish Times* book pages (two every Saturday, with a 'Book
of the Day' on weekdays) are another place where literature,
history and politics rub shoulders, though without necessarily
communicating. Since 1961 there have been only three literary
editors: the novelist Terence de Vere White (until 1977); Brian
Fallon, chiefly known as an art critic; and, from 1988, another
novelist, John Banville. This contrasts with greater mobility in
London, where, even if some editors stay put, most of the eggs
are not in one editorial basket. This underlines the difference
that, for good or ill, an individual can make in a small country.
    Many contingencies, not always under the literary editor's
control, shape a particular set of reviews on a particular day.
Also, general book pages have to cater for politics, the visual
arts, science, children's books and so on. Banville has been
accused of devoting both too much and too little space to Irish,
and especially Irish-published, books. The latter charge, however, is brought more frequently. His own aesthetic has always
been anti-local and devoted to the premisses of international
high modernism. He said in 1979: 'I never really thought about
Irish literature as such. I don't really think that specifically
"national" literatures are of terribly great significance. Perhaps
for a country's self-esteem . . . if I were to look about for a
stream to be part of I would certainly look to America or
Europe.'[47] This produces some internal conflict on the book
pages. It also produces infuriated letters from Irish publishers.
The map of fiction reviews favours novelists who are not from
'these islands' or in thrall to traditional narrative. Poetry from
abroad gets less coverage.
    I monitored the *Irish Times*'s Saturday book pages for three
months, from the end of August to the end of October 1995.
The most 'Irish' week featured five Irish publishers out of eleven,
or out of twenty-two if you count 'Paperback Choice': an

---

[47] Interview with Ronan Sheehan, *Crane Bag*, 3/1 (1979), 76–84, quoted in
Rudiger Imhof, *John Banville: A Critical Introduction* (Dublin 1989), 10.

anthology of women's poetry, and four novels swept into the category 'Recent Fiction from Irish Publishers'. However, there were also long reviews of Jennifer Johnston's *The Illusionist* and Heaney's *The Redress of Poetry*—a better-informed review (by Brian Lynch) than anything in the English press; and, an instance of significant reciprocity between the national and international, Banville himself reviewing Milan Kundera's *Testaments Betrayed*, in a tone possibly directed at recent fiction from Irish publishers: 'This is a bracingly ill-tempered book . . . a spirited defence of the autonomy of art against meddlers, hopeless do-gooders such as Kafka's friend Max Brod, and critics who imagine that the work of art should be an unmediated slice of life.'[48]

Thanks to market forces, crude slices of book-life now get on to the literary pages of the *Irish Times*: the photographs sent out by publishers of show-biz biography, best-seller lists, the need to cram brief notices into 'Paperback Choice'. One Saturday there were photographs of Prince Charles, Salman Rushdie and Linford Christie. The space for 'reviews' is shrinking. In the same week, John Boland's column reported on a wonderful example of unhealthy collusion between the English and Irish literary environments, and between varieties of publicity-seeking. Under the heading 'Bloodaxe Bags the Taoisigh [plural of Taoiseach]' we are told: 'Next Wednesday in the [former] House of Lords on College Green, Taoiseach John Bruton will be launching Micheal O'Siadhail's latest book of poems . . . the following Monday . . . former Taoiseach Charles J. Haughey will launch Brendan Kennelly's new collection . . . This reception is being sponsored by Allied Irish Banks.'[49] This could either testify to the high public profile of poetry in Ireland or to its accelerating corruption. The hype, mercifully, did not influence the *Irish Times* reviews.

When I examined another two months of *Irish Times* book pages (April–May 1996), much the same pattern emerged. One Saturday featured five Irish-published books; another, seven Irish books from British or American publishers. 'Paperback Choice' continued to be monopolized by Penguin *et al.* Up to a point, aside from the paper's need to cover non-Irish books, it is

---

[48] *Irish Times*, 16 Sept. 1995.   [49] Ibid.

leading Irish writers themselves who (by publishing in Britain) make things difficult for Irish publishers. Further, while the pool of reviewers during 1995–6 included Banville himself, John McGahern and Denis Donoghue, the critical edge is blunted by Banville's tendency to rely on staff journalists; to allow the same reviewers to keep reviewing the same kind of books; and to assign poor collections of Irish-published verse to a soft reviewer rather than make connections with the criteria for evaluating Derek Mahon or Medbh McGuckian. There *is* lively critical debate with reference to contemporary Irish literature. It can be picked up here and there, among writers, among some academic critics, in some magazines. But it does not always make the book pages of the *Irish Times*.

Irish poetry presses can usually count on reviews in little magazines (not only Irish magazines); fiction tends to be less fortunate in this respect. Yet *Poetry Ireland Review*, which is on a par with *Poetry Review* (London) and whose editor, usually a poet, changes every year, shows signs of a crisis of confidence. There is explicit and implicit anxiety about critical standards. The critic Terence Brown began his editorship by stating: 'The problem of criticism in Ireland remains to be solved'; Peter Denman by promising: 'I hope to have reviews of as many books of Irish poetry as possible.'[50] Richard Hayes, having indexed issues 1–20, concluded that criticism had, indeed, been marginalized, that there had been 'inadequate review space for new collections by Irish poets', and that 'the separation . . . of scholarship and . . . criticism from poetry has been a silent sub-text to *PIR* from the beginning'.[51] The incidence of reviews has increased, although their depth and rigour varies. This seems to be correlated with editorial permissiveness in the selection of poems. Like the London *Poetry Review*, *Poetry Ireland Review* must make up for newspaper neglect, and juggle the following elements: poems (submitted in huge numbers), reviews, longer articles or review-articles, recognition of poetry from other countries,[52] topic-based issues (e.g. 'Poetry and Politics'). Irish-

[50] *Poetry Ireland Review*, 14 (Autumn 1985), 6; 34 (Spring 1992), 1.

[51] See Richard Hayes, '*Poetry Ireland Review*, Issues 1–21: A Review', *Poetry Ireland Review*, 36 (Autumn 1992), 53–66.

[52] The degree of engagement with poetry from elsewhere varies from editor to editor, but coverage is less extensive than in *Poetry Review*. There have been occasional special issues, such as an excellent North American issue, 43/44

language poetry, today enjoying a revival, also has to be represented. Nevertheless, Hayes's identification of an uneasy subtext hits the mark, especially when he also notices unexamined 'national' assumptions or a phase of complacent insularity. As in *Poetry Review*, some reviewers subscribe to the descriptive, everybody-welcome, school of criticism—amateurish reviews of amateur poets: 'a major and long-awaited event in Irish poetry'; 'These books all imagine journeys'; 'Some of X's most engaging poems grow out of his identification with place.' Poets reviewing other poets worry about their own critical reception, and everyone watches their tongues more closely in a small and tribal country. These inhibitions compound the universal problem defined by Nuala Ni Dhomhnaill: 'If you talk in a negative way about someone's poem you're really attacking primary narcissism.'[53] That appeared in the critical backbone of *Poetry Ireland Review*: 'Pickings and Choosings', Dennis O'Driscoll's column of *obiter dicta* on poetry taken from many sources.

There is also tension, not unique to Ireland, between the desire to promote what might be a dying art and the need to expose it to bracing critical winds. Further, the centre that is failing to hold is precisely the doubly critical ground where literary journalism keeps poetry at a wary distance from the academy. A brash new English poetry magazine, aptly named *Thumbscrew*, is a healthy sign. Some academics, however, ominously want reviewers to have more truck with theory. In *New Relations: The Refashioning of British Poetry 1980–94*, David Kennedy takes up Anthony Easthope's agenda:

The poetry scene, in fact, wants the endorsement of the Academy but thinks it can avoid the fundamentals of contemporary critical enquiry: the exposing and upsetting of undeclared and unanalysed assumptions; the refusal to ignore the problematics of discourse brought into play, when, for example, one gender writes in the persona of the other; or an alertness to questions of sexuality or nationality.[54]

Throughout his study, designed to complement the Bloodaxe anthology *The New Poetry* of which he was co-editor, Kennedy

---

(Autumn/Winter 1994), ed. Chris Agee, which includes Irish poets writing about American poets whose work they admire.

[53] *Poetry Ireland Review*, 38 (Summer 1993), 110.

[54] David Kennedy, *New Relations: The Refashioning of British Poetry 1980–94* (Bridgend, 1996), 13–14.

defers to 'poetries', thus atomizing art and ceding evaluation to
ethnicity, gender, class. (His theoretical correctness does not
make him especially alert to Irish contexts.) The real issue for
both literary scholarship and literary journalism is how to take
account of 'contemporary critical enquiry', in its more sensitive
guises, without abandoning either aesthetic discrimination or all
contact with poetry's common readers. And the academy, as
audience, often fails to analyse its own influential assumptions
in the light of local particularities. For instance, Irish literature,
having been caught before, usually tries to struggle out of
ethnicity, not back into it. And Kennedy's 'problematics of
discourse' sounds rather like an Irish censor anxious to prevent
intercourse on the page between poets and their unconscious.

Irish literary studies involve a distinctive nexus of relations
between older and newer critical approaches, one further complicated by internal strains, probably evident in this essay, and
by the interpretive diaspora. To put the matter negatively: there
is a difference between the sentimentality about Ireland that
may visit the true-born English reviewer, Irish expatriates, and
born-again Irish-in-Britain or 'Irish Americans'. The American
academic journals that review Irish poetry, fiction and associated critical texts are *Eire/Ireland*, *The Recorder: The Journal of
the American Irish Historical Society*, and the *Irish Literary
Supplement*. It is symptomatic that the latter's title mimics the
TLS, without its actually being a supplement *to* anything. In
these periodicals American academics who write in a more or
less traditional manner mingle with Irish academics of similar
inclinations, and the tone is generally upbeat, although a few
honourable exceptions bring themselves to criticize an Irish
writer.[55] Elsewhere I have argued that the export-market (in
books and authors) and cultural tourism, now attached to Irish
literature, have coalesced with the blandness of which Dana
Gioia accuses American poetry criticism; and that even when
critics based in Ireland review for American audiences, they are
tempted to pull their punches and join in what Yeats called 'the

---

[55] For instance, James Scruton questions some 'unexamined' pronouncements in
Eavan Boland's collection of essays, *Object Lessons*, *Irish Literary Supplement*,
14/2 (Fall 1995), 8; and Nicholas Grene and David Krause probe the reasons for
the comparative artistic failure of Brian Friel's play, *Molly Sweeney*, *Irish Literary
Supplement*, 14/1 (Spring 1995), 25.

old gush & folly'.[56] More awkward critics have had their copy spiked by the *Irish Literary Supplement*.

The dynamics are different in Britain, since it is closer to home—not that every Irish writer or critic would admit this—and the quarterly journal *Irish Studies Review*, sponsored by the British Association for Irish Studies, quite successfully combines theoretical awareness and inter-disciplinarity with an accessible reviewing style. It also multiplies the angles by drawing on a range of expatriate reviewers and presenting a pluralistic critical mix from both islands. *Irish Studies Review* is less anxious than its American counterpart to advertise or celebrate 'Irishness'. With Irish Studies continuing to develop in Britain, contemporary Irish writing may be reviewed both as books and as 'Irish' books. As in the US, on the first count there may be too little context; on the second, too much. There remains the need to communicate, critically and culturally, between audiences, between specialist and non-specialist readers. Some recent 'Irish' issues of American journals—*Poetry Chicago, Southern Review*—are, in certain respects, almost as indulgent as the established Irish Studies channels. Besides providing information and a showcase, they might also have focused the sharp eye of distance. It is ironical that Irish poets of the 1960s should have looked to America, and that John Banville should question the priority of the national, when the wider world appears so vulnerable to Celtic seductions. 'Poetries' is bad news for Yeats's desire to make Irish criticism as 'international' as possible, even while promoting a national literature. To back this up with a statistic from literary scholarship: Michael Allen has edited a Macmillan 'New Casebook' (1997) on the poetry of Seamus Heaney. Most of the material he includes is by Irish academic critics. There are several essays from England; nothing from North America, despite the output there. I would add a brighter coda to all this: in some cases, as in discussion of Paul Muldoon's poetry, contemporary Irish writing influences theory and criticism—a contrast with Kennedy's demand for theory to influence contemporary writing and reviewing. Which is the cart, which the horse, does not appear to be so clear-cut.

The unbalanced critical economy also, of course, has to do

[56] See Edna Longley, 'Irish Bards and American Audiences', *Southern Review*, 31/3 (Summer 1995), 757-71.

with confused signals, vocabularies, and definitions emanating
from Ireland itself. On the academic front, we are only beginning to question the historical relevance of Anglo-American
literary criticism, or to analyse relations between American
modernism and Ireland, let alone weigh the usefulness of more
recent theoretical imports. There is also an interdisciplinary
argument between historians and literary critics which pivots on
narratives of history. Dispatches from these various fronts continue to appear.[57] Two factors have prevented academics and
literary intellectuals from advancing the argument on such
issues as rapidly as they might. One is not so much ideological
difference in itself as the adversarial, implicitly sectarian struc-
tures that theology and politics have put in place. When trying
to build his 'bridge' of communication, Hubert Butler said: 'Too
many people would sooner be silent or untruthful than disloyal
to their side . . . there is always a drift towards crisis, a gentle,
persistent pressure towards some simple alignment of Good and
Evil, Friend and Enemy.'[58] In Ireland 'Who speaks?' has been a
long-standing question, and sometimes the only one asked
about a critical or political proposition.

The second factor is, once again, 'little room'—where not
only politics induce claustrophobia. Ireland's microcosmic potential for the writer, as the case of Patrick Kavanagh indicates,
can be offset by affiliations from which it is hard for criticism to
detach itself. 'Interpretive communities' have not yet floated free
of communities. While keeping alive the will o' the wisp of a
literature and criticism in touch with an entire society, this also
encourages, in Gerald Dawe's words, 'deference to received
wisdom', given the weakness of any civic, post-Enlightenment
'tradition of opposition . . . to political, religious, or cultural

---

[57] See, most recently, Ciaran Brady, ed., *Interpreting Irish History: The Debate on
Historical Revisionism* (Dublin, 1994); Edna Longley, *The Living Stream: Literature
and Revisionism in Ireland* (Newcastle on Tyne, 1994); Declan Kiberd, *Inventing
Ireland* (London, 1995); Terry Eagleton, *Heathcliff and the Great Hunger: Studies
in Irish Culture* (London, 1995); Patricia Coughlan and Alex Davis, eds., *Modernism and Ireland: The Poetry of the 1930s* (Cork, 1995); Luke Gibbons, *Transforma-
tions in Irish Culture* (Cork, 1996); George D. Boyce and Alan O'Day, *The Making
of Irish History: Revisionism and the Revisionist Controversy* (London, 1996);
Richard Kirkland, *Literature and Culture in Northern Ireland since 1965: Moments
of Danger* (London, 1996).
[58] Butler, *Grandmother and Wolfe Tone*, 65.

orthodoxies'.[59] Hence the Irish coinage and currency of the word 'begrudgery'. To give some examples: an *Irish Times* editorial warned against begrudgery when Seamus Heaney won the Nobel prize (although the warning would have been more to the point when it was won by Yeats); when Gerry Adams launched *Before the Dawn: An Autobiography* in Dublin (September 1996), he noticed 'a few begrudgers' among the audience. More hearteningly, the composer Raymond Deane has written an article called 'In Praise of Begrudgery', which argues that 'In Ireland the standards by which we evaluate art are based almost exclusively on mercantile premises, and on a repertoire of vainglorious delusions about "how others see us"'.[60] 'Begrudgery', then, not only signals low expectations about the disinterested exercise of judgement, but can also be deployed to intimidate judgement: to pre-empt any unwelcome criticism as subjective or ideological. It thus denies, as do other conditions I have discussed, the possibility of taking on the responsibilities of criticism. Ernest Boyd's warning, uttered before the Easter Rising compounded the problems that he diagnoses, remains to the point: 'We cannot expect others to show more discrimination than ourselves.'[61]

---

[59] Gerald Dawe, 'Rights of Passage: Poetry and Teaching', *Poetry Ireland Review*, 35 (Summer 1992), 64.

[60] Raymond Deane, 'In Praise of Begrudgery', *Irish Times*, 24 Sept. 1996.

[61] See epigraph to this article, from Ernest A. Boyd, *Ireland's Literary Renaissance* (Dublin and London, 1916), 397–8.

12

What We Don't Talk About When We Talk About Poetry: Some Aporias of Literary Journalism

MARJORIE PERLOFF

Grub Street and the Ivory Tower: as earlier essays in this book have demonstrated, the worlds of literary journalism and literary scholarship have been, for at least the past two centuries, much more closely allied than is commonly thought. But what about the third term in the equation, the literary itself? Specifically, how does 'literary journalism' confront the poetry written in its own time, along with the scholarly reception and theorization of that poetry?

Writing about poetry and poetics has for a long time occupied an anomalous place in the larger humanistic discourse in which it is embedded. Take, for example, two long reviews that appeared just a few months apart in *The Times Literary Supplement*. The first is a review by Richard Sennett of four books on contemporary architectural theory (18 September 1992, 3–4), the second, one by Glyn Maxwell of eight books on contemporary poetry and poetics (29 January 1993, 9–10).

Richard Sennett is a well-known social critic, currently Professor of Sociology and Humanities at New York University, whose most recent book, *The Conscience of the Eye* (1991) is subtitled *The Design and Social Life of Cities*. The books under review in this, a special issue on 'Cities', which also featured articles by Gavin Stamp, David Rieff and Saskia Sassen, were Jean-Louis Cohen's *Le Corbusier and the Mystique of the USSR: Theories and Projects for Moscow, 1928–1936*

A different version of this essay appears in Marjorie Perloff's *Poetry On and Off the Page* (Northwestern University Press, 1998).

(Princeton, 1991), Robert Harbison's *The Built, the Unbuilt, and the Unbuildable* (Thames and Hudson, 1992), Beatriz Colomina's collection, *Sexuality and Space* (Princeton, 1992), and Anthony Vidler's *The Architectural Uncanny* (MIT, 1992). Sennett wrote about these books as an informed insider: he has himself been active in the symposia held at the Princeton University School of Architecture, where some of the material in question had been aired. His essay takes it as a given that urban spaces are now largely disaster areas but argues that architects neither are to blame for this state of affairs nor can be expected to come up with blueprints for some kind of Utopian renewal. Rather, he suggests, in sympathy with the theorists under review, that what is needed at the moment is perhaps a better understanding of how these spaces actually work, how buildings, streets and open spaces relate to the human body.

Cohen's book on Le Corbusier supplies Sennett with his historical frame, for it details the great architect's design for the proposed Palace of the Soviets in Moscow, a design based on the attempt to integrate, inside and outside, the built form to its surrounding space so as to downplay ceremony and create a truly popular architecture. The rejection of the plan by the authorities in 1932 'in favour of a standard-issue monument in neo-Palladian style by Zhotovsky' is taken, both by Cohen and by Sennett, as emblematic of the difficulties of trying to invent a genuinely 'popular' form of architecture. Perhaps, then, as Robert Harbison and the contributors to *Sexuality and Space* argue, the best that buildings can do is to create what Harbison calls 'fictions of value'. Harbison 'sees the experience of industrial ruin as inviting a radically innovative response'; in the case of Richard Rogers's Lloyd's Building, for example, the elaborate 'mock-ruins' unexpectedly built from steel and glass have a curious way of altering our sense of time. And Anthony Vidler's *Architectural Uncanny* (a book that has since become celebrated in discussions of the postmodern arts) carries this notion one step further. To counter the deadness of contemporary neutralized urban spaces, Vidler suggests, one must open oneself to the 'uncanny' of crossings, must try to break down the existing borders between suburb, strip and urban centre and see what their intersection will produce. Loss, dislocation, invasion: these become positive values.

Another reviewer might have been less sympathetic to the works under review than Sennett, but I think most readers would agree that his is an interesting, sophisticated, well-informed piece that helps one to understand what's going on in recent urban theory. And Sennett's knowledge of the social context, his own participation in the debate on what to do with urban spaces, makes him an excellent expositor.

Glyn Maxwell sees his role rather differently. The books that he was assigned to review are, in fairness to him, as curious an assortment of apples and oranges as one can imagine.[1] First, two critical studies of established poets: *The Art of Derek Walcott*, a collection of essays edited by Stuart Brown (Seren, 1989) and James Booth's monograph *Philip Larkin, Writer* (Harvester, 1992). Next, a biography, A. T. Tolley's *My Proper Ground: A Study of the Work of Philip Larkin and its Development* (Edinburgh, 1992). These were followed by three more theoretical works: Linda Reinfeld's *Language Poetry: Writing as Rescue* (Baton Rouge, La., 1992), Charles Bernstein's *A Poetics* (Harvard, 1992), and Anthony Easthope and John O. Thompson's *Contemporary Poetry Meets Modern Theory* (Harvester, 1991). These three books are related: the poet Charles Bernstein's manifestos, theoretical prose poems and cultural explorations collected in *A Poetics* stand behind Linda Reinfeld's analytical history of the Language Poetry movement in the US, and Easthope and Thompson, for their part, have brought together a variety of critics who hold the common view that the more radical poetries today have much in common with poststructuralist theory. The three, in any case, have nothing in common with the Walcott and Larkin studies on the one hand or with Robert Pack's *The Long View: Essays on the Discipline of Hope and Poetic Craft* (Cambridge, Mass., 1991), on the other. Pack is an American poet who has been around for a long time and is best known as an anthologist. His essays are avowedly personal, impressionistic and casual. Finally, the review includes a study of Emersonian-Jamesian poetics, *Poetry and*

---

[1] The choice of books to be reviewed, here as elsewhere, is of course the assigning editor's. But we should bear in mind that, in the case of omnibus reviews, the reviewer normally reserves the right to omit specific items (and could in any case decline the commission). In what follows, then, I attribute responsibility to Maxwell rather than to the *TLS* editor.

Pragmatism (Faber, 1992), by one of the most distinguished academic critics in the US, Richard Poirier.

Unlike the four books reviewed by Sennett, which are closely related, both historically and ideologically, Maxwell's list thus has no rationale, except that somehow all eight books (published, incidentally, over a four-year period) have some bearing on contemporary poetry, whatever that is. One should note that Maxwell was given some four columns to cover eight books, as against the six columns allotted to Sennett. More importantly: whereas Sennett is on a par with the authors he reviews, having written comparable books and essays as a fellow-worker in the field, Maxwell seems to have been assigned this review in his capacity not as a published poetry critic or scholar or theorist (none of which he is) but as a poet. Indeed, it has become increasingly common in literary journalism for theoretical and historical studies of poetry like Reinfeld's and Poirier's, to be reviewed—when they are reviewed at all—by certified poets. (A certified poet is one who has published a book or two of poems with a mainstream publisher and has received a few respectful reviews in the mainstream press.) The parallel, in the case of the architecture books, would be to have an architect, perhaps a partner in a respected firm that specializes in office buildings on Park Avenue or in suburban tract housing, review Anthony Vidler's *Architectural Uncanny*.

Maxwell begins with a set of assumptions: (1) the 'great poem' induce[s] strong, conflicting emotions in every reader who reads it in its language; (2) 'it is always instantly memorized'; (3) once its author is dead, it quickly gets overinterpreted, has meanings read into it, and a myth of its author comes into being that threatens to displace the 'authentic' poet who wrote it; (4) 'Poets know what is worth saying about other poets'; and (5) the concept of 'schools' is 'especially unhelpful'. All these theorems are put before us as if they were simply a matter of common sense, even though critical theory of the past half-century has dismantled, step by step, the notion of the authentic *ur*-poem, destroyed by later misreadings, the poem as catharsis of 'conflicting emotions' (shades of I. A. Richards), best understood by other poets. As for the memorability criterion, which Maxwell puts forward as if it were the second law of thermodynamics, it does not allow for free verse (hard to memorize), prose poetry or visual poetries—all of them very prominent and exciting today. Memorability depends, of course, on rhyme and metre; it's much easier to memorize *Don Juan* than *The Prelude*, Emily Dickinson's short hymn stanzas than Whitman's long poems, Robert Frost than William Carlos Williams. And how would one 'memorize' Ian Hamilton Finlay's poetic compositions? Or Susan Howe's?

Maxwell doesn't worry about such thorny issues. He knows what he likes and the books on Walcott and Larkin are deemed worthy, not because their contributors are doing anything special, but because Walcott and Larkin are worthy. The reviewer doesn't worry much about them, nor about Pack and Poirier (the latter gets rather short shrift), his witty barbs being reserved for the so-called language poets discussed by Linda Reinfeld, by some of Anthony Easthope's contributors, and by Charles Bernstein, himself one of the founders of the movement. Maxwell doesn't like the concept of the movement or school, which animates Reinfeld's discussion of language poetry, but he never bothers to investigate if the poets in question—Bernstein, Howe, Michael Palmer, Lyn Hejinian, Clark Coolidge, Ron Silliman—do, in fact, constitute one. Never mind: the main thing is that these, to Maxwell, self-evidently worthless poets continue to write about each other 'long after the magazine that gave them their name [$L=A=N=G=U=A=G=E$] has disappeared, along with any likelihood of anyone else taking an interest'. And further: theirs is a poetry of 'complete and deliberate impenetrability', a poetry that 'jettison[s] the notion that language can communicate'. The twin goals of poetry—to teach and to delight—are thus totally violated.

Unlike Richard Sennett, then, Glyn Maxwell has no commitment to the approaches taken by his subjects. On the contrary, he gives no evidence that he has ever read a single poem by Charles Bernstein or the other poets Reinfeld discusses; indeed, it is doubtful that he has so much as looked at *A Poetics*, since Bernstein's arguments are cited only from Reinfeld's book, as if her account, which is after all an interpretation of Bernstein's theory, were simply equivalent to it. As for the Easthope-Thompson volume, I can testify to the fact that he hasn't read my own essay in that collection, of which he writes, 'Elsewhere, Marjorie Perloff celebrates the brick wall of Steve

McCaffery's work by invoking Ezra Pound—odd how these radical, dethroning writers will gulp whole the dicta ("Make it new!") of an old apologist for fascism.' My essay on McCaffery's *Lag* never mentions Pound's name nor do I say anything in it about 'Make it new!'. But even if I did, the assumption that a Pound echo in McCaffery would somehow link this poet to Fascism takes one's breath away. And, incidentally, how and why is McCaffery's poem a 'brick wall'? Is it enough merely so to pronounce?

Maxwell's is thus a review that blithely ignores the facts, not to mention the poetic principles involved. The reviewer's assertion that 'no one' takes an interest in the language poetry movement is belied by so many articles, books and symposia, not only in the US but also in the UK (as in France, China, Japan, and Australia) that the statement hardly warrants serious rebuttal. Indeed, this review would hardly be worth talking about, were it not so typical. For the fact is that whereas *TLS* reviews of books on architectural theory, on feminist studies, on the Elizabethan theatre, or on philosophy (the same issue included a brilliant, excoriating piece by Arthur Danto on Charles Taylor's *Ethics of Authenticity*) are largely responsible pieces, written by experts in their various fields, the journal's discourse about contemporary poetry (perhaps about contemporary literary forms in general) is largely impressionistic, uninformed and philistine. And the *TLS* is by no means the worst offender.

Here, for example, is Anthony Libby, a poet-critic who teaches at Ohio State University, on Stephen Dunn's *New and Selected Poems: 1974–94* (Norton, 1994) and Stephen Dobyns's *Velocities: New and Selected Poems, 1966–1992* (Viking-Penguin, 1994) in the *New York Times Book Review* (*NYTBR*) for 15 January 1995:

Are all the best poems about loss? They are not, probably, about happiness or love's sweet contentment, and the poet who aims to traverse those pleasant territories takes a hard road. . . . The heart of [Dunn's] collection records a long struggle to develop a voice true to Mr. Dunn's simple affirmations and proof against the cynical reader's resistance. . . . [As for Dobyns], his is a more traditional style of masculinity, somewhat cool or repressed, angry, torn by constant awareness that 'we are the creatures that love and slaughter'. . . . The triumph of Stephen Dobyns's poetry may be that it keeps that sense of play intact, without denying horrors. . . . His quirky imagination affirms by celebrating itself, if not the dark and clouded world.[2]

What is this supposed to mean? Why should the 'quirky imagination' of our time 'celebrate itself'? Why do we want poetry that conveys a 'somewhat cool or repressed masculinity'? And do we in fact need poetry to tell us that 'we are the creatures that love and slaughter'?

Or, to take a third example, consider the poet David Kirby's review of Marilyn Hacker's *Selected Poems, 1965–1990* (Norton, 1994), again in the *NYTBR*. Kirby begins by announcing, 'The history of recent literature is the history of the phrase "Only connect." Writers and readers have taken these words from E. M. Forster's *Howards End* as an exhortation, with "only" meaning "merely" or perhaps "exclusively".'[3] Those of us who don't quite subscribe to the notion that American poetry in the 1990s is written under the sign of E. M. Forster needn't worry. The reference functions merely as an acceptable literary lead-in, and Kirby quickly moves on to his more personal impressions: 'At a time when so many writers seem to be measuring life from a considerable remove, it is invigorating to watch Marilyn Hacker glad-handing her way through the world with a warm facility. And a formalism so colloquial as to undo any readerly stereotypes.'

The *NYTBR* has been castigated for not devoting enough space to poetry. For the period January–June 1995, of approximately 500 reviews, only five—1 per cent—deal with new poetry. But quantity is not the answer. Indeed, if journalistic discourse on poetry can't be better than these examples, one might prefer a moratorium on the half-hearted attempt to include, for the sake of some residual notion of 'culture', the occasional poetry review along with the occasional poem, the latter invariably presented inside a box as if to cordon it off from more important matters. But my modest proposal is not as pessimistic as it may sound. For I also want to suggest that the abysmal state of poetry reviewing is not, paradoxically, hurting the cause of poetry itself, which is, to my mind, extraordinarily healthy at the moment. Rather, there seems to be a mechanism at play that is making 'literary journalism' irrelevant so far as

---

[2] *NYTBR*, 15 Jan. 1995, 15.   [3] *NYTBR*, 12 Mar. 1995, 6.

contemporary literary production is concerned. It is this mechanism I want to explore.

History Lessons

Was poetry reviewing better in the Good Old Days? Is it only in recent years, thanks to the increasing commodification of our culture, that poetry has seemed to have no place in the public arena? Conservative critics like Dana Gioia would have us think so,[4] but a statistical survey of actual book reviewing tells us otherwise. My examples here are taken from what are generally regarded as the two leading book reviews in the United States: the *NYTBR*, at this writing exactly a hundred years old, still the review that can make or break a book so far as sales are concerned, and the *New York Review of Books*, which began publication in 1963 in response to the extended strike at the *New York Times* and quickly established itself as the intellectuals' book review of choice.

The first issue of *NYTBR* appeared on 10 October 1896 as what was then called the *Saturday Book Review Supplement*. Its avowed purpose, according to the introductory essay for the Arno Press Reprint (1968) by the then *Book Review* editor Francis Brown, was 'to bring to readers news of books, news of authors, news of publishing, literary news of all kinds'.[5] In 1896, this last category included such things as 'reports on the state of Oscar Wilde in Reading Gaol'. Indeed, there are continuing reports, throughout 1897, on Wilde's condition, which is declared 'beyond human endurance', and his consequent turn to spirituality (see Rowland Strong in the 12 June 1897 issue). Reviewing was thus a form of reporting, its aim being, as Brown puts it, 'to help the reader and buyer, not the writer or publisher'. The reviewer, Brown suggests, had the interests of the non-specialist reader in mind; he (the pronoun is used

---

[4] See Dana Gioia, *Can Poetry Matter?* (New York, 1992). Gioia claims that until 1960 or so, poetry had a wide circulation—it appeared in newspapers and popular magazines, along with political journalism, humour, fiction and reviews—and it was widely reviewed and discussed in the leading papers. But the quality of that 'it' is open to question, as I argue here.

[5] Brown's introduction (unpaginated) is reprinted as the headnote to each of the 72 Arno Reprint volumes, followed by Alfred Kazin's *A Sense of History*.

generically) functions as his reader's guide, philosopher and friend. It is his business to say of new books what there is in them in such wise that his reader may learn whether the book under notice will probably interest him. Knowledge, equity and candor are the chief elements in the equipment of the book reviewer. Two assumptions govern these and related statements. First, it was assumed that objective judgements on books could be made by more or less anonymous professional reviewers. (In the early years, the front-page leader was in fact anonymous.) And second, it was taken for granted that a review of 'literature' was just that—a review of novels, poems, plays, perhaps *belles-lettres*, not, as is prevalent today, primarily books on political, historical, psychological, anthropological subjects, on current events, biographies and memoirs. Reminiscing about the pre-First World War years, Brown writes:

In retrospect these were great literary years. . . . In verse, names were being made that would dominate for a long time to come: Yeats and Masefield, Ezra Pound, William Carlos Williams, Edward Arlington Robinson. In the novel it was the age of Conrad and Thomas Mann, Galsworthy, Anatole France, the still unappreciated Dreiser. Willa Cather wrote *Pioneers* [sic], D. H. Lawrence, *Sons and Lovers*, and there was always Mrs Wharton. Kipling in 1907 received a Nobel Prize at 42.

The canon would not be described all that differently today. And Brown is also proud to note that in 1922 *NYTBR* pronounced Joyce's *Ulysses* 'the most important contribution that has been made to fictional literature in the twentieth century' and that Proust's *Swann's Way* received high marks. In the 6 February 1897 issue, Paul Lawrence Dunbar's *Lyrics of Lowly Life*, published by Dodd, Mead & Co. with an intoduction by W. D. Howells, received extravagant (and anonymous) praise for its wit, keen satire, subtle humour, and 'rich colours'. Richard Le Gallienne, reviewing Dunbar's complete poems on 18 January 1914, went even further: the poems, he declared, 'have a certain classical rank in American literature by virtue of an excellence which is in need of no allowances on account of the poet's race'. Dunbar's is an 'authentic achievement which must give him a high and permanent place among the dialect poets of the world', and such poems as 'The Debt', written in standard English, are also singled out for praise and cited in full. One would be hard put to find an African-American poet today who has received this sort of attention in the *Times*.

But lest we wax nostalgic, it was also true that reviewing as spreading-the-word (more blurb than critique) ran into trouble as the volume of books increased sharply after the First World War. Indeed, not just their volume, but their variety. In 1909, after all, F. T. Marinetti had managed to get his first Futurist manifesto published on the front page of the Paris *Figaro*, where its competition was little more than the race-track news, the stockmarket quotations and the society news. After the war—a watershed for book reviews as for so much else—a larger literate (and voting) population demanded more from reviews, as from news articles and editorials. At the same time, the new Modernist poetry was often intentionally difficult and demanding. *The Waste Land* (1922), for example, could not be processed as readily as could the collections of short lyric poems to which audiences were accustomed, even if those poems were, like Dunbar's, by a black man. Eliot's long collage-poem, with its foreign phrases and fussy footnotes was not reviewed at all in *NYTBR*. By this time, in any case, books no longer meant just literary books. On 6 January 1924, for example, the front page of the now larger (thanks to increasing advertising space) book review was devoted to a French memoir, the former premier and war minister Paul Painlevé's *Comment j'ai nommé Foch et Petain*. The same issue has a review of Count Burian's memoir of the Kaiser Franz Joseph and of Bertrand Russell's *ABC of Atoms*. And by the early 1930s, the basic blueprint and layout that characterize the *NYTBR* to this day were in place. The lead article (on the cover, usually with a large photograph at the centre) tended to be a review of a 'major new novel' or of a substantial historical/social critique. On 14 January 1934, for example, the leader is a review of Pearl Buck's *The Mother*; on 28 January, Sinclair Lewis's *Work of Art*, on 4 February, Phyllis Bentley's *A Modern Tragedy* (with the headline 'A Novel that Clarifies Our Age'); and on 11 February, Oswald Spengler's *The Hour of Decision*.

Big novels, big ideas! What happens to poetry or to the more avant-garde literary productions in this context? Poetry could hardly be eliminated, a neo-Victorian, neo-Romantic culture continuing to demand its 'higher' presence, even as it does in today's *New Yorker*, *New Republic*, or *Atlantic*. But as slender books of poems continued to proliferate, the group review became normative, one of the reviewer's chief tasks thus being to find a common thread like Kirby's 'Only connect'. The reviewers tended to be themselves minor poets or, as in the founding days of *NYTBR*, professional journalists. Certainly there was no precedent for asking a poetry specialist (an academic critic or theorist, for example) to review these books. For poetry—and this bias is still with us—had come to be considered a category of writing to which the usual questions of expertise did not apply. As Pierre Bourdieu has demonstrated in his study of literary reception:

Poetry, by virtue of its restricted audience. . . . the consequent low profits, which make it the disinterested activity par excellence, and also its prestige, linked to the historical tradition initiated by the Romantics, is destined to charismatic legitimation. . . . Although the break between poetry and the mass readership has been virtually total since the late nineteenth century . . . poetry continues to represent the ideal model of literature for the least cultured consumers.[6]

Jimmy Carter's recent poetry venture is a case in point. 'I have always found it possible', said Carter on the publication of his best-selling *Always a Reckoning* (1995), 'to say things in my poems that would have been impossible to say in prose.' Things like how sad he was to have to kill his aged dog:

> Yesterday I killed him. I had known
> for months I could not let him live. I might
> have paid someone to end it, but I knew
> that after fifteen years of sharing life
> the bullet ending his must be my own.[7]

Try saying that bit of blank verse in prose! The newspaper reviewers, evidently impressed by the sheer disinterestedness of the former President's efforts, did not wish to be harsh. And

---

[6] See Pierre Bourdieu, 'The Field of Cultural Production, or: The Economic World Reversed' (Amsterdam, 1983), trans. Richard Nice in *The Field of Cultural Production: Essays on Art and Literature*, ed. Randal Johnson (New York, 1993), 51 and cf. figure 2 on p. 49.

[7] Jimmy Carter, 'Sport', *Always a Reckoning* (New York, 1995), 23.

soon Jimmy Carter was embarking on a book tour around the US and to Dylan Thomas's Wales.

The 14 January 1934 issue of the *NYTBR*, described earlier, typically has a full-page article on 'Six New Books of Verse by a Diversity of Poets'. Among the poets are Kimi Gengo, Adelaide Love, C. Arthur Coan, and Mary Owens Lewis. The reviewer, Percy Hutchinson, praises the poems in Adelaide Love's *The Slender Singing Tree* (its 'highly engaging title' is remarked upon) which are 'written with skill against a background of deep thought'. He cites 'The Lien':

> Relentless press of little things;
> Eternal haste to do them all;
> The prior claim upon our days
> Relinquished to the trivial.
>
> Our obligations never paid
> But endless and imperative.
> O life, why must you always leave
> So little time to live?

Somehow [*remarks Hutchinson*] this seems to us the possible utterance of a disciplined Emily Dickinson. Not, of course, that the real Emily could ever have been disciplined, either as to thought or poetic utterance . . . But . . . the Amherst spinster-poet must ever stand symbolically for her sex's expression of itself in poetry. Thus it seems to us that Adelaide Love carries on what might be termed the Emily Dickinson tradition, that is, she expresses herself fragmentarily while seeing with inclusive vision, and plucks at the heart-strings, but always with the most gentle touch, perceiving and transferring beauty.[8]

From our vantage point sixty years later, we can laugh at the very idea of Adelaide Love's little jingle being favourably compared to the work of the, alas, 'undisciplined' Emily Dickinson. But the problems of poetry reviewing confronting Percy Hutchinson were not all that different from those experienced by David Kirby in his review of Marilyn Hacker or even by Glyn Maxwell in his omnibus piece for the *TLS*. The mandate—to say something telling and original about five or ten unlike and generally unexceptional volumes of short personal lyrics—is not easy to fulfil. We can see this even in the more specifically

[8] *NYTBR*, 14 Jan. 1934, 14.

literary journals like the *Georgia Review* or the *Hudson Review*. Consider an article in *PN Review*, 80 (1991), in which T. J. G. Harris discusses Michael Hulse's *Eating Strawberries in the Necropolis* and Andrew Motion's *Love in a Life*, along with the first book, *Tale of the Mayor's Son*, by the very same Glyn Maxwell, who, being the newcomer in this group, gets one long paragraph:

Glyn Maxwell combines strictness of form with abrupt arbitrariness, a kind of headlong, thrown-together, jagged improvisation that, if it often has small attraction for the ear, certainly has, as Joseph Brodsky remarks on the back of the book, a 'propulsion . . . , owing in part to his tendency to draw metaphor from the syntax itself'. But the propulsion is not so often real as apparent, and one has the frequent impression that a device (a tricky self-reference or address to the reader, a drawing of metaphor from syntax, a blatant obscurity of one kind or another—of which there are far too many) has been thrown in not so much to keep something going as to stop it from flagging. The 'propulsion' also makes reading this book, which would have been better shorter, a wearying—and not, as it should be, an exhilarating— experience, since everything starts sounding the breathless, edgy same as it whoops and echoes in the ear's labyrinth. Maxwell needs an editor. But he is good at creating an atmosphere of arbitrary urban or suburban menace, and he can be funny. One senses a definite and characteristic style coming clear in this, his first book.[9]

This may have a more sophisticated patina than a comparable review in *NYTBR*, but what do we really learn about Glyn Maxwell's poetry from Harris's review? Primarily that the book has the imprimatur of Joseph Brodsky, which probably accounts for its having been published by Bloodaxe in the first place. What else does Harris tell us? Well, that Maxwell uses 'strict' forms (presumably rhyming metrical stanzas) to contain his 'jagged improvisation'. But since 'improvisation' is by definition a form of extempore composition, designed to look natural and unrehearsed, why is it better served by 'strictness of form' than by, say, free verse or Marinettian *parole in libertà*? Further: if Maxwell is, as Harris implies, tricky and needlessly obscure, how and where is he 'funny'? But the most gratuitous phrase in this review is the reference to that 'atmosphere of arbitrary urban or suburban menace', which Maxwell is evidently so

---

[9] T. J. G. Harris, 'In the Labyrinth', *PN Review*, 80 (July/Aug. 1991), 71.

'good at creating'. Does this mean he is not good at creating an atmosphere of rural menace? Lambs stolen by vicious vagrants? Cows on speed jumping over fences? Or does he mean that Maxwell does not take on the menace of wild, untrammelled nature? Of fire and flood and earthquake? But then what English poet today does write about these subjects? Urban or suburban—that about covers the menace most of Maxwell's readers are likely to have experienced.

The fault here is not, of course Maxwell's, nor is it strictly speaking that of his reviewer, T. J. G. Harris. It is the assignment, the demand for the one telling paragraph, that is the problem. The reviewer simply doesn't have space to define his or her terms. Even in somewhat longer reviews, this haziness of vocabulary, coupled with the need to make definitive judgements, poses problems, as when Katha Pollitt, in a full-page review of Robert Pinsky's *The Figured Wheel: New and Collected Poems, 1966–1996* for *NYTBR*[10], praises the long poem 'Essay on Psychiatrists' because it 'really is an essay, that moves from a group portrait of psychiatrists as a bourgeois social type . . . to a large and fully earned conclusion: "But it is all bosh, the false/Link between genius and sickness".' Like Harris's 'urban or suburban', this assessment cannot withstand scrutiny. For why do we want a poem 'really' to be an 'essay'? Surely we have enough essays around. Secondly, if an essay really came to the 'it is all bosh' conclusion cited above, wouldn't most readers find the analysis rather facile, given the large library of works that have probed the relation of genius to madness?

The *New York Review of Books*, to which I now turn, does not go in for this sort of empty impressionism. Its own solution (and that of the *LRB* is similar) is to limit the list of reviewable poets, confining itself to a very small circle and then to devote long, individual reviews to its members. From its inception in 1963, *NYRB* has limited itself largely to the poetry of Robert Lowell (the then-husband of Elizabeth Hardwick, one of *NYRB*'s founding editors) and to the Lowell circle that includes John Berryman, Elizabeth Bishop, Randall Jarrell, Sylvia Plath and James Merrill. Auden is an elder statesman who belongs to

[10] 18 Aug. 1996, 9.

the group as is, at the other end of the age scale, Adrienne Rich. A few British and Irish poets—Seamus Heaney, Philip Larkin, Thom Gunn, more recently James Fenton—have been invited to join the club along with Americans on the circle's fringes like Theodore Roethke, W. S. Merwin and Howard Nemerov. Helen Vendler, a regular *NYRB* reviewer, has tried to bring John Ashbery into the fold, but Ashbery seems not to be taken very seriously by such other *NYRB* poetry reviewers as Denis Donoghue and Frank Kermode; a number of his recent books have not been reviewed in *NYRB* at all.

To whatever extent this parochialism might have been justified in the 1960s and 1970s, when, incidentally, the *NYRB* ignored the Objectivists (Louis Zukofsky, George Oppen, Carl Rakosi, Charles Reznikoff, Lorine Niedecker), the Beats, the Black Mountain and San Francisco poets, as well as John Cage, Ian Hamilton Finlay, and any number of Dada, Surrealist, and Fluxus poets, it has become, in the mid-1990s, a way of denying poetry its very life. For most of the above are now safely dead, and where are the young who should replace them? Has time simply stopped so that 'poetry' can mean no more than a review of Elizabeth Bishop's posthumously published letters or an obituary essay about James Merrill? Much of today's 'literary journalism' would have us believe so. In a recent article in *The Economist*,[11] for example, we are told that '[America']s poetic voice has shrunk to a whisper', that 'Since the death of Robert Lowell in 1977, America seems to have lacked a major poet. In fact most people are not even aware of the concerns of American poets these days. It has declined into a minor art, subsidised principally by universities.' The occasion for these ruminations is the publication by prestigious Faber & Faber of three younger (actually not so young) American poets: Charles Simic, Chase Twitchell and August Kleinzahler. But since these are (rightly, to my mind) discovered to be not all that remarkable, the anonymous *Economist* writer feels the point has been proved.

The reasoning here is purely circular. If Chase Twitchell 'represents' the New American Poetry, then the New American Poetry can't be very good. And since many of us would argue that even Robert Lowell can't represent great American poetry

---

[11] 8 July 1995, 82.

quite as convincingly as did Walt Whitman or Emily Dickinson or T. S. Eliot, things must be really bad. Thus, while the *NYRB* and *TLS* pay careful attention to the New Historicism, the New Gender Criticism or the New Cultural Studies, they pay no comparable attention—indeed, no attention at all—to the New Poetics. Let us consider why this is the case.

Poetry Degree Zero

Suppose a reviewer is assigned to write a piece on Renaissance New Historicist studies. He or she knows (or quickly learns) that the founding father of this movement is Stephen Greenblatt, a professor at Berkeley, whose new book is to be discussed in the review along with others by Thomas Laqueur, Richard Helgerson and Nancy Vickers. The reviewer reads 'background' material, considers opposing views, and is ready to write the piece. A similar process takes place when a reviewer takes on, say, the most recent book by Jean-François Lyotard or Hélène Cixous.

But—and here's the rub—what *is* poetry anyway? Does anyone have a clear idea? The problem is not insurmountable if the review is to be of studies of Milton or Eliot or even HD, for these canonical authors at least partially provide the aesthetic norms against which books about their *œuvre* have been and will be judged. But Charles Bernstein, Charles Wright, Charles Simic? Who knows what is to be looked for in the case of their books?

A further complication has been produced by the relative positioning of poetry and theory in the university curriculum of the past few decades. We expect graduate students in English or Comparative Literature to be familiar with Saussure's distinction between signifier and signified, Roman Jakobson's distinction between metaphor and metonymy, with Lacan's elaboration on that distinction, and Paul De Man's related discussion of irony and allegory. The 'death of the author', as defined by Barthes and Foucault is now a common topic of discussion. Judith Butler's notions of 'gender performativity' are regularly cited, as are Fredric Jameson's interpretations of consumer culture and Homi K. Bhabha's theories on the hybridity and porosity of nations. But when the book to be discussed is a book of poems, the reader suddenly seems to forget everything he or she has learned about *literariness*, about the cultural construction of the subject, the naturalization of ideology, or the relation of genre to gender. The fairly simple principle that the choice of verse form is never merely arbitrary, that one doesn't just 'at will' write sonnets on Monday, fragmented free verse on Tuesday and prose on Wednesday, is largely ignored, as is the twin question why poet X—say, Philip Larkin—never wrote prose poetry. And beyond the individual poet, what about period style? National or ethnic styles? Are the 'affirmations' of a 'quirky imagination' the same in 1990 as they were when Wordsworth wrote 'Resolution and Independence'?

A sense of history and a sense of theory: these are the twin poles of criticism missing from most poetry discourse today and hence missing in the typical poetry review. Poet X, we read regularly, 'has found his voice'. But is his voice worth finding? Poet Y never lets her formalism get in the way of the colloquial. But why do we want poetry to be colloquial? 'There is a distinct world in Michael Longley's poetry', writes his fellow poet Eavan Boland. 'He has created it from a sense of lost values, out of lyric irony, and with a considerable fortitude.'[12] But in most discourses today the very idea of a 'distinct world' is suspect, and as for those 'values' to be recovered with 'considerable fortitude', maybe it would be better if they were 'lost'.

The poetry review (one poet reviewing another) comes, directly or indirectly, out of the poetry workshop, and the poetry workshop (or, for that matter, the creative writing workshop in general) is still dominated by a regressively Romantic concept of the poet as a man speaking to men (or woman speaking to women—the principle is the same), by the notion that poetry is emotion recollected in tranquillity, the poet speaking for all of us—only more sensitively, perceptively and expertly. And how could the workshop be otherwise without going out of existence? How could it not be based on the assumption that a given student just might have 'talent', that that talent needs to find a conduit of expression and then he or she can become a certified poet? One writes on a given subject or uses a given verse form,

---

[12] Eavan Boland, 'Identities and Disguises' (review of Michael Longley, *Poems 1963–1983* and E. A. Markham, *Living in Disguise*), *PN Review*, 55 (1987), 95.

the instructor and one's fellow students provide constructive criticism and, if one is diligent and lucky, poems are born—and published in *American Poetry Review.*

Ironically this workshop/journalism discourse is wholly at odds, not only with the discourses of architecture, anthropology, social science and philosophy, but also with the amazing body of writing on poetics (often by poets themselves) throughout our century. From Roman Jakobson's brilliant study of Khlebnikov called *New Russian Poetry* (1921), Ezra Pound's *How to Read* (1928), and Gertrude Stein's *How to Write* (1931), to the Concrete Poetry manifestos of the 1950s, produced by the Noigandres group in Brazil, to John Cage's *Silence* (1962) and *A Year From Monday* (1969), Ingeborg Bachmann's *Wir mussen wahre Satze finden* (1983), and Susan Howe's *The Birthmark* (1993), we have an exciting body of poetics, a discourse on poetry impressive in its richness and excitement. This is not to say that there is large-scale agreement between individual poet-theorists, but what can be said is that, from Futurism and Dada on down, the international poetic impetus has been constructivist rather than expressivist: it is committed, in other words, to the basic theorem that poetry is the language art, the art in which the 'what' cannnot be separated from 'how', in which the said exists only in the saying. In his widely discussed 'Artifice of Absorption' (reprinted in *A Poetics*), Charles Bernstein calls this quality the 'non-absorbability' of poetic discourse. But then Yeats had already said as much when he declared that 'Our words must seem to be inevitable'. At the same time—and here is a corollary principle about which there is little disagreement in the arena of poetics (as compared to the arena of poetic journalism)—poetic language is never simply unique, natural, and universal; it is the product, in large part, of particular social, historical and cultural formations. And these formations demand study.

There is, then, no good intellectual reason why poetry reviewing in, say, the *TLS* couldn't be just as useful and interesting as reviews of urban or gender studies. But it's not likely to happen in our culture because, to put it bluntly, there isn't enough at stake. As long as self-proclaimed poets appear on the scene in every city and small town in Britain or America—and, oddly enough, poetry still has enough cultural capital for this to be the case[13]—as long as the editors of *NYTBR*, *NYRB*, *TLS* and so on have to choose books to be reviewed from a wide variety of disciplines and areas, there is no way to weed out the dross, which is about 90 per cent of so-called poetry publication. Who, we say democratically and bravely, is to decide which of the countless poets now plying their trade are worthy of attention? And why is one set of poetic principles—say, the ones I've just adumbrated above—any more 'valid' than another?

Notice we never say this about historians or anthropologists—or even architects—perhaps because certification in these fields is a complex process. A given architect or architecture critic might, for example, personally dislike the work of Frank Gehry or of Denise Scott-Brown. But that work won't be dismissed by reviewers as simply unimportant or irrelevant. In poetry journalism, however, it happens all the time: witness James Fenton's 'Getting Rid of the Burden of Sense', a review of John Ashbery's *Selected Poems* (1985) in *NYTBR*.[14] The poet, declares Fenton, 'ask[s] of the reader impossible feats of attention . . . yielding only a minimum of reward'. And he confesses that 'There were times during my reading of this *Selected Poems* (a gathering from 30 years' work) when I actually thought I was going to burst into tears of boredom.'

New Thresholds, New Anatomies

What, in the face of such arbitrary and subjective judgement, can be done to strengthen critical writing about poetry? A lot, actually, but perhaps no longer in the popular literary press. In the last decade or so, thanks to the world of the Internet and hyperspace, of desktop publishing and small press production, poetry, as even the newspapers keep telling us, is once more a widely practised and popular art form, and the discourse about it is becoming much more interesting. A case in point is a large, glossy-paged volume called *Exact Change Yearbook no. 1: Yearbook 1995*, edited by a young poet named Peter Gizzi (who

---

[13] For an excellent sociological account of how and why poetry still occupies this privileged position, in name if not in fact, see Pierre Bourdieu, *Field of Cultural Production*, ch. 6, 'Principles for a Sociology of Cultural Works', 176–91.

[14] 29 Dec. 1985, 10.

received his training in the Buffalo Poetics Program from Charles Bernstein, Susan Howe and Robert Creeley) and published jointly by Exact Change in Boston and Carcanet Press in the UK. Its elegant and perhaps too extravagant layout has been executed by a team of production assistants and printed in Hong Kong. *Yearbook 1* features Michael Palmer, glamorously pictured on the book's cover and represented by an excellent interview with Peter Gizzi and a twelve-page selection from his work. And—signs of the times—the *Yearbook* includes a CD of readings by twelve poets from Palmer to Ted Berrigan[15] and is available for $35 in the US and £19.50 in Britain.

In their prefatory 'Publishers' Note', Damon Krukowski and Naomi Yang (who doubles as the book's designer) write that they wanted to replace the now defunct *New Directions* annual (edited for some forty years by James Laughlin) with 'a large miscellany of avant-garde work, both contemporary and historical, chosen less to represent a particular "school", and more in the spirit of learning what's out there.' To this end, the publishers asked Gizzi 'to help us find a range of contemporary work that draws on the tradition we publish in our books of Surrealist and other early twentieth-century experimentation . . . To what came back we added work by Exact Change authors [Stein, Cage, de Chirico, Aragon], as well as a few other discoveries we were eager to share.'

What makes the project unusual is that it juxtaposes avant-garde poets and artists from the US (ranging chronologically from the *Imaginary Elegies* of the late Jack Spicer and Fanny Howe's presentation of extracts from John Wiener's very moving journal *707 Scott Street*, to a 'Gallery' of younger largely unknown poets like Paul Beatty, Tory Dent, and Jennifer Moxley), with their counterparts abroad—specifically, in Britain, France, Germany, China, Russia—and, closer to home, in the Caribbean and Canada. And as if these juxtapositions weren't enough, we can also read, say, Clark Coolidge or Susan

[15] The CD is disappointing, there being no explanation of the eclectic mix of poets represented, many of whom (e.g. Alice Notley, Kenward Elmslie) are not in the book at all and some, like the Jack Spicer 'Imaginary Elegies' (1957), and John Ashbery's ' "They Dream Only of America" ' (1962), stemming from earlier decades. One could argue that the aim here, as in the book, is to produce telling juxtapositions, but in practice, the sequence from Michael Palmer to Ted Berrigan creates more confusion than insight.

Howe against Gertrude Stein's *Before the Flowers of Friendship Faded Friendship Faded*, which is printed for the first time (as Julianna Spahr explains in her headnote), together with Stein's source text, Georges Hugnet's 'Enfance', exactly in the form they were originally published in the journal *Pagany* (1930). Or again, we can read Barbara Guest's lecture 'Poetry the True Fiction' against Hugo Ball's 'Grand Hotel Metaphysics', the 'Radio Happenings' of John Cage and Morton Feldman against Erik Satie's 'Dried Embryos', Michael Palmer against Louis Aragon's 'Peasant's Dream' or the 'Fragments' of De Chirico.

Such collaging gives, me at least, a sense of—forgive the taboo word—transcendence. For instead of the usual anthology wars (who's in, who's out, which editor is sufficiently multicultural?) the *Exact Change Yearbook* offers the most convincing evidence I've seen to date that our own radical poetries are not (as Maxwell or Fenton would have us think) some kind of local aberration, spawned by a bunch of theory-crazed, left-wing poets in New York and San Francisco, and perpetrated by *les jeunes* at Buffalo and other out-of-the way stations—poetries that deserve simply to be ignored. Indeed, what Gizzi's juxtapositions of US and foreign portfolios suggest is that the attention to the materiality of language I spoke of above, to syntactic disjunction and visual constellation, and especially to the reconfiguration of lyric as speaking, once again, not for the hypothetical 'sensitive' and 'authentic' individual ('Here's a vision I had as I was weeding the garden yesterday') but for the larger cultural and philosophical moment—that all these are now characteristic of poetries produced around the globe.

Take Jeff Twitchell's portfolio of the 'Original Chinese Language Group'. As Twitchell explains, 'Original, not in the sense of unique, but because of their interest in the earlier meanings and associations that can be read in the Chinese written character. . . . So, too, the recuperation of the original impetus of poetry as the play in language.' The 'Original Poets', Twitchell notes, go beyond their predecessors, the so-called 'Misty' (because branded 'obscure' by the official critics) poets of the late 1970s, of whom the best known in the US is Bei Dao. The 1988 'Original' Manifesto, reproduced here, comes out strongly against the localism, ethnocentrism, and nationalism that bedevilled Communist China until quite recently. The aim

is to make contact with 'modern Western art', and the vehicle
for such contact, the manifesto declares, is the written character,
which, compared to spoken language, is 'less polluted and
pre-judged'. 'We do not avoid', they declare, 'the phrase "word
games" which already has aroused great misunderstanding. We
even like it. "Game" [*yóuxi*] is a word, connoting the profound,
eerie spirit of art and philosophy.' And the text gives way to the
visual image of a large black cross which represents the intersection of 'swim' [*yóu*]—to get in touch with reality—and 'play'
[*xí*].

   Twitchell's portfolio is taken from the selection that appeared
in the British journal *Parataxis*, 7 (1994), edited by the poet
Drew Milne. In translation, the poems themselves—by Che
Quian-Zi, Zhou Ya-Ping, Yi Cun, Huang Gan, Xian Meng,
and Hong Liu (the one woman in this group)—don't quite live
up to that manifesto.[16] 'Word games', in the sense of Steve
McCaffery's or Charles Bernstein's paragrammatic play, are less
common than neo-Surrealist imagery and the casting of a sharp
eye on the 'direct treatment of the thing' in the Poundian Imagist
sense. Just as Pound's fabled 'invention of China' turns out to
have little to do with the classical Chinese models which were
his source, so the Original Poets' version of 'language poetry' is
more graphic and precisionist than, say, Lyn Hejinian's or Bob
Perelman's. Here, for example, is Part III of Zhou Ya-Ping's
'Vulgar Beauty':

> An afterbirth is unfolded, taking the shape of an umbrella.
> The ridges of an umbrella along yellow lines.
> A fetus like a coal cinder has long been reared in it,
> Lit by me, it will give off light.
> A white crane, unexpectedly covered by a black string-net
> A snake, bound with a copper wire, body
> Like a tightening spring, soft parts flashing.

We must remember that in the Mandarin Chinese, as J. H.
Prynne notes in his 'Afterword', the 'iconic deployment [of the
language] by stroke play and contexture makes a traffic with the

---

[16] Ming-Quian Ma, a Chinese doctoral candidate at Stanford, who has published
essays on Carl Rakosi, George Oppen, Susan Howe and Lyn Hejinian, and who is
working on further translations of the 'Original' poets with Jeff Twitchell, tells me
that in Mandarin, the poems in question are much more non-syntactic and disjunc-
tive than in these translations.

eye worked by a different ground-plan'. At one point, the translators planned to include some of the Chinese text so as to show how the tactile element works, but the Originals themselves countered this idea because, as Prynne puts it, 'it would suggest exoticism or extraneous willow-pattern ornament; to them, we are the exotics, with our credit-card view of the speech act'.

That 'credit-card view' is satirized in Prynne's own poems in *Bands around the Throat*, the entire chapbook, originally published in Cambridge in a limited edition, reprinted in the *Exact Change Yearbook*. And Tom Raworth's 'Anglo-Irish Alternative', a portfolio printed elsewhere in the anthology, provides a rich context in which to understand Prynne's work. Such contextualizing (one should certainly read Rosmarie Waldrop's Berlin portfolio 'against' Raworth's) provides a kind of information that is absent from the short review, however elegant, of the individual poet. And Gizzi's juxtapositions have their counterpart in a number of recent anthologies. Since 1993 alone, the following have appeared: Eliot Weinberger's *American Poetry Since 1950: Innovators and Outsiders* (Marsilio, a bestseller in Mexico in a Spanish edition), Paul Hoover's *A Norton Book of Postmodern Poetry* (Norton), Douglas Messerli's *From the Other Side of the Century: A New American Poetry 1960–90* (Sun & Moon), volume 1 of Jerome Rothenberg and Pierre Joris's *Poems for the Millennium* (Berkeley, Calif.), and, most recently, Maggie O'Sullivan's *Out of Everywhere: Linguistically Innovative Poetry by Women in North America and the UK* (Reality Street Editions). Some of these anthologies have barely been reviewed, and yet, in what is a surprising development, they are already being assigned for classroom use and discussed at conferences. Romana Huk, a professor at the University of New Hampshire, for example, has organized an international poetry festival called 'Assembling Alternatives', largely based, in the case of Anglo-American poetry, on such yet-to-be-reviewed anthologies and small-press books, many of which she came across during a fellowship year in the UK.

But how, it will be asked, is such work disseminated if not via reviews in the major papers? Here is where electronic discussion groups and the Internet come in. On the Poetics Discussion Group sponsored by the Poetics Program at the State University of New York at Buffalo and open to anyone who hears about it by word of mouth and cares to join, the daily conversation now contains an average of 1200 lines and includes postings from all over the world. Much of the 'talk' is trivial: who said what to whom where, what X meant when she said Y, and so on. But there have lately been extended conversations on the nature of free verse, on 'close reading' (Peter Quartermain began this one when he asked, on the net, 'Why the animus against close reading? Do we want distant and/or careless reading?'), and on the relation of language poetry to other contemporary movements. Bob Perelman's new critical book *The Trouble with Genius: Reading Pound, Joyce, Stein, and Zukofsky* (Berkeley, Calif., 1995) has been discussed in a series of postings; indeed, the argument as to what Perelman's book does and what its implications might be, acts as a kind of supplement (in the Derridean sense of substitute as well as addition) to the more conventional book review.

Buffalo also sponsors the Electronic Poetry Center where one can call up, say, an 'Authors' file and access an impressive list of poets, each one represented by a photograph, followed by selected poems, prose writings, bibliography and so on. Then, too, the Electronic Poetry Center publishes its own journal, *Rif/t*, which contains poems, fictions, critical essays and reviews as does the on-line Postmodern Culture, published at the University of Virginia. A new group has just been formed in San Francisco that discusses concrete poetry, visual poetics and language-art relationships; this one is called *Majordomo* and is accessed by subscribing to something called Wr-eye-tings; a related group is Silence, devoted to the work of the late John Cage; this group is extremely active, sharing information about Cage scores, recordings, musical interpretations, poetic texts, and so on. James Pritchett's recent book on *Cage's Music* (Cambridge, 1994) was discussed and debated in a series of postings.

The 'reviewing' that occurs on such lists and in the new *e-zines* is by no means ideal. Internet reviewers are not as accountable as are their counterparts in the print media, and editors are not likely to ask for substantial revisions or fact-checking. The immateriality of the digital medium controls the discourse: one flick of the finger—and this is a very easy mistake to make—and the text disappears from the screen, perhaps not to be found again. Then, too, on-screen discussion of poetry and poetics is designed for a limited (and largely younger) audience that is at home with the new technologies.

And this raises the spectre of the nominal 'public' that, for the past hundred years, has ostensibly depended on reviewers to help it decide what poetry books to read. Doesn't a weekly paper like *TLS* owe something to this non-professional public, and isn't it therefore better to 'cover' a range of books, even as Glyn Maxwell does in his omnibus piece? Two books on Larkin, one on Walcott, some theoretical treatises from the US: why not let the reader decide which ones are worthwhile?

My own sense is that this middle-class poetry public no longer exists, that poetics is now at least as specialized as is architectural discourse; indeed, the latter actually speaks to a much wider audience than does poetry, given that everyone lives and works in specific buildings and hence takes an interest in the look and feel of the built environment. In the case of poetry, however, the *rapprochement* with the university may well be a *fait accompli.*[17] And thus it is that the *TLS* or *NYRB* review may well be on its way toward becoming obsolete.

Take the case of Charles Bernstein's *A Poetics*, the book Maxwell dismissed so offhandedly. This 1992 collection of 'essays' (the first and longest piece 'Artifice of Absorption' is, strictly speaking, a verse treatise, written in what is predominantly iambic pentameter) was reviewed neither in *NYTBR* nor in *NYRB*, nor in the *New Republic*, the *Village Voice Literary Supplement*, or the *Washington Post Book World*, to mention just the most obvious daily and weekly papers. Yet within two years of its publication, it appeared on course syllabuses across the US (and many in the UK and Australia as well), has become a popular item on Ph.D. qualifying exams, and is cited, along with Bernstein's earlier collection of critical prose, *Content's Dream* (Sun & Moon, 1986), with increasing frequency. The relation of 'absorption' to 'anti-absorption' in poetry is

---

[17] One should bear in mind that in the US, almost 50% of the appropriate population attends university and that university campuses draw in a larger public that shares the concerns of particular departments, attends lectures and readings and so on. But this public, though surprisingly large, is by no means equivalent to, say, the general *TLS* or *NYTBR* readership.

discussed in learned journals. And *A Poetics* has now sold some 5,000 copies and has gone through two printings and numerous translations. How does the process of dissemination work in a case like Bernstein's? How is the readership for such a book constructed? Can the Electronic Poetry Center and other e-zines, together with the more traditional scholarly journals and small poetry magazines in which *A Poetics* has been reviewed,[18] really make the difference? Or is distribution dependent on word of mouth on the campus and at the ever-burgeoning number of conferences? Or controlled by a particular group of fellow poets, professors, and editors? These are questions I can't yet answer satisfactorily. But what I can say is that literary journalism, as we used to know it and as many of us still practise it, has had little to do with the case.

---

[18] To date, in the US, *A Poetics* has been reviewed in the following mix of scholarly journals and little magazines: *Agni Review, American Literature, College Literature, Common Knowledge, Comparative Literature Studies, Contemporary Literature, Harvard Review, Modernism/Modernity, Sulfur, Virginia Quarterly Review, West Coast Line, World Literature Today.*

13

Teachers, Writers

KARL MILLER

It would seem to be part of the point of institutions that they don't get on, or at any rate, that the members of an institution are apt to attach importance to being seen as separate from the membership of other institutions in the vicinity. This has often been true of the two of which, for many years, I enjoyed a simultaneous experience: the humanities as pursued in the university system and the loose confederation represented by novelists, poets, critics and biographers. The literary community is not like the Norwich Union. It is as much a small world, or a diaspora, as it is an institution. But the term can be used here without undue discomfort. The literary community has, institutionally enough, its Society of Literature, its Society of Authors, its Public Lending Right, its cadres of poets, novelists and journalists, its honours, ceremonies and clubs, and its conventions of solitude and dissent.

Members of the two institutions in question have been and still are given to declaring their hostility or indifference to one another. F. R. Leavis's strategy as a polemicist was to set himself at an equidistance from the activities of the old-fashioned don (belletrist or textual editor) and those of the London literary journalist; but it could also be said of him that he delivered an attack on 'journalism' which rested on a desideratum—that of an improved, a critically-educated academy—and which was the work, as Stefan Collini has argued here,[1] of a man who was both a journalist and a don. During my years as a university teacher, I was sometimes to hear it said that a particular writer— generally one with university affiliations who had become well known to the world at large—was 'not one of us'. Meanwhile,

---

[1] See above, Chapter 9.

for their part, writers and journalists have long been in the habit of distancing themselves from donnish behaviour, from what they considered to be the pedantry and hidebound professionalism of the universities. This mutual suspicion can be very keenly felt. But there are times when it can appear to belong to a rhetoric primarily motivated by attitudes quite remote from any concern with academic propriety or journalistic vivacity. I shall turn presently to a case in point.

The Sunday-paper reviewer and Bloomsbury star, Raymond Mortimer, ringingly referred to 'the acrimony of the learned' in the course of a discussion, in 1952, of a book by Leavis, who was, in one of his aspects, an enemy of learning, and yet undoubtedly acrimonious. But then Raymond Mortimer was being acrimonious himself, on the subject of this book by Leavis, 'the most combative of scholars'. 'I always delight in the acrimony of the learned', he wrote in the *Observer*. It made him cross, and it also made him smile. But Leavis's was more comical than usual, he felt, because, in his 'pharisaic rigour', 'he abstains from all levity or wit'. The rivalry and mutual antipathy implied by Mortimer's review was something that I saw about me, or thought I saw, in some abundance, when I was young (it was said, incidentally, that sales of *The Common Pursuit* soared after Mortimer's review). Since then, times have changed; readers may now be more familiar with the acrimony of the ill-informed book-reviewer than with that of the learned. But it has not been a simple change, and it was to include an enlarged contribution by writers to university teaching and (until recently) by teachers to journals and Sunday papers.

Such contributions had, of course, always been apparent, with the second sort more apparent than the first. If the two institutions have often appeared to be at stand-off, there have been times when friendship broke out and mergers occurred, when critics performed as teachers and academics did some of their teaching in the public prints. Elsewhere in this book, John Sutherland writes about a nineteenth-century collaboration of this kind, when University College London let in journalists, and one of the country's best journalists, David Masson, was also one of its best scholars.[2] There have been periods when there

---

[2] See above, Chapter 4.

was more than enough in the way of interchange between the academic and the literary worlds to make it possible to wonder how it could ever be otherwise, and to make it possible to doubt the existence of a cold war, as opposed to a sometimes desultory continuous process of collaboration. Masson's successor at Edinburgh University was George Saintsbury, the bookman professor, his two roles inextricable in their simultaneity. Soon after Saintsbury, in the south, there arose, among others, Geoffrey Grigson, with whom I was eventually to work, never for any length of time an academic, but an editor and journalist with an impressive record as a scholar, innovator and creative anthologist: someone publicly wounding and personally friendly, a combination of attributes not uncommon both among journalists and among dons. Nevertheless, over the past 150 years, there has been a strain of suspicion, rivalry and reciprocal neglect, which has yet to die away and may never do so. There are good reasons, on both sides, why this should have happened, reasons which can be readily understood in terms of the two different sets of professional constraints which operate in this area. But there have been good reasons, too, for doing something about it.

During the 1970s—when Stephen Spender taught there—and the 1980s, University College London resumed its ancient ways. It was one of the places in the university system where collaboration can be said to have occurred. In the 1980s the English department had three, and at times more than three, teachers who were also imaginative writers; and a number of teachers doubled as literary journalists or as one or other sort of editor, besides making themselves responsible for the authorship of more than one sort of book. The novelists A. S. Byatt and Dan Jacobson were not 'in residence' merely: they were full-time tenured members of staff, and were rated internally as no more specialized, and as no more ephemeral or peripheral, than those colleagues whose skill lay in the field of textual editing or grammar.

It follows from what I've been saying that there must have been those who felt that this was not a healthy state of affairs, and when I went to the department to serve as its head, I expected that some people would be shocked. At the point when I was interviewed, Frank Kermode, my predecessor in the post, was kind enough to support my candidature, while warning me that one or two in the department were worried at the thought that they might be joined by a person who had spent the previous twenty years as an editor of journals. Once I arrived, I can't say I felt unwelcome, and I was to discover in this English department excellent company and a team of dedicated teachers. During the months that followed, though, I was told of three expressions of concern outside the College. The three concerned men were all prominent writers, whom I had published. They were also prominent academics, and in that capacity they said that I was not, as the saying goes, 'one of us'. Of one of the three the same thing is reported to have been said at an earlier point. Their complaint was, in part or in sum, that I hadn't ascended the promotion ladder in the normal way, and the implication that writing for and editing journals is different from and inferior to teaching in a university is unlikely to have been altogether missing from what they had to say. It would be the worse for intellectual journalism if that implication were felt to be universally valid. The anxieties that accompany such work have been a deterrent to some of those who were equipped to do it well, and the implication could be thought to add insult to insecurity, to lend itself to deterrence and deterioration, and to obscure the fact that a high proportion of the most valuable and truthful literary criticism has appeared, not in books initially, or ever, but in journals.

I went to the College as Lord Northcliffe Professor of Modern English Literature in 1975, a few months after resigning the editorship of the *Listener*. I founded the *London Review of Books* in 1979. And I gave up both my academic post and my editorship of the *LRB* thirteen years later. The English department at University College is large and long-established. The syllabus runs chronologically from Old English to the present, with an emphasis on periods and topics held to be of outstanding interest, and on language study. In my day, there were some twenty teachers, 200 undergraduates and a dozen research students. We were no different in scope and structure from many other departments of English: more conservative, more traditional, than most, according to some observers. There was no separate course or satellite group which studied creative writing, the creative writing of the student enrolment, though space was found for such studies, on an optional basis, in later years. What I'm writing about here is, in a sense, the opposite of that: I'm discussing the incorporation in a multi-faceted representative English department of imaginative writers and literary journalists, qualified to teach the history of literature and the skills of reading and writing. Very few members of such departments are qualified to teach every bit of the syllabus: in that respect, the writers and critics at University College were no different from their colleagues. Nor was that all there was in the way of collaboration. In addition to the presence of writers and critics, there was the *LRB* in the vicinity—a vicinity of five minutes' walk—to which staff members contributed.

The arrangements I am describing are grounded in the idea of a traffic between the literary and the academic communities, and their justification must lie in the hope that they might do a little to sustain and improve standards on both sides of the tracks— hesitant though one may be, at this point, to use the word 'standards', a word so often subject to dogmatic misuse. Talk of standards can frequently appear to involve the fiction of a past superiority, and it would be inappropriate to depend heavily, in this case, on such a fiction—to imagine a golden age when the two communities were at peace and reviewers were all well-informed and self-critical. And indeed there is some excuse for thinking in terms of a familiar joint deficiency. On the one hand, the faults of reviewers have never gone unnoticed. On the other, the university study of literature has been prone to a hermeticism detectable in the guise both of scholarship and of literary criticism, and far from unrecognizable in the guise of theory; it has shut itself off from too much of what goes on outside the universities; and it has done less than it should to continue the work done in schools, and to defend the higher literacy. There is no reason to suppose that the types of collaboration I am discussing are unfit to supply a corrective touch in both respects.

Over the last fifty years, attempts have been made—and assailed in certain quarters—to broaden the curriculum, to secure 'relevance' by the introduction of Media Studies and the like. The arrangements I have been outlining with reference to University College are something else again, but it may be that they could be assailed on some of the same grounds. The case against such arrangements, so far as I have come to know it, can resemble the objection that used to be made to the placing of contemporary literature on the university curriculum—that it's wrong for interested parties to try to study what is still happening. The case would appear to suggest that writers, as opposed to teachers, are experts on what is happening: but that they should not be allowed to teach it, any more than they should be allowed to teach the past. Writers may one day get onto the university curriculum but shouldn't contribute their persons to the staff of English departments. The argument omits the possibility that many of the difficulties which affect the teaching of the present also affect the teaching of the past, and that there may even be advantages in teaching to the moment, so to speak, where there is the will and the capacity to attempt it.

It has become harder to obtain the funds that allow young people to go on to research and to enter the profession. Good people are being kept out, and deterred. The sort of arrangements I am discussing would permit some of them to come back in at a later stage. Financial stringency, however, together with the need to secure and protect young teachers, has begun to discourage or prohibit the effort required to make the necessary 'mature' appointments—appointments, that's to say, of people who have been out in the world practising some allied trade, doing what they could, as opposed to teaching it, to make use of that invidious distinction. I have the impression that a closing of the ranks, a tighter professionalism, has supervened.

These arrangements are still of interest, though, to the department at University College, and I don't believe—as, admittedly, an interested party—that, in the 1980s, they did any harm. No division emerged between the interlopers and the rest of the staff, no difference of outlook more intractable than the one which occasionally manifests itself in relations between language and literature teachers in traditional departments of English. Neither the undergraduates nor the graduate students showed great interest in the journal I was editing, though there were always one or two who read it and more than one of them wrote for it. There were members of staff, however, who took an interest and were among its regular contributors. The teaching of the department was not transformed by the launching of the journal, but there was a flow from it into lectures and tutorials, and out of lectures and tutorials back into the journal, and there were occasions when it was pleasant to feel that reading and writing and learning were proceeding together.

In the *LRB* of 3 October 1996, there was a review by John Sutherland which offered an example of collaboration and versatility in this field. The review was of books on educational policy and classroom performance by George Walden and standard-bearing Melanie Phillips, and it was by a professor of literature who is also a university admissions officer, abreast of what sixth-formers now know and don't know, and a journalist able to address a general public on the subject. The university entrants he was writing about, moreover, were there in the classroom to talk to him, if they wanted, about what he had written about them. I'd have to say that more might have been done in my own time to bring about departmental discussion, to bring about investigation and challenges, in response to arguments presented in the *LRB*. I took there to be an argument in favour of a tactful restriction of the journal's visibility in the College. In its early days especially, this was not difficult to achieve, but it was, perhaps, an odd approach for an editor to pursue, and for someone to pursue who thought that his two worlds should be in touch. Tact, and also taboo, an atavistic compunction, may have entered into it.

An important amphibian—in the sense of these remarks—is Conor Cruise O'Brien. He can scarcely be employed to settle, single-handed, the case for having literature and the academy send up 'all one mutual cry', in the words of Shakespeare. But his career is an illustration of what can be done by crossing boundaries, and a guide to the ironies that can attend such transgressions. He has straddled the two worlds of literature and academic life, and has excelled in a plethora of vocations. He has been a diplomat, a literary critic, a historian, a politician, a Vice-Chancellor, an editor-in-chief. He began with a highly technical, extravagantly footnoted book on Parnell and his party—Namierite in its stress on quantification and the political rank-and-file.[3] Then came a book on the Catholic imagination in the rebarbative modern world; a vivid account of his involvement, as a United Nations representative, in the Katanga seces-

---

[3] *Parnell and his Party, 1880–1890* (Oxford, 1957).

sion, and a study of the 'theatre' of United Nations transactions and displays; an eloquent defensive history of Zionism, and a political life of Edmund Burke.[4] And there are collections of reprinted essays. In recent times, there have been books on the Irish Nationalist heritage, the new millennium, and on the odious French Revolutionariness (or 'bloody' millenarianism) of Thomas Jefferson.[5] This is a man who was said by a London academic, faced with the prospect of O'Brien's coming to my college to lecture on Burke, to be 'not one of us'.

Published in 1992, O'Brien's book on Burke embodies a repudiation of the dismissive line taken, in relation to Burke, by the don's don, Lewis Namier, for whom Burke was insufficiently rank-and-file, insufficiently representative of the governing élite, while also a lackey of its magnates, and a snob. He was not one of a number in George III's House of Commons: his importance could not be counted, therefore—could not be assessed in terms of the parliamentary arithmetic that might have made up for his failure to attain high office. O'Brien attacks this line by means of a political veteran's shrewd investigation of Burke's career. He points out that Namier's strategy, in the attack on Burke in his books, is rarely to mention him. But O'Brien does not mention a review by Namier published in the *Spectator* of 19 December 1958, during my time there as literary editor (which overlapped with O'Brien's time there as a contributor), a review in which 'the character of Burke' is discussed at length.

The review is striking and outspoken, by no means a bad advertisement for reviewing; it gives full expression to Namier's dislike and deserves the close attention of any student of the eighteenth century. Burke is called contradictory, egocentric, a 'poor observer'. He has in him 'a streak of persecution mania'. An ethnic note might seem to be struck. Burke is emotional, and 'rootless': a 'solitary, rootless man who preached party', and a

---

[4] *Maria Cross: Imaginative Patterns in a Group of Modern Catholic Writers* (London, 1963); *To Katonga and Back. A UN Case History* (London, 1962); *The Siege, the Saga of Israel, and Zionism* (London, 1986); *The Great Melody, a Thematic Biography and Commented Anthology of Edmund Burke* (London, 1992).

[5] e.g. *States of Ireland* (London, 1972), *Godland, Reflections on Religion and Rationalism* (Cambridge, Mass., 1988), *Ancestral Voices: Religion and Nationalism in Ireland* (Dublin, 1994), *On the Eve of the Millenium: the Future of Democracy through an Age of Unreason* (New York, London, 1995), *The Long Affair: Thomas Jefferson and the French Revolution* (London, 1996).

party politician with 'a minority mind'. It might appear that a high-born Jewish refugee, with an emotional approach to the English aristocracy, is seeing off this unstable Irish upstart. Namier was, as O'Brien says, a 'rigorous' man. The general editor of the ten-volume edition of Burke's correspondence is described in the review, in a parenthesis, as 'not a professional historian'. Namier does, however, grant him his professorial title.

There are journalists who can show themselves, when they write books, to be more donnish than any don, and there are passages in O'Brien's study of Burke when that thought comes to mind; it might even suggest a reason for his omission of the Namier review. The study of Burke is a long but severely-focused book. So political a biography is this that it says nothing about Burke's influential early treatise on aesthetics, and very little about his personal life. It has been extolled, and it has been challenged. A politician I know thinks it egocentric, and a professor I know thinks that it too much identifies with Burke. O'Brien explains that Burke cared deeply about the Irish Catholics from whom he was descended, and about the sufferings occasioned by their experience of the Protestant hierarchy in which Burke rose to eminence and which he eloquently praised. O'Brien sees Ireland in Burke's successive campaigns on behalf of the American colonists and of India's exploited peoples, campaigns which confronted oppressions practised by Burke's adopted tribe, the Hanoverian élite; and he sees Ireland, too, though more refractedly, in Burke's attitude to the French Revolution. These three preoccupations of his—with America, India and France—elicited the 'great melody' of Burke's principal eloquence.

This expression, the 'great melody', which furnishes the title of the book, is drawn from a poem by Yeats, from an awkward corner of that poem:

> American colonists, Ireland, France, and India
> Harried, and Burke's great melody against it.

Burke is down in the poem as a hater of Whigs (though he was a Whig himself for a while), and Whiggery is seen by one of the poem's interlocutors as 'a levelling, rancorous, rational sort of mind'. The 'it' in these lines may be thought to refer to the harrying that starts the second of the lines (with France then having to be seen as harried by its levellers). O'Brien thinks of this 'it' as the abuse of power. But it might be Whiggery, and it might also be more than one, or all, of the three.

Another professor who has responded to the book thinks that the 'it' in question is Whiggery, and rebukes O'Brien on the point. But this is the least of the rebukes contained in the review of the book by the historian, journalist and novelist Seamus Deane—himself a boundary-breaker—which appeared in the *Irish Literary Supplement* (Spring 1993), a journal read by Irish Nationalist Americans. The review speaks of its 'amateurisms', and of 'tabloid journalism'. 'Amateur' is a hard word to apply to the author of the Parnell book, an enduringly respected work of history done at the outset of O'Brien's career. And 'tabloid journalism' is a familiar academic conflation, for polemical purposes, of one variety of journalism with another: someone who writes for journals and broadsheets can thereby become a tabloid journalist. Antipathy functions here, or imagines itself here, as an offended academy. The review also speaks of O'Brien's 'paranoia', causing him to resemble Namier's Burke, and makes the following claim:

> this disturbed attempt to rewrite the story of Burke as a version of the story of Conor Cruise O'Brien—Irish, not British, heroically consistent in his principles and not a venal hack, sympathetic to the Irish Catholic cause, opposed to the Protestant ascendancy, as prescient as he is passionate, the enemy of ideologues and revolutionary cabals, the friend of inherited wisdom and affections—will be a fascinating document for those interested in O'Brien and somewhat less enthralling for those interested in Burke.

It goes on: 'Burke's reputation will survive O'Brien, but I don't think O'Brien's will long survive his Burke.' And it ends: 'O'Brien is writing a disguised autobiography. In doing so he has reduced Burke to his own dimensions. That is, in its way, a remarkable achievement.' It can only be a remarkable achievement if O'Brien's reputation is tiny or tainted, and only a bitter enemy is going to believe that.

The review is an episode in the academy's war with the outside world. But it is also a piece of Irish rigour, or rancour. Seamus Deane is of Republican stock, and has recently published a fine work of fiction, *Reading in the Dark* (1997), which deals with his family background, while O'Brien has long been a strong opponent of IRA Republicanism (an opponent very unlikely to have used the Burke book in order to deny or obscure the fact, if that is what Deane is suggesting at one point) and has recently appeared among Ulster's Protestants as a Unionist. It is possible to think, therefore, that a political anti- pathy has moved Deane to portray O'Brien, in stereotypical fashion, as underqualified professionally. There's talk of an inconsistency in the matter of footnotes and of a neglect of certain books on Burke—familiar gambits on occasions of academic displeasure. And it's true that O'Brien has been known to miss, or to miss out, writings—such as the Namier review—that could be thought relevant to his purposes, and that an element of identification and special pleading can be attrib- uted to his book on Burke. These are qualities, however, which are by no means incompatible with distinguished achievement in literature and in historical scholarship—Namier's, for instance. The author of this book could not be excluded from any self- respecting seat of learning. But the fact that he has spent time in other places has helped to make his book the success I think it is. It succeeds because it is rich in instruction and in excellent prose, and because he has been where Burke has been—in the eye of the political storm.

Asked to say what I feel I learned by going back to the university, I'd be bound to reply that in one sense I feel that I'd never been away. I didn't need to go back in order to feel impelled to take care with what I wrote—not that the effort has always been sufficient or successful; academics would seem to compare well, in this respect, with most varieties of journalist, but there are many academics who are no more careful than the members of other institutions are. It's also true, however, that going back made me more appreciative of the interesting techni- calities of literary study, and put me in closer touch with new scholarship than I might otherwise have been, while giving me time to read lots of interesting old books. It did not rescue me from the difficulty I have found in addressing two different publics, one of which is more disposed than the other to be beguiled and entertained. I've always wanted to be amusing without always knowing how, and I was determined, when I became a teacher, to keep on trying, and not to mind too much if other teachers found me culpably amusement-prone.

The difficulty is one that induced the thought that within the institutional relations I have been discussing may lie a radical incongruity, the lineaments of an irreducible difference of outlook, which may need to be conceded by those who object to the phobic demarcations and exclusions which have characterized these relations. It would certainly be unwise to predict an early end to the tendency of historians to be repelled by the literary qualities which readers will continue to expect of them, and to refuse to acknowledge as such the works of art which some of their number will continue to produce.

14

Living on Writing

LORNA SAGE

Book-chat (Gore Vidal's phrase) always gives writing a character. In Grub Street people's distinguishing marks are important, and for reviewers authors are first and last people who write. Many novelists and poets are book-reviewers themselves, or have jobs with publishers, or on the literary pages. Regular reviewers of new novels (or plays or poems, but I speak from experience only of fiction) are part of the daily life of letters, they write on the run, in the present tense, they have to live writing—read (say) ten new novels every fortnight and write about two or three of them—in order even partly to live on it. You swap words for money, you reprocess reading into writing and commentary. You describe, paraphrase, quote, reperform, 'place' and help sell (or not) the books you're reviewing. Reviewing is in an important sense *reading out loud*, rather like not being able to read without moving your lips. What literary editors like is an excited, vivid, dramatized response, whether it is positive or negative is less important than its power to arouse interest, to make the book in question twitch and show signs of life—for it's a dead blank to the real reader at this stage, so you can *galvanize* it by giving it a character with quirks. Reviewers can never—or very seldom—afford to say one of the most pressing things they know, which is that most of the writing they read is neither bad nor good nor distinctive but just part of the mulch of the contemporary literary imagination, part of on-going articulate life. Reviewers (whose own words are of course even more dispensable) are bound to relish, and deny, the ephemeral nature of writing, its continuous generation and decay. To write reading you must spot and exaggerate and semaphore all the signs, insert yourself between author and real reader, make over long texts into short alliterative sentences, perform reading as surrogate and advocate, and at all costs help to keep the trade in words alive.

This journalistic reader is, I want to argue, very different from the academic kind. But it's a difference of relatively recent origin, and what I am calling 'writing reading' used to look like a continuum. George Steiner, for instance, writing almost twenty years ago on ' "Critic"/"Reader" ' could still say with some conviction that, though 'philosophical criticism' was a branch of aesthetics,

performative or mimetic criticism is one of the multiple forms of applied rhetoric. At a guess, one would say that this form comprises nine-tenths of the craft. It stretches from the iceberg mass of daily reviewing—the 'art critic', 'the book critic', 'the music critic' in the media—all the way to such undoubted pinnacles of judicial re-enactment and summation as Samuel Johnson's discourse on Shakespeare or T. S. Eliot's on Dante. . . . Can anything useful be said of a phenomenology so various that it includes . . . I. A. Richards on Coleridge at one end, and the pandemonium of daily academic-journalistic market quotations at the other? The inchoate plurality is undeniable.[1]

One useful thing that *can* be said is that this continuity is no longer at all so evident in the 1990s: 'inchoate plurality', with its carnival associations, has nowadays a nostalgic sound, academic criticism and literary journalism have grown further apart. Steiner himself, in a 1995 postscript to this same essay, puts it succinctly. Reading is no longer the critic's main concern: 'Deconstructive, postmodernist, feminist, gender-oriented treatments of literary texts (where these are accorded any distinct status at all) are an industry.'[2] The gap between what Roland Barthes called the *readable* and the writable, or writerly, conception of the text—the one with avant-garde gaps, which flatters critics by making them into diviners supplying what's *not* there—has become thoroughly institutionalized.

Now, 'performative or mimetic criticism' belongs largely to the media, not to the Ivory Tower. Reviewers collude with authors as they always did. Even when they abuse them, they single them out, pay them attention, characterize them and

---

[1] ' "Critic"/"Reader" ' (*New Literary History*, 1979) reprinted in *George Steiner: A Reader* (Harmondsworth, 1984) and in *Real Voices on Reading*, ed. Philip Davis (London, 1997), 15–16 and 3–37.

[2] *Real Voices*, 35.

make a noise about them. Reviewers read, or try to, the author's other books, they sketch some sort of continuity. The piece will sometimes have a photograph of the author. And it may well be supported on other pages with an interview with the author, or—more grandly—a profile, or a 'feature' of some sort connecting the author with the topical commentary, or the real estate, or the food, or the clothes that fill up the 'life-style' sections of papers and magazines. Zest, curiosity, voyeurism, vicarious *paper*-living enter into book reviewing, there's no real boundary around the books, and indeed book pages merge more and more into features, and there's a constant rearguard action being fought by literary editors to keep their space, and to find ways of allowing books to look like books without losing their 'living' appeal. Literary prizes help, but they also hinder in almost equal measure, since they assimilate books to 'news' and authors to the general topos of fame-and-luck-and-lottery. Thus, for example, Kate Atkinson, who won the Whitbread First Novel Prize for 1995 with *Behind the Scenes at the Museum*, got caught up in a 'story' belonging to an archetype of the lottery winner—chambermaid and single mum writes prize-winning novel. But then again, novelist and literary journalist Hilary Mantel wrote a very good piece analysing and exposing this treatment in the *London Review of Books*: the world of book-chat was not yet a tame supplement to the rest of the journalistic world.

But the inevitable bias of book-pages is towards lives-of-letters. And more and more the present tense of dialogue amongst those who subsist on the literary scene favours the allotment of space not to reviews of what we clumsily call literary fiction, but to reviews of 'non-fiction' genres: travel writing, memoirs, biography and (especially revealingly) literary biography. In a sense this confirms my reading of the subtext of reviewing—that it is interested in the life of the author. Grub Street embraces literary biography, for example, because it makes long-dead authors, whose work and reputation are public currency, live over again, so that you can review them without having to start from scratch. And—even more satisfyingly and temptingly for the 'features' people—you can recapture their 'life-styles', tastes in clothes, houses, love-affairs, manners with money, eating habits and servant problems. In their Lives they become eminently consumable, their œuvres constitute secondary but bigger stories, the epic and intimate narratives of their lives-as-writers. The rise and rise of literary biography in the age of the (theoretical) death of the Author cannot be attributed to the influence of literary journalism, but it's certainly true that Grub Street has welcomed it, given it space and helped it to happen. The person of the author has never been more on display than it is now, and the popularity of Virginia Woolf's term 'life-writing' is explained by the extraordinary variety of kinds of writing now barely covered by the biography label. Woolf in *The Common Reader* advised, 'Do not dictate to your author; try to become him',[3] and the contemporary collusion between Grub Street and literary biography has produced some sophisticated and self-conscious examples of just this.

The biographer, like the profile-writer, lives by disrespect, as Janet Malcolm in her 1994 book on Sylvia Plath titled *The Silent Woman* (which started life as a *New Yorker* profile) 'confessed': 'breaking into a house, rifling through certain drawers . . . tiptoeing down the corridor . . . to stand in front of the bedroom door and try to peep through the keyhole'.[4] In fact, Malcolm upped the stakes considerably (her metaphor) by looking into the lives and motives of Plath's biographers too, characterizing them, interviewing them, quoting their letters. Her argument is that such writers-on-writers are really trying to make space for the self—including, not to put too fine a point on it, themselves. The canonized writer is a representative figure, the object of desire and envy, the epitome of the self as self-fashioner. We all want to be writers in a way . . . Malcolm's *ad hominem*, *ad feminam* line produces a narrative of infinite regress, generating always more characters and more narrative. For her the affinity of biography with Grub Street makes sense because they both appeal to an appetite for life, which by no means stops with the writer's death. Indeed, as with Plath, death often makes the subject a lot more interesting, after all in most legal systems you cannot libel the dead. The Author is doubly dead for this irreverent writing; the mission of biography is a form of intrusion on

---

[3] Virginia Woolf, *The Common Reader* (London, 1932), 268.
[4] Janet Malcolm, *The Silent Woman: Sylvia Plath and Ted Hughes* (London, 1994), 9.

that finality too: 'a room so dark and gloomy that one has a hard time seeing one's hand . . . The air in the room is bad. . . . Through the door one can see an open coffin.'[5] Malcolm herself is a most ambitious writer, calling on Borges[6] to aid her in describing the claustrophobic excitements of coming after. With such 'quotations' she means to give the lie to those who think of biography as a cosy, because 'readable', kind of writing.

Malcolm reminds us, then, that for biography (and Grub Street) writers, unlike the Author, are undead, their deaths are part of the continuing narrative of their Lives. Reviewers are quite often called on to write obituaries, too, short-order reviews of a whole life's work. The reviewer (this is one aspect of what it means to work in Grub Street) writes to the moment, whatever the moment supplies. It is an addiction for some, including myself. I've moonlighted as a book-reviewer for nearly all of my academic life: I wrote reviews, profiles, columns instead of writing academic articles and books throughout the 1970s and 1980s, not exclusively, but nearly so; and for part of that time I reviewed new fiction in bulk, first for the *TLS* in its last anonymous days, then for the *Observer*. The expertise in contemporary literary culture I acquired this way became my academic stock in trade, and though I started off writing a thesis on seventeenth-century poetry, I mostly write as an academic on contemporary fiction, and that's also the field in which I'm asked to examine theses. So in a way my career in Grub Street has been my career, which demonstrates that the boundaries between the two worlds are more permeable than they are made out to be. This is a development I deplore even while I benefit from it, I realize, for I have much enjoyed working in two worlds officially ignorant of each other. But really, they never have been sealed off from each other: witness the development of 'Writing' programmes in British universities. These bring poets, novelists and dramatists into literature departments, and make them look (even) a little like Grub Street.

To come back to the place of the author on the daily surface of contemporary literary life: add in readings (accompanied by book-signings), and the proliferation of book festivals (backed

---

[5] Janet Malcolm, 41.   [6] Ibid. 73.

by regional Arts Boards, who don't much like the private character of writing and reading, and love to sponsor public 'community' events), and the living author becomes even more
ubiquitous. Writing fiction is an art that undoes the singularity,
the monological character of speech, and even when it's
mimetically noisy 'throws' the author's voice in all directions,
removes the person speaking, but readings—however teas-
ingly—put the writer back in the frame. It's customary for
writers, and writers on writers, to treat the author-tours that are
now built into most contracts writers make with publishers, as
extraneous bally-hoo. But they are now an integral part of what
authorship means, and those who don't and won't take part—
like Thomas Pynchon—become interesting by that fact; Salman
Rushdie's readings, during the darkest days of the threat of the
fatwah, unadvertised and attended by bored special-branch officers in bulgy overcoats, were important to proving he was still
alive as a writer, as well as in the more literal sense. And indeed
you can see the effects of this 'reading' culture *inside* many
contemporary novels and stories, in which avatars of the author—inset 'I' figures, tale-tellers, performers—are given a voice
on the page which can readily become a script for performance
when occasion arises.

But the death of the Author has been foundational for the Ivory
Tower of literary studies. Almost every major critical 'school' or
'ism', from Russian Formalism to Richards's experiments with
anonymized passages for analysis in Practical Criticism, to New
Criticism, Structuralism and since, has insisted that serious criticism must address itself to the text, even though that has been
defined very variously, sometimes consisting of the individual
poem or novel or play, sometimes of a whole genre, sometimes
of a great tradition, sometimes of a whole literature. The main
shift here, over the post-war period, has been that instead of
insisting, as modernists and their critical commentators had
done, on the integrity, richness, autonomy and self-reference of
the text, postmodernists and deconstructionists have opened it
up, emphasizing the continuity of literary and non-literary discourses, the ragged edges of textuality and its inner indeterminacy. The death of the Author Barthes and Foucault were calling
for at the end of the 1960s meant this: the death (as Foucault

said) of the *author-function*, which had outlived assaults on the
Intentional Fallacy, and on romantic notions of creative genius.
This function survived in modernist and avant-garde thinking as
a transcendental anonymity, and it was this last refuge of the
(God-like) point of origin that was under attack. This function
worked to guarantee the authority and wholeness of the canonized Work. Remove it and you remove the imaginative and
conceptual separateness, the ontological priority, of literary
texts. This is the move that brings about the contemporary
divorce of critic and reader, and renders old-fashioned 'close
reading' redundant.

Where mimetic criticism celebrating, describing and 'replay-
ing' works of literature survives at all, it is largely in the prag-
matic revisionist projects (recovering and revaluing neglected
authors and their work) of women's studies, black studies, gay
(literary) pride. And it does so by arguing apologetically, with
ingenuity and circumspection, working hard to make space for
a surviving subject, who is still constructing himself/herself,
through 'an ironic manipulation of the semiotics of performance'. The words belong to Nancy K. Miller, and come from a
much reprinted essay, 'Changing the Subject'. Miller argues that
feminism needs to negotiate a reprieve for the author-function,
however deconstructed, because women and men have had different histories, and unequal access to authorship: 'women . . .
have not, I think, (collectively) felt burdened by *too much* self,
ego, cogito, etc. Because the female subject has juridically been
excluded from the polis, hence decentred, "disoriginated",
deinstitutionalized, etc., her relation to integrity and textuality,
desire and authority, displays structurally important differences
from that universal position.'[7]

It's less often noticed that this effect works across the whole
field of contemporary writing, where the deconstructive doctrines aimed at demystifying the great (past) figures of the canon
leave no real room for contemporary writers who are trying to
make themselves a character and a space. In other words, the
present is already accounted for. The quality of the attention
given to contemporary writers and writing by the inhabitants

---

[7] 'Changing the Subject' (*Subject to Change*, New York, 1988), reprinted in
Maurice Biriotti and Nicola Miller, eds., *What is an Author?* (Manchester and New
York, 1993), 19–41, 34, 23.

of the Ivory Tower suffers in consequence. Writing on 'the postmodern' softens and disguises and carnivalizes this state of affairs, so that it looks as though there's a great deal of celebration of contemporary fiction—its use of parody, pastiche, reflexive jokes of all kinds, and its recyclings of others' texts, and rewritings of the past. A lot of contemporary texts and names get mentioned in passing. However, this style of critical writing is still a long way from offering particularizing accounts of individual writers and works, and indeed doesn't aim to. Reading contemporaneity in this spirit you tend to locate particular novels in a story of fragmentation and reflexivity (the postmodern condition) and you abstract diversity into a condition of all texts. A lot of theses that look from their titles as though they are about particular writers in fact follow this model, and embed their subjects in the language of theory. Particular novels, for instance, are seen not in the context of the writer's other books, or of other contemporary fiction, nor in relation to their past or present objects of parody or rewriting, but in relation to the history and development of critical formulations of intertextuality, the carnivalesque and so on. This way of handling the work of contemporaries leads to a very depleted canon, since the real 'newness' is associated by such readers and critics with critical discourse, not fiction-making.

On one level, the reasons for this are self-evident: academic status and worth are measured by publication, one must publish in order to be mobile and promotable, in order to survive at all. Academic critics more and more live in their own writing, then (even though the books and articles themselves very seldom make money), so that their 'secondariness' as commentators on and analysts of others' works is to a degree obscured. However, the more interesting implication lurking here is that it is the *academic critic* not the novelist or poet who is the heir to the avant-garde literary project of making it new, art which (as in the case of the *nouveau roman* in the 1940s and 1950s) took the form of utopian anti-art and demystification. Poststructuralist critical writing—elusive, shadowy, self-renewing, prolific— becomes a new, rival genre, and literariness itself, the work of representation in fiction, for example, is seen as an anachronism. Two critical/creative encounters—radical feminist Suzanne Kappeler on Angela Carter and post-colonialist and feminist critic Gayatri Spivak on Salman Rushdie—may help to show how this works. Carter and Rushdie are theory-friendly fiction-writers, who (one might think) are readily assimilable as 'magical realists' and 'postmodernists'. But no, at least not for their most exigent deconstructionist critics.

Carter's posthumous canonization has perhaps helped us forget how thoroughly some radical feminist criticism marginalized or rejected her work in the 1970s and 1980s. Like many writers before her, she was obliged to labour to create the taste by which she was to be savoured, and a major move in that game, in conjunction with the founding of Virago Press (where she was an early adviser) was the publication in 1979 of *The Sadeian Woman* (by Virago) and her collection of rewritten fairy stories, *The Bloody Chamber*. These books constituted between them, one polemically, the other imaginatively and by example, a kind of manifesto for a new women's writing which would set itself against traditions of passivity, modesty and victimization. Both books used parody, pastiche and ironic 'performative' devices, though the fairy tales exuded charm and the Sade book abused 'bankrupt enchantments'. By taking on (in the aggressive sense) the genres of pornography and fairy tale, Carter was aligning herself against high-minded views on the disinterestedness of art: 'If nobody, including the artist, acknowledges art as a mean of *knowing* the world, then art is relegated to a kind of rumpus room of the mind'.[8] However, she wanted to rewrite literary images, not erase them, and for Suzanne Kappeler in *The Pornography of Representation* that was a piece of retrograde illogic:

> Carter, the potential feminist critic, has withdrawn into the literary sanctuary, has become literary critic. . . . Like good modern literary critics, we move from the author/writer to the œuvre text which by literary convention bears his name. . . . Sade's pornographic assault on one particular patriarchal representation of woman—the Mother— renders him in the eyes of Carter, a provider of a service to women. . . . Women, of course, neither produced nor sanctified the mothering aspect of their patriarchal representation. . . .'[9]

---

[8] Angela Carter, *The Sadeian Woman: An Exercise in Cultural History* (London, 1979), 13.
[9] *The Pornography of Representation* (Oxford, 1986), 134.

What is at stake is the meaning of the 'literary': for Carter genres like pornography and fairy tale are not at all edged with piety, they are already desecrating 'the literary sanctury'. Later she would write: 'fairy tales . . . are anonymous and genderless . . . Ours is a highly individualised culture, with a great faith in the work of art as a unique one-off, and the artist as an original. . . . But fairy tales are not like that nor are their makers. . . . Think in terms of the domestic arts. "This is how *I* make potato soup." '[10] Kappeler thinks that representation *in itself* is powerfully impure and voyeuristic. Carter agrees. But this is where they part company, for Kappeler wants to do away with literariness, destroy the images, and have people speak for themselves without artifice in the name of truth, whereas Carter wants to see everyone as potentially a liar or fiction-maker, and vindicate women's creative role past and present. The blameless woman is for her the unimaginative woman. In other words, she was giving a formal, fictive and 'untruthful' answer to a political and theoretical question, and that meant she was frequently convicted of heresy.

My second example, Gayatri Spivak's 1989 essay 'Reading *The Satanic Verses*', is a great deal more well-mannered and circumspect. She does indeed 'read' Rushdie's novel with sympathy: for her Rushdie is very much the postmodern writer, that is 'a reader at the performance of writing'.[11] This enables her wittily to cast Khomeini in the role of Author: 'the late Ayatollah . . . can be seen as filling the Author-function, and Salman Rushdie, himself caught in a different cultural logic, is no more than the writer-as-performer'. However, as reader-writers she and Rushdie diverge, since she is engaged in reading not only his text, but also the texts of the cultures outside it: 'The point is not necessarily and exclusively the correct description of a book, but the construction of readerships.' This is not a 'contextualizing' move. Spivak the theorist and Rushdie the novelist are both engaged in acts of *representation*, and for her Rushdie's fiction is (still) a relatively closed-off style of discourse—'fabricating decentred subjects as the sign of the times is

---

[10] *The Virago Book of Fairy Tales* (London, 1990), p. x.

[11] 'Reading *The Satanic Verses*', first version published in *Public Culture*, 2/1 (Fall, 1989) reprinted in Biriotti and Miller, *What is an Author?* 104–34, 106.

not necessarily these times decentring the subject'.[12] That the
novel—with eery prescience—addressed the issue of censorship
doesn't for her change the overall impression of its closedness to
aspects of 'these times'. Her own critical narrative, for instance,
brings into the picture a figure—an Indian Muslim woman
Shahbano, whose 'case' stands for a whole world of the silenced,
the censored and self-censored—who (this is the point) has no
voice, no story really, is not a 'character' . . .

Writing like Spivak's affords both the pleasure and the pain of
the text, in abundance and in itself. But this means in turn that,
despite its nostalgia for a writing without character, without
'fabricated subjects', her text inscribes its own limits. It's sometimes assumed that to grant criticism any creativity is to make
it into a meta-genre, levitating out of the various binds it
describes, but actually it becomes levelled to partiality. Thus
Spivak's piece is in an odd way very *personal* writing. It's no
accident (for instance) that she has an ironic and acrobatic
parenthesis on herself as one of Rushdie's characters. (This is a
way, as I read her, of telling us who Gayatri Spivak is, but letting
Rushdie do the crass business of representation.) 'As a post-
colonial migrant, "a tall, thin Bengali woman with cropped
hair"[13] like Swatilekha—the "real" name of the woman playing
the lead character in Ray's film version of Tagore's *The Home
and the World*—an "actress" acting out the script of female
Anglicisation—read emancipation—by male planning in the
colonial dispensation, I am part of Rushdie's text, after all.'[14]
Such writing describes, through its labyrinthine indirections, its
displacements, where the writer 'comes from'. Its message is
'after all', that all representation is misrepresentation, only I
represent myself.

So doing performative or mimetic criticism, re-enacting the
pleasures of reading dense, elaborate, playful, polyglot texts,
what I have called *writing reading* is low down on this agenda,
largely a thing of the past. This is Edward Said, dislodging the
readable text:

Much of what was so exciting for four decades about Western modernism and its aftermath—in, say, the elaborate interpretative strategies of

---

[12] 'Reading *The Satanic Verses*', 107, 116, and 113.
[13] Salman Rushdie, *The Satanic Verses*, 536.
[14] 'Reading *The Satanic Verses*', 111.

critical theory or the self-consciousness of literary and musical forms—seems almost quaintly abstract, desperately Eurocentric today. More reliable now are the reports from the front line where struggles are being fought between domestic tyrants and idealist oppositions, hybrid combinations of realism and fantasy, cartographic and archaeological descriptions, explorations in mixed forms (essay, video or film, photograph, memoir, story, aphorism) of unhoused exilic experiences.[15]

In fact, however, this list sounds very much like the programme of a 1930s avant-garde, which rather undermines the argument from contemporary political geography. And in practice, one of the main effects of such a move has been *reflexive* and self-conscious, as in Spivak's piece, sending the critic back to where he or she stands, reporting from the front line of the self: the unhoused exilic experience of *writing this way*, in this new non-genre.

More and more of the Ivory Tower theoreticians who banished the Author have been producing various kinds of life-writing of their own. Christine Brooke-Rose, who—as an experimental novelist and a critical theorist—had always inhabited two worlds, reflected on some of the ironies of this when she moved into the third world of liminal life-writing with *Remake* in 1996. The book is described on the jacket as 'an autobiographical novel' which 'uses life materials'; inside the covers we are told with rather more confessional baldness that 'The old lady's publisher has asked for an autobiography. But the resistance is huge. The absorbing present creates interference, as well as the old lady's lifelong prejudice against biographical criticism, called laundry-lists by Pound. Only the text matters, if the text survives at all . . .'[16] Brooke-Rose has a serious quarrel with most forms of life-writing, but that is a matter of their traditional links with realism and family romance. She wouldn't be seen dead inhabiting such a Life, but there is a mode of life-writing, telling the story of her love-affair with words, that she can countenance. *Remake* is a palimpsest-text, using quotations from letters, period pastiche (neo-romantic 'poetry' for desire 1940s-style—'The red underground becomes blood thundering under London's skin'[17]) and even some reflections on life-writing borrowed from the novelist Jenny Diski—a neat piece of

---

[15] Edward Said, *Culture and Imperialism* (London, 1993), 400.
[16] *Remake* (Manchester, 1996), 6.   [17] Ibid. 139.

intertextuality—exasperatedly reviewing a batch of autobiographies in the *LRB*.

And in the summer of the same year the *New York Times* magazine hailed the conversion of theory-obsessed academe to memoir-writing: 'Down at Duke, always a reliable harbinger of the zeitgeist, lit. crit. has been virtually banished from the campus in favour of what the literary journalist Adam Begley has dubbed "moi criticism": the private confessions of professors.'[18] One case in point was Frank Lentricchia, expert on Eliot and international modernism. In *The Edge of Night* (subtitled 'A Confession', 1994) he wrote his way back into his second-generation Italian-American origins in Utica, NY, back into the bookless household he'd left behind in the 1950s to go to school after school. Once upon a time there were 'meanings without ideas, flesh and blood . . .'[19] For Lentricchia the family romance is a romance of work, above all (his father was a house-painter, his mother worked on an assembly line) and *The Edge of Night* exorcizes some of the guilt of being an intellectual by visceral, demotic, anti-abstract writing—a kind of writing, of *work*, that he confesses he loves: 'Don't let *this* end, whatever this is . . . This activity. These selves. Writings.'[20] His self-consciousness remains of course ineradicable.

Lentricchia is more typical of the contemporary academic elision of theory with practice I'm describing than Brooke-Rose. She can confidently proclaim 'Only the text matters', because she has long been a novelist, and moreover a novelist of the cosmopolitan experimental kind whose books are constructed, made-up things. Brooke-Rose thinks like a modernist and a structuralist, in other words, while Lentricchia, in his excursion into hybrid, unmade, embryonic, half-truthful semi-fiction (he has gone on to write two 'novels' castigating himself as a 'weak word-maker') is more representative of the new generic territory I'm sketching out. In the 'Confession' he brings on his teenage daughters to mock him: 'Are these stories supposed to be put-downs of your university friends? We get the point. You're not a wimp. They're all spoiled WASPs.'[21] For Lentricchia the *work* of literature is a kind of doubtful pun.

---

[18] James Atlas, *New York Times* magazine, 12 May 1996.
[19] *The Edge of Night* (New York, 1994), 145.
[20] Ibid. 173.   [21] Ibid. 143.

So who in the Ivory Tower 'represents' the contemporary writers of fiction (poetry, drama)? True to the times I think increasingly the answer is: they themselves. Not novelists who also practise literary criticism like Brooke-Rose, but those who teach Creative Writing. I have been describing the Ivory Tower as if it were inhabited fairly exclusively by poststructuralists, but it's not, though they have set the tone over the last twenty years or so. Even the recent national Research Assessment, which set out to judge the productivity of academics in the UK, acknowledged this fact by including Creative Writing as a *form* of research into English Literature. Increasingly, and not only in the United States, where Creative Writing is usually a separate department, the business of analysing the workings of words on the page is in the hands of writing teachers. And many of them would say that what they really teach is reading, and that they have become (thanks to theory's domination in criticism) the main custodians of the canon, too. But they don't write this down, they do it orally, in classes. And because this is an activity that doesn't generally advertise itself in books and journals it's easy to underestimate its importance. But *Teaching Literature* edited by Judy Travis (1996), a collection of interviews with mainly American and Irish Writing teachers, writers as diverse as Grace Paley, Edmund White, Andrei Codrescu, Tom Mullins, Guy Davenport and Katha Pollitt, reveals a remarkable consistency of approach, in which reading out loud (for instance) figures very prominently. These writers see themselves in part as handing on the secrets of a craft to other potential writers, but also as training readers, creating audiences. They reminisce, some of them, about their own teachers in terms that insist on waywardness and individuality ('My Shakespeare professor . . . was a short chubby man, wall-eyed and with a pointy nose, and he would burst into long quotations') and all of them in one way or another would echo Grace Paley's happy admission, 'We in the writing department . . . we're in a situation where the English department is always mad at us.'

The Creative Writers are not reflexive theory's only significant others, however. Many academics don't in fact write criticism very much at all, but instead—for example—literary biography. Nowadays someone who didn't want to write theory (as I so much didn't twenty-five years ago) might perhaps turn to biography rather than literary journalism, and lead a rather less schizophrenic life. I still think, though, that that leaves the question of how to write *reading* other than as a literary journalist problematic. Barthes's famous saying went: 'The birth of the reader must be at the cost of the death of the Author.' But the Author's death has led to the birth of endless lower-case authors. If you want to speak with authority as a reader, in other words, you do it by first saying that you are a writer. I have always preferred to be a hack, it seems less of a mystification.

It's arguable I think that our current interest in literary journalism—not just in doing it, but in writing about it—is an admission that many academics have been missing the personalities of writing, writing's character, the stories of how books are structured, received, sold, understood or not, *made*. At the same time, this new respectability of Grub Street worries me, I don't want literary journalists to turn into 'writers', to join in the conspiracy of reflexiveness. Reviewing used to seem so safely low-life, so hand-to-mouth, so ephemeral, so focused on other people's work, that it was a refuge from the self-consciousness of academe. But now I'm not so sure.

Notes on Contributors

Bridget Bennett is a lecturer in the Department of English and Comparative Literary Studies at the University of Warwick. She is the author of *The Damnation of Harold Frederic* (1997) and the editor of *Ripples of Dissent: Women's Stories of Marriage from the 1890s* (1996).

Stefan Collini is Reader in Intellectual History and English Literature at Cambridge. His books include *Liberalism and Sociology: L. T. Hobhouse and Political Argument in England 1880–1914* (1979), *That Noble Science of Politics: A Study in Nineteenth-Century Intellectual History* (with Donald Winch and John Burrow, 1983), *Public Moralists: Political Thought and Intellectual Life in Britain 1850–1930* (1991), and *Matthew Arnold: A Critical Portrait* (1994). He has edited works by J. S. Mill, Matthew Arnold, C. P. Snow, and Umberto Eco. From 1986 to 1993 he was co-editor of *The Cambridge Review*. He is working on a book on intellectuals in Britain.

Valentine Cunningham is a Professor of English Language and Literature at Oxford and the senior Fellow in English at Corpus Christi College. His books include *British Writers of the Thirties* (1988) and *In the Reading Gaol: Texts, Postmodernity, and History* (1994). He is a regular contributor to a range of newspapers and journals.

David Finkelstein is Co-Director of the Scottish Centre for the Book at Napier University, Edinburgh, has written extensively on nineteenth-century literature and publishing history and is editor of *Sharp News*, the quarterly bulletin of the Society for the History of Authorship, Reading and Publishing. His publications include *An Index to Blackwood's Magazine 1901–1980* (1995) and, as part of the Victorian Fiction Research Guides series, *Philip Meadows Taylor* (1990). He is working on a study of the Edinburgh publishers William Blackwood and Sons.

Zachary Leader is Professor of English Literature at the Roehampton Institute, London, and the author of *Revision and Romantic Authorship* (1996), *Writer's Block* (1991), and *Reading Blake's Songs* (1981), and co-editor with Ian Haywood of *Romantic Period Writings 1798–1832: An Anthology* (1998). He reviews regularly for the *TLS* and *LRB* and has written for the books pages of the *Observer, Independent* *on Sunday*, and the *Sunday Times*. He is editing the *Selected Letters of Kingsley Amis* and the Oxford Authors *Shelley*.

Hermione Lee is Goldsmiths' Professor of English Literature at Oxford. She has written and edited a number of books, the most recent of which is *Virginia Woolf* (1996). She is well-known as a critic and broadcaster.

Grevel Lindop is Professor of Romantic and Early Victorian Studies at the University of Manchester. His books include *The Opium-Eater: A Life of Thomas De Quincey* (1981), *A Literary Guide to the Lake District* (1993), *The Path and the Palace: Reflections on the Nature of Poetry* (1996) and three collections of poems. A frequent contributor to the *TLS* over twenty years, he is the General Editor of the forthcoming edition of De Quincey's works.

Edna Longley is a Professor of English at Queen's University, Belfast. She has written extensively on twentieth-century Irish and English poetry, and on Irish culture. Her most recent works are *The Living Stream: Literature and Revisionism in Ireland* (1994) and *Yeats Annual 12 'That Accusing Eye': Yeats and his Irish Readers* (1996), co-edited with Warwick Gould. A new collection of essays on poetry will be published in 1998.

Karl Miller founded the *London Review of Books* and edited it for ten years. He was previously literary editor of the *Spectator* and the *New Statesman* and editor of the *Listener*. From 1974 to 1992 he was Lord Northcliffe Professor of Modern English Literature at University College London. Among his books are *Cockburn's Millennium* (1975) and *Doubles and Authors* (1985).

Marjorie Perloff is Sadie Dernham Patek Professor of Humanities at Stanford University. She has written many books and essays on twentieth-century poetics and poetry, including *The Poetics of Indeterminacy: Rimbaud to Cage* (1981) and *The Futurist Moment: Avant-Garde, Avant-Guerre and the Language of Rupture* (1986). Her most recent book is *Wittgenstein's Ladder: Poetic Language and the Strangeness of the Ordinary* (1996).

Lorna Sage is a Professor of English Literature at the University of East Anglia, where she has also been Dean of the School of English and American Studies. She has reviewed for many newspapers and journals, including the *TLS*, the *New Statesman*, the *Observer*, the *New Review*, *Vogue*, *Marxism Today*, the *Guardian*, the *New York Times*, and the *LRB*. Her books include *Women in the House of Fiction* (1992) and *Angela Carter* (1994). She is currently writing an autobiographical book and editing the Cambridge *Guide to Women's Writing in English*.

John Stokes is Professor in the Department of English, King's College London. He is the author of *In the Nineties* (1989) and *Oscar Wilde: Myths, Miracles, and Imitations* (1996), and co-author of *Bernhardt, Terry, Duse: The Actress in her Time* (1988) and *Three Tragic Actresses: Siddons, Rachel, Ristori* (1996). Together with Russell Jackson he is now editing Oscar Wilde's journalism for Oxford English Texts. He writes frequently for the *Guardian* and the *TLS*.

John Sutherland is Lord Northcliffe Professor of English at University College London. He is a prolific writer and regular reviewer. Among his books are *The Longman Companion to Victorian Fiction* (1988), *Mrs Humphry Ward, Eminent Victorian, Pre-eminent Edwardian* (1990), *Is Heathcliffe a Murderer? Great Puzzles in Nineteenth Century Literature* (1996) and *Can Jane Eyre be Happy? More Puzzles in Classic Fiction* (1997).

Jeremy Treglown is a Professor of English at the University of Warwick and Chair of the Warwick Writing Programme. From 1982 to 1990 he was editor of the *TLS* and he has contributed to a range of newspapers and journals including the *New Yorker* and (as co-editor) *Liber: A European Review of Books*. Among his books are an edition of the correspondence of John Wilmot, Earl of Rochester (1980), a selection of Robert Louis Stevenson's essays (1988) and a biography of Roald Dahl (1994).

Jenny Uglow is a biographer, critic and publisher. Her books include *George Eliot* (1987), *Elizabeth Gaskell: A Habit of Stories* (1993), *Cultural Babbage: Time, Technology and Invention* (with Francis Spufford, 1996), *Henry Fielding* (1996) and *Hogarth: A Life and a World* (1997).

Index

publicists 202 n.
publicity 104
publishers 17, 86, 116 n., 118, 125, 139, 148; American 96, 106, 125, 231; bookseller 6; First World War period 92, 94 n., 96, 102, 106, 107; Irish 202 n., 203, 206 n., 211–13, 214 n., 217, 218; male-dominated 121; poetry 78, 88, 232, 236, 238, 243
puffery 201; 'clique-' 76, 118, 129
Pynchon, Thomas 267

Quain, Frederick 64, 67, 68, 69
Quarterly Review 49, 78, 79 n.
Quartermain, Peter 247
Queen's College for Women, London 74
Queen's University, Belfast 207 n.
Quennell, Peter 146
question-and-answer magazines 6
Quiller-Couch, Sir Arthur 95, 109
Quirk, Randolph 69, 70

radical intellectuals 48, 214
Radio Ulster 201 n.
RAF (Royal Air Force) 140
Rakosi, Carl 238, 245 n.
Raleigh, Sir Walter (navigator) 72–3
Raleigh, Sir Walter Alexander (critic) 63
Ralph, James 2, 8, 9
Rattigan, Terence 185, 189
Raworth, Tom 246
Ray, Satyajit 272
Read, Herbert 146
'recognition' 161
Recorder, The 220
Red Cross 110, 140
Redgrave, Vanessa 194
Reid, Thomas 43
Reinfeld, Linda 226, 227, 228
Research Assessment ix, 275
Review, The 136 n.
reviews/reviewers 2, 3, 18–21 *passim*, 69, 76, 86, 113, 120, 121, 130, 160, 179, 276; American 157; anonymous 150; architectural 225–6; brain prostitution' 129; culturally conservative/politically right-wing 174; essays, journalism and 113; female 147; friends 118–20; Internet 247; Ireland, problems and contexts 200–23; Jewishness of 137; living on writing 262–76; photographs/illustrations in 174; poetry 49, 53, 141, 224–49; political books 142; pressures 79–80, 124; psychology of 197; Sunday-paper 251; Tynan's description 178
Reznikoff, Charles 238
Ricardo, David 41
Rich, Adrienne 238
Richards, I. A. 67, 227, 263, 267
Richardson, Samuel 16, 19 n.
Richmond, Bruce 119, 121, 138, 139, 146
Richmond Lecture (Leavis, 1962) 160, 163, 164–5, 169

Rieff, David 224
Rif/t 247
Robbins, Lionel C., Baron Robbins of Clare Market 164
Robins, Elizabeth 120
Robinson, Edward Arlington 232
Robinson, Ian 156, 157
Robinson, Lennox 207
Robinson, Mary (Irish president) 212
Robinson, Mary (poet) 33 n.
Roethke, Theodore 238
Rogers, Pat 1 n.
Rogers, Richard 225
Rothenberg, Jerome 246
Rothermere, *see* Harmsworth
Rowe, Nicholas ix
Royal Court Theatre 198
Royal National Theatre 177, 190, 193, 195, 199
Royde-Smith, Naomi 146, 147 n.
RTE (Radio Telifis Eireann) 201 n.
Rushdie, Salman 217, 267, 270, 271–2
Ruskin, John 60
Russell, Bertrand, 3rd Earl 233
Russell, George, *see* 'AE'
Russian literature/poetry 143, 243; Formalism 267

Sackville-West, Vita 119 n., 147
Sade, Marquis de 270
Sadleir, Michael 146
Sage, Lorna x
Said, Edward 272–3
Saintsbury, George 86, 252
St Andrews University 49
St Clair, William 27, 28 n.
St James's 10
St John's Gate 1
sales 1, 6, 8, 92, 103, 108; difficult and unpopular books 126
Salkeld, Cecil 207
San Francisco poets 238, 244, 247
Sanders, M. L. 93 n., 94 n., 96.
Sassen, Saskia 224
Satie, Erik 244
satire 9, 16, 68, 77, 80, 129, 142
Saturday Book Review Supplement, see *New York Times Book Review*
Saturday Review 88
Saurat, Denis 140
Saussure, Ferdinand de 239
Savage, Richard 15
Scandinavian literature 87
Scandinavian Studies 66
Schelling, F. W. J. 51
Schiller, J. C. F. von 27, 45
scholarship 24, 41, 42, 49, 50, 52, 56, 57, 71, 203, 221; allied to literary journalism 224; antagonism between journalism and 170; anti-Semitism in 140; 'undesirable amusement to learned world' 88–9
science 46, 52, 56
Scientific American 57